D1545796

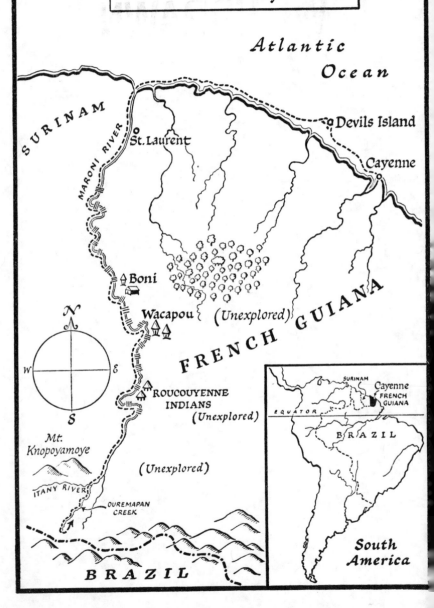

THE
Hassoldt Davis Expedition

Atlantic
Ocean

SURINAM

MARONI RIVER

St.Laurent

Devils Island

Cayenne

Boni

Wacapou

(Unexplored)

FRENCH GUIANA

N

W E

S

ROUCOUYENNE
INDIANS
(Unexplored)

Mt.
Knopoyamoye

(Unexplored)

ITANY RIVER

OUREMAPAN
CREEK

SURINAM

Cayenne
FRENCH
GUIANA

EQUATOR

BRAZIL

BRAZIL

South
America

HASSOLDT DAVIS

The Jungle
and the Damned

WITH PHOTOGRAPHS BY RUTH AND HASSOLDT DAVIS

Introduction to the Bison Books Edition
by Lawrence Millman

UNIVERSITY OF NEBRASKA PRESS
LINCOLN AND LONDON

INTRODUCTION

Lawrence Millman

"I was home again, in the dank discomfort which I loved." So writes Hassoldt Davis of French Guiana at the outset of *The Jungle and the Damned*.

Like many other celebrants of discomfort, whether of the dank, dry, or hypothermic variety, Davis grew up in relatively cushy circumstances. His father, a greeting card magnate, provided his family with all the amenities, including an estate in the fashionable Boston suburb of Wellesley Hills and a roomy summer house on Maine's Penobscot Bay. Young Bill (he used Hassoldt, his mother's maiden name, as a kind of nom de plume) tried to escape such amenities from the beginning. The *very* beginning—at birth he refused to breathe, whereupon a nurse anointed him with alcohol, and he bawled with life.

Books offered him a world quite different from both his family's world and the gray puritanical world of early twentieth-century New England. Especially Tarzan books. He became so obsessed with Edgar Rice Burroughs's arboreal hero that he even tried to look like him; he took a Charles Atlas physical-culture course and did in fact win a magazine prize for being "The Best Developed Boy in America." This wasn't enough though. At the age of thirteen, he packed a slingshot, maps, and a compass, and set off for Africa. He got no closer to the Dark Continent than Tremont Street in downtown Boston. Even so, he established a paradigm for his subsequent travels: shoot for the proverbial moon, for the risky, the distant, and the exotic, rather than the cozy world next door.

Romantic interests inevitably replaced his urge to swing from tree to tree. When he was nineteen, he traveled to Paris and promptly took up with an artist's model named Dodo. His father wouldn't have approved of Dodo. So much the better. Meanwhile, Davis was writing a novel about *l'amour* and taking artistic photographs of prostitutes. The bohemian idyll ended when he joined a public protest against the execution of Sacco and Vanzetti and was expelled from France as an undesirable alien. Back at home, he entered Harvard, boxed, and wrote poetry. Then came the incident that changed his life: he took some nude photographs of his seventeen-year-old sister, Aline.

Actually, the pictures are pretty tame, even by the standards of their time. Made with a lens screen and opal printing paper, they show Aline wearing a scarf around her waist and balancing a hoop, her back demurely to the viewer. But his father, a man very possessive of his daughter, found them totally indecent and kicked Bill out of the house. Thus began his career as an author and perennial wanderer.

First Davis went to San Francisco, where he worked as a freelance journalist, although he achieved more fame—or at least notoriety—as a maker of death masks. Then he booked passage for Tahiti, where he met Nordhoff and Hall (authors of *Mutiny on the Bounty*), the great documentary filmmaker Robert Flaherty, Paul Gauguin's son, and any number of obliging native women. Inspired by his friend Flaherty's tales of even more exotic islands, he was suddenly on a ship again, visiting Fiji, the Celebes, and Bali; whatever the destination, he would travel deck class in order to experience the rough edges of shipboard life. Footloose and seemingly fancy-free, he wrote to Aline: "The future will take care of its bastard self."

From these early travels came the first Hassoldt Davis book, *Islands under the Wind*. Brimming with purple, nay, ultraviolet prose, *Islands under the Wind* is not a particularly good book. Apart from a splendid description of a shark fight in the Celebes, it is chiefly remarkable for its sexual frankness; its author both kisses and tells, a combination somewhat unusual in a travel book and even more unusual for a travel book published as long ago as 1932.

There's often a fine line between travel and exploration, and Davis crossed that line in the late 1930s when he signed on as a writer, still photographer, and self-styled whipping boy with the Denis-Roosevelt Asiatic Expedition. Led by filmmaker Armand Denis, the expedition spent eight arduous months in the most isolated parts of Burma, northern India, and Nepal. Davis wrote up this experience in *The Land of the Eye*, a book vastly superior to his first. Here for the first time he exercises his passion for the bizarre and the grotesque, a passion that was to become one of his trademarks. He describes what it's like to have hundreds of gorged leeches clinging to your skin; he reports on an aphrodisiac composed of owl dung, powdered snakeskin, and bone dust; and he gives a blow-by-blow account of the ritual decapitation of water buffalo in Nepal, after which "my moccasins squished with blood."

Writing does not seem to have been Davis's favorite pursuit. "You sit by yourself all day long," he says in his 1957 autobiography *World without a Roof*, "and, if you get tight enough, half through the night, living with the ghosts of memory or the imagined ones of fiction, hoping the telephone will ring, that your most calamitous friend will drop in on you, forgetting your work to call up women you really don't give a damn about . . ." Like Ernest Hemingway, who later became his friend (they would ring each other up and complain about their relationships with women), he considered himself a man of action at least as much as a writer. And to a large extent he was a man of action, perhaps more so than Hemingway.

Unlike Hemingway, who went to great lengths to prove that he was a war hero, Davis actually was a war hero, albeit in a French rather than an American uniform. In 1941, he joined the Free French forces of General Leclerc in French Equatorial Africa and was soon serving as a combat captain with a crack Spahi (Moroccan cavalry) regiment. He saw action all over Africa and, eventually, in Europe. His wartime memoir, *Half Past When*, describes his many brushes with "Papa Death," a phenomenon he seems to have been more than half in love with. Still, *Half Past When* is an uncommonly modest book. If you blink while reading it, you might miss the fact that its author won both the Legion of Honor and the Croix de guerre (twice) for conduct under fire. Maybe its author won something else, too—the knowledge that he was no longer a villain in the eyes of the country that had once expelled him.

After the war, in New York, the much-decorated soldier met a professional photographer named Ruth Staudinger. Ruth was a blonde, and Davis had once stated in print that he didn't care for blonde women because they smelled like boiled milk. Ruth was different, however. She smelled like caramel and hot rum, or so he says in *World without a Roof*. Likewise she was adventurous, a first-rate cameraperson, and very attractive. She became the second Mrs. Davis (the first was a temperamental Russian woman named Hinny, about whom he wrote: "We didn't want each other, but loneliness was the colder choice.").

"Where were you to turn, Explorer, in a world so shrunken by war—mapped, exposed, foul? . . ." Davis now inquired of both himself and Ruth, newly adopted as an explorer. To the Francophile and aficionado of dank discomfort, the answer came almost immediately: French Guiana. Ruth, to her credit, was not put off by the idea of a honeymoon in what her husband cheerfully referred to as "rotten country."

France has always been a bit peculiar about what it chooses to colonize—what other nation would have tried to colonize the Sahara? Pestilential, bug-ridden, and covered with impenetrable jungle, French Guiana is hardly less daunting in its own way than the Sahara. Its infamous penal settlements were at least situated on a group of offshore islands. Known as the Iles du Salut (Islands of Health), they got their name not because they were healthy—perish the thought—but because the colony's interior was so unhealthy.

It was this interior that Davis wanted to explore. He proposed to paddle up the five-hundred-mile Maroni River and then trek into the remote Tumuc-Humac Mountains, the presumed location of Sir Walter Raleigh's lost city of gold, El Dorado. This plan had certain risks. For one thing, the Maroni boasts eighty or so rapids, most of them whitewater with a vengeance. For another, the local Indians had a reputation for being not very good hosts—the Oyaricoulets, for example, had killed all but one member of a recent expedition to the Maroni's headwaters (the lone survivor had been asleep in a tree). But travel, for Davis, wasn't satisfying unless it had an element of risk.

The Davises arrived in French Guiana without their provisions, which had been held up by a dock strike in Martinique. Having little else to do, they began gathering information about the colony's convicts, many of whom were on restricted parole. One convict cut Davis's hair without, he was happy to note, also cutting his throat. Another would sing hymns of praise to his blanket, the only thing in the world that was truly his. Yet another was a disgruntled author who'd killed his publisher.

In *The Jungle and the Damned*, Davis seems to devote an inordinate amount of space to these convicts—the "damned" of his title. A reader impatient for vicarious thrills and death-defying adventures might be inclined to say, "Get on with it, give me some action, enough about these bloody prisoners . . ." Davis was a writer always willing to bend a narrative out of shape to accommodate a good story, and the convicts' stories are often very good indeed. Yet I suspect there's another, more personal reason why he gives so much attention to the convicts: he identified with them. Kicked out of his home, he was a societal reject, a sort of convict, too. And in telling one story after another about unrepentant felons, he may have been telling his own story.

At last their provisions came, and off went the Davises into the colony's interior. Their paddlers were Boni, descendants of African slaves who'd escaped to the bush years earlier. Later they hired a group of brightly painted Roucouyenne Indians to serve as guides. For Ruth, who was filming the expedition, the daily presence of these two relatively traditional ethnic groups was a photographic boon. But there were not many other boons on a trip that seemed to go from bad to worse with each successive paddle stroke. The Boni constantly threatened mutiny, the expedition's cook was demented, and the guides were untrustworthy . . . and this was just the small stuff. "I sat snarling at the fire," writes Davis of one particularly bad day, "wishing I had brought along just one person whom I could sock in the teeth from time to time."

But a book is not the same as the experience it recounts, and *The Jungle and the Damned* offers triumphant proof that the world, rather than being shrunken, is a bountiful, expansive, often quite marvelous place. It takes a trip from hell, so-called, and turns it into something rich and strange, not to mention frequently very funny. In reading about such trips, you find yourself saying, "Thank God I stayed at home, but thank God the author didn't."

After the French Guiana trip, the couple returned to New York.

Ruth edited her film, which Warner Brothers later picked up and released, much to her disgust, as *Jungle Terror*. As for Davis himself, he wrote, lectured, helped with the film, and grew increasingly bored. He could tolerate neither domesticity nor staying put, so he began planning another expedition, this time to West Africa.

Less than a year after they got back from Guiana, he and Ruth landed at Abidjan, capital of the Ivory Coast, and then set off into the bush in search of a reputed school for witch doctors. With its unreliable guides, tropical maladies (Davis came down with what he called "shaking-like-a-bloody-aspen-leaf malaria"), and arcane rituals, the trip had a quality of déjà vu about it. In fact, *Sorcerer's Village*, the book Davis wrote about this trip, can be read as a sort of sequel to *The Jungle and the Damned*.

And then they were home again. But since home, for Davis, was anywhere but home, his Fifth Avenue apartment was not so much a residence as it was a repository for his travels. He filled it with African tribal masks, Tibetan trumpets, prayer wheels, poison arrows, tom-toms, leopard skins, and hundreds of other artifacts. Pets included a large rattlesnake and a tortoise named Consuela, whose shell he regularly shined with shoe polish. As a gesture toward permanence, he kept a French perpetual soup on the stove; every week or so, he would clarify the soup with egg, throw in vegetable waters and marrow bones, and then set the pot to simmer again. The soup sat on his stove for years, scrupulously tended by friends when he was away.

As Davis grew older, his whims seemed to grow more peculiar. For instance, he developed an urge to taste human flesh, not having done so on any of his trips to cannibal lands. So when a doctor friend brought him a hand snatched from an unclaimed corpse in the city morgue, he eagerly cooked and ate it, pronouncing it excellent: could the doctor bring him its mate?

I can't help but think that there was a quality of *épater* about such behavior. But since the person whom he wanted to outrage, doubtless his father, had long since died, Ruth got the brunt of it. In the early years of their marriage, she put up with her husband's eccentricities, but now she found herself resenting them, particularly when he mixed them with alcohol, of which he was a devotee.

Every morning he would drink orange juice crowded with vodka (he claimed he couldn't have food on an empty stomach). At last she divorced him. She returned to Africa and made a name for herself by running a gallery that showed only the work of untrained artists.

Davis once described Ruth as "an excellent jungle wife." It's not obvious that he wanted a wife whose talents extended beyond the jungle; even so, he felt her loss keenly. Jokingly, he talked about the need for an organization called S.A. (Satyrs Anonymous) that would "cure us chronic addicts of love." His other addiction, liquor, was no joke; he was now drinking more or less all the time. His work floundered. He took a trip around the world on a tramp steamer but wrote almost nothing about it. Perhaps the trip was unadventurous by his standards; or perhaps he was no longer at home even when he was away from home, and no longer at home with himself.

There is a certain symmetry about Hassoldt Davis's life. Alcohol helped him enter the world, and alcohol dispatched him to his grave. On 15 September 1959, he died of its effects. One might regret the fact that he was only fifty-two at the time of his death, but I suspect he would have preferred it that way. For it's unlikely he would have tolerated the infirmities of age or indeed anything else that would have kept him from lighting out for the farflung Territory.

To
L. H. D. C.

CONTENTS

I
The Damned

Sunset over Devil's Island, seen from Royale Island

Royale Island road leading to port. (*"This road forbidden to Convicts"*)

A convict and leper. Soon he will be freed, to go to a civil leprosarium

Ruth Standinger Davis holds the mummified head of an executed Indochinese

Better-privileged convicts were permitted enough light to see the vampire bats

Bunk of boards in the solitary confinement cells. The iron crossbar is the dreaded instrument known as the *fer*

Captain Hassoldt Davis with Afokati, his headman, in the upper reaches
of the Maroni River

On the upriver journey the canoes were poled and portaged for four
months

The bed of the river was strewn with jagged rocks

In the more severe rapids baggage was hauled with heavy vines, which
the natives preferred to rope

The Poligodou Falls, among the worst on the Maroni River

The women of the Boni tribe are tattooed as their relatives in Africa are. The hair-do in spikes is another West African survival

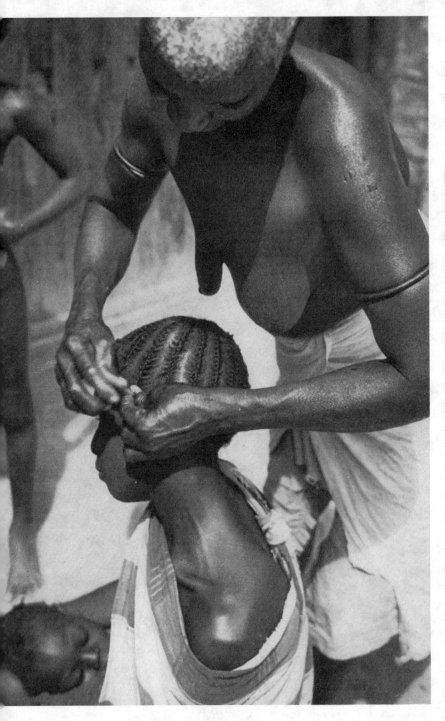

This is the melon-cut coiffure

Roucouyenne Indians applying a wasp mat to the chest of an Indian,
to test his courage

ai girls are expert paddlers

Dancing after the ceremony

WE KNEW that this darkness was Cayenne because the car had stopped. It was 10:15, and not a light in a window anywhere when we reached the Hôtel des Palmistes.

We knocked up, as the British say, the pajama-ed proprietor, and walked upstairs over a number of ancient dogs. We were led by Ruth, who sees in the dark; the lights of Cayenne go on at 6:10 in the evening automatically, and go out again at 10:10 without your raising a hand to help them with a switch.

The room, the swaying, punctured ghost of a mosquito netting, the moon through a latticed window, the chamber pot, the mildew, the frowsty candle, the twitter of bats echoing beneath the roof of corrugated iron, the sweat in the eyes smarting, and the taste of it, were curiously good again. The colonies I had lived in were blended of these. I was home again, in the dank discomfort which I loved.

❧

This was rather a different expedition from those I had had for the last twenty years, excepting the war years which I had spent in the French Army. Most of the good companions of the Denis-Roosevelt Expeditions were dispersed by now, and Bali and Nepal and Africa were no longer places one could inquire into and write about and film. They were uppity places now, with their own explorers, thank you, and no need for the likes of us, the abstract journeymen; and we were uneasy about prying into the past or attempting to divine the future from the signs and omens of science, which for them — and for us, indeed — had no political interest at all.

The world was reduced. An atom could find you anywhere. You could find Communists in Inner Mongolia, where the errant Sven Hedin had abandoned his honest theodolite beside the bones of Genghis Khan. Or the sailors of the Pacific navies could show you photographs of inner New Guinea to confound your ethnology. Where were you to turn, Explorer, in a world so shrunken by war — mapped, exposed, fouled as a pellet in an atom's pocket?

There was French Guiana. The French Ministries of Health, Colonies, and Information decided at last to send me for a report by film and book upon their oldest colony, which most of their own people were still confusing with New Guinea in the Pacific or French Guinea in Africa.

My new-wed wife, Ruth, of course, **was** coming along. The services of a professional photographer, which she was, would be indispensable, but I should have to swallow a number of public utterances to the effect that women on expeditions were a pest (they argued; they asked *why* when you desperately were wondering *how;* their heroism was mistimed and misplaced; they said, "Why, nothing, nothing at

THE DAMNED

all is the matter"; they riled or encouraged your adversaries; they drank your liquor up; they were back-seat drivers flagging their half-dried nail polish at busy intersections.)

UNESCO, the Explorers' Club, the New York Botanical Gardens, the Caribbean Commission — all backed us cordially. We had very little money for a jaunt like this, and we were grateful for the help which various companies gave us in exchange for honest reports on the qualities of their products under conditions which were unusual and usually severe. Those that held up poorly shall honestly be nameless here.

There were two excitements in French Guiana then which were not in my province at all: the liquidation of the penal settlement, the *bagne*, sensationally and erroneously known as Devil's Island; and the jolting change of the territory into a Department of France. I should stick to the customs of the few but various native peoples, two thousand at the most, who lived in the El Dorado which had cost Sir Walter Raleigh his head.

∾

It was my hope to pole and portage up the Maroni River into the Territory of Inini, which is nine tenths of French Guiana, continuing along the Awa River into the Itany River and finally branching into one of the creeks, still going south, until we reached the fabulous Tumuc-Humac Mountains on the border of Brazil.

This long, low range, almost entirely unexplored, was once thought to be El Dorado, the legendary lost land of the

[5]

golden cities and the lake called Parimé, where the Incan kings, fleeing from the brothers Pizarro, had built a tiny state. So very wealthy were they that each morning they dusted themselves with gold, and each evening washed it off in Lake Parimé.

This was the equivalent of headline news in the sixteenth century, promulgated, supposedly, by a Spanish officer named Martinez who possibly sailed with Columbus in 1498 when he reached the mouth of the Orinoco on his third visit to the New World, or possibly sailed with Vicente Yáñez Pinczón along the Guiana coast in 1500. His story attracted a number of freebooters and commercial explorers like Laurence Keymis and Sir Walter Raleigh.

Sir Walter, casting his cloak and later his head before Fortune, as before the Queen he too briefly beguiled, set an example in publicity which many an explorer has employed with sponsors ever since. Convincingly he wrote of the Guianas:

> The sandy soil is compact and makes marching easy for horses and men; deer cross every path; birds sing in the evening from a thousand different trees; herons and egrets, white, pink or dark red, perch at the edges of the waterways; the air is always fresh with the gentle breeze from the Orient, and every pebble one touches is warm with the promise of silver or gold. . . .

This was pretty good promotion, with its sandy soil of the reeking swamps, its hypothetical horses in the tangled wood, its fresh breeze through one of the hottest and dampest countries of the world.

And Sir Walter continued, chanting:

The flesh of the earth has never been torn, nor its fecundity sterilized by the laborer; the tombs have never been scavenged for the treasures within them; the mines have never known the sledge; the temple idols have not been overthrown and melted. Ah, this land has never been invaded by men in armor, nor conquered, nor in any way possessed by a Christian Prince. . . .

Then Raleigh added a touch, describing the banquets of the King, the Grand Cacique, in the mythical city of Manoa on Lake Parimé:

The guests are completely nude, their bodies anointed with certain balms, and the King's servants, having pounded gold to the finest powder, blow it upon the notables through hollow tubes of cane until their bodies glisten from head to foot, and thus gilded do seat themselves at their sumptuous tables by twenties and by thousands. . . .

Thus Raleigh, our Elizabethan forerunner.

Our expedition was more modest in its expectations and aims. We wanted to see whatever few people lived between the last French outpost and the Tumuc-Humac Mountains, and to know of their customs. Lover of the world's fleshpots that I was, gourmand, miser, I should shy from Lake Parimé if ever I should see it blazing in the hills, said I to Ruth — who contradicted me.

I had lost the habit of exploration, for through the war ·
I had been guided too long, and so I was impatient with the
politicians' papers, the false starts, the backing and filling,
the decisions decided and revised which were the normal in-
gredients of all expeditions, no matter how expertly managed.

Governor Peset, young and not in the best of health, welcomed us and took us sadly across the hills of Cayenne, along
the good roads he had faithfully made, along canals bordered
with fromager trees, and with cannonwood — a sorry tree
which drops the little gray corpses, like dried mice, of its
leaves along the path, and explodes in anguish when you put
it into the fire. We perceived that the land was resentful of
us. The clay tripped us up. Plants swung in the wind to
sting us. In these hills we were thirsty, and the Cane du Congo
with its red bulb of a flower and the water in its stem was
always just beyond our reach among the thorns.

Dr. Floch of the Pasteur Institute trudged moodily along
with us.

"Watch the goats," he said, "and the dogs — their thin
legs. No bones at all . . . no calcium in the soil."

The governor grinned boldly and led us down the hill.
He was another of the many who had come here and striven
with all their hearts to activate the country; he too would be
gone tomorrow.

Our wait in Cayenne at times seemed as limitless as mean-
ingless. There were confused and confusing messages about
our impedimenta, so necessary to any progress we might

make upriver; there were hints of bureaucratic disapproval, even more confusing in the face of the documents and letters from high officials and other credentials which we carried.

At one point Ruth was graciously given permission to leave French Guiana; this from a politican whom she had flattered in film for several days. "You," said he to Ruth, "may go away."

He may have picked up this idea from the crowd of loungers and local social commentators, who did not approve Europeans or Americans or "imperialists" or "adventurers" or "outsiders." They murmured at us as we passed the tables in the cavern of the bar of the Hôtel des Palmistes. Always, after our dispirited drives around Cayenne in the jeep — during which we held hands and talked of our damned blind love of France, and longed for the clean woods somewhere ahead of us — we walked smartly through the hotel bar when we got back, hurrying past the counterpoint of talk, the insults tossed into the air and meant to land on our necks.

All this was inauspicious, we said quietly to each other, for what should be a small link in the continuing fraternity of France and the United States; it was unquestionably awkward for me, who was still, by courtesy of General Leclerc, in the uniform of the French Moroccan Spahis.

The sun came suddenly here, for we were about two degrees north of the equator. It would bloom in our windows abruptly and shafts of it would shoot through the larger holes of our grimy mosquito net, catching me in the eye invariably, and spotlighting the freckles of Ruth's golden back. The Deputy's secretary's typewriter below us was slapping away nagging at us, and the cook's wooden sandals went *clink-clonk, clink-clonk* along the flagged pathway to her foul den. Smoke came gray from it against the green and scarlet of the hibiscus bushes, and the cook's helper, a *libéré*, sent forth his morning chant: "Upon the head of my mother, upon the head of my only child, I swear . . ." (It was a common chant.) Then he would be silent for a while as he drank a shot of the lowly rum called "taffia."

The divisions of convicts and ex-convicts in French Guiana were complex, but four of their denominations were enough for us. The *transportés* were murderers; the *relégués* were thieves with more than four convictions; the *libérés*, either murderers or thieves and frequently both, had served their time and were now free in the colony, but would be kept there until they had stayed a number of years equal to the term of their former prison confinement. The fourth group — *déportés*, political prisoners of the Dreyfus and Ullmo sort — was a race apart, rarely seen.

All the convicts were class-conscious; the *libéré* was superior, of course; and the *transporté*, who had committed murder only, perhaps in a moment of passion as you or I might do, despised the habitual thief.

Convicts were easily recognizable, in or out of uniform, for those still lodged in prison but free to work outside wore the traditional pajama suit of red and white stripes. Pajamas of blue and white, or green and white, were cherished by the convicts as relics of the lean years of the penal settlement, when clothing was scarce. There was a curious masochistic pride about these effigies of men; their penance was their boast, they vaunted their afflictions: "Twenty-two welts they gave me; look at these scars. . . . Six months of the solitary cell. . . . Thirty years I've had of it. . . ."

The *libéré* in civilian clothes was nearly as easy to distinguish, and you would know him anywhere, in any crowd. There were exceptions, of course, but the *libérés* of French Guiana were mostly of two physical classes. One was skeletal, vulpine, bony over the antrums and sinuses, with cautious pale eyes set close together, a beaked nose from which most of the cartilage had shriveled, the aspect of a man tossing a glance over his shoulder like a pinch of salt for luck, and at the same time looking with one eye straight ahead to discern only infinite darkness. Usually his teeth were missing as a result of malnutrition, beatings, or the commerce in gold teeth with the boatmen who sold them for a percentage in Cayenne.

The other was a swarthy type, always impeccably dressed, lipless, and with eyes so deep they gave you the impression that the hard small light in them was piped from the daylight at the backs of their heads. Usually they were *garçons de famille*, rented as family servants by the administration; they loved little children and all animals; they cared for the sick most tenderly, as they did all things weaker than themselves; Sacher-Masoch and the Marquis de Sade and

the characters of Krafft-Ebing were wan in contrast to
them.

☙

Fifty-two thousand of these men in clowns' clothing had
passed through the *bagne*, the penal colony, since its inauguration in 1854. Their paths were various; most of them
prematurely died. Eighteen hundred *libérés* were still stag-
gering around French Guiana waiting on the paper work of
the officials, which might permit them to go home again. The
wise ones knew they never would go home again; and the
physicians counseled them to stay in French Guiana with
their thinned blood and to count their corpuscles like pearls.

The Arabs among them were the most determined to get
home; they must die in Moslem land at any price, even
honestly gained; and the last shipload of Arabs to Africa, in
April 1947, had sent ahead of them some fifty-four million
francs by postal money order.

The Arab — murderer though he might be and usually
was — was a conservative, a practical man who paid his debt
of crime and returned to forget it and till his land. He despised the soil of French Guiana, which was infinitely superior
to his own, the gold in it, the fruits still blooming above plantations which were abandoned two centuries ago. Unlike the
political Negro, who has abrogated the name of "Creole"
in French Guiana, the Arab was a gentleman assassin.

One of these gentlemen assassins, not very surprisingly
named Mohammed, was delegated to our expedition by the

French authorities; he was to function as our cook and servant.

On one of the nights we spent waiting in Cayenne, Mohammed, who was not especially eager to go with us, sat down on our hot veranda. The stripes of his convict pajamas faded before the fluorescent glow of my Totelite (the city lights had been turned off promptly at 10:10). A banjo somewhere was clanking its metal teeth.

"Have you a pin?" he asked. "I should like to be pricked."

Ruth cauterized a pin for him and he jammed it into his forehead. Mohammed winced. "I suppose I shall have to come along with you," he said. "But I will try again."

Ruth gave him another pin and he balanced it back and forth like a harpoon and plunged it into a mound of scaly skin just over his solar plexus. He jumped just like any man who has had a pin plunged into his solar plexus.

"No good," he said. "They'd never believe me. I shall have to go along with you. I couldn't pretend to be a leper at all." The Arabs were honest men.

We were allowed three trips to Devil's Island; to Devil's Island itself, not only the neighboring islands of St. Joseph and Royale, which are the closest that previous investigators came to the island whose name they have always used to denote the penal colony as a whole. Devil's Island was the happiest of this group. There had been, comparatively, very little horror there. The *déportés*, the adverse politicians, the greater traitors, had been lodged there fairly comfortably by their unsure wardens, who felt that some man like Dreyfus might someday be freed to condemn them, or that an Ullmo might write of them when he returned to France.

Slowly and as on a rocking horse we teetered over the waves which separated Cayenne from the Islands of Health; that is the official name of the three islands, and truly named they are, if climate alone is to be considered. The anopheles mosquito which carries malaria is unable to cross the strait.

We heaved and we ho-ed, and we hove into port beneath the dark green hills of Royale Island. We backed and filled again, held our tail high to the waves, and came rushing giddily back to the quay of granite blocks at the foot of the terrible little hills where the prisoners had lived. No one was here now but the wardens and a few incorrigible murderers, who tended the lighthouse and the boats arriving.

They waited for us at the quay, three lean men looking like all their fellows, with thin lips, high cheekbones, sunken eyes, and that glance over the shoulder. They helped us ashore without a smile. They had the faces of men who after twenty years of imprisonment have not a dream or a hope to disturb them.

There was a long hard road up the escarpment to the hills —and harder it must have been for the ants of men who built it fifty years ago. It was a gray ramp of flagstone curving a quarter of the way round the island, mounting through shadows beneath the cliffs where the *surveillants'* houses were set. Once a thousand men had toiled and sweated and bled on it. Little pink flowers grew in the wall, and you could imagine a convict turning with a snarl to these dimpled things and talking to them.

"There's no work in thee," he would say. "Thou hast not a muscle in thee. Could'st thee lift a shovel or tear off the hair by handfuls from the head of thy neighbor's wife? Pah, I should knock thy smirk away!"

But he wouldn't. Ruth and I knew murderers more intimately than we knew anyone else in French Guiana; they despised everyone and everything that was weaker than they, but their solicitude for the weak was deep and inevitable; they would threaten the guard who had beaten them and then nurse him like a mother when he was ill; they would mend hurt dogs; a flower might snicker at them and they would curse it because it was weak and free, and not strong and confined as they pretended to be, but they were such cowardly sentimentalists that they would likely kill another man to keep it from harm.

On these three Islands of Health there were usually about twelve hundred prisoners in the heyday of the penitentiary which was called Devil's Island. Its sensational renown began during the imprisonment of Dreyfus. The name was dramatic, and the *évadés*, the convicts who escaped from one or another of the many camps in French Guiana, always boasted that they had escaped from "Devil's Island," which harbored only the élite. Devil's Island itself never had a murderer — or a visiting journalist — on it. It was a soft asylum for traitors and politicos.

I was impressed at first and then made uneasy by the gentleness of the two guardians, one white and one black, who were still on Royale Island in charge of the dozen remaining convicts. Their words were honeyed, their gestures as soft as plumes in the breeze, as we walked quietly around the island, wineglass in hand, admiring the excellent weather, having the church and the hospital pointed out to us as examples of beneficence. They even showed us the funnels and the cylinders of stone where those who had committed a *bêtise* (a foolishness) had been confined until they went mad or died. These were small individual dungeons lighted and aired almost imperceptibly by a three-inch hole high above. And in them, said our guardians, those foolish boys were kept, alone, clamped by the *fer* (the iron horseshoe) to the tilted bed of boards, with no companions but the vampire bats.

A condemned man couldn't see the bats in that darkness, and even had he not been shackled he never could have struck them with his flailing arms. These little bats, rarely more than a foot in wingspread, would make contact with him only while he slept and they were in need of blood. Their system of bloodletting was as evil as that of the prison itself, which would grind a man's morale to fibers, not quite killing him, then let the rest of him putrefy and slough away. The vampires would hover above his bare feet, never touching him until their teeth made the painless needle-sharp incision so they might suck a minute quantity of blood; the fearful thing was that they injected simultaneously a noncoagulating agent into the bloodstream, which would leave the wound flowing until the convict awoke in the morning with a quart or more of his blood drained onto the floor.

The cells were so dark that Ruth changed her film in them; their doors stood open now, three inches thick, some of them with holes gouged from the inside by the shackled men, and some from the outside so that the warders could flash a light and observe the mania of their patients.

We filmed the open doors by government command.

The black *surveillant* smiled at Ruth and said in his lullaby voice, "Beatings? Ah, yes, some of them required it, particularly the *évadés* who tried to meet *La Belle* — that was their name for escape — and at least four fifths attempted it. They were ingenious and very brave to tempt the sharks in these waters. Many of them made rafts of coconut husks. One, a trusty, built his own narrow hut where he was to stand watch as sentinel, but this was so cunningly constructed that one night, in the space of half an hour, he converted it into a boat and sailed away. He deserved his freedom!"

He shook his head reminiscently. "I myself literally escaped from my duties here to join the Free French during the war. Damned glad I was too. The prisoners died like flies under the regime of Vichy; and any Gaullist, even a free citizen, who was discovered, was flung into the murderers' blockhouses. Here's one now."

We had approached a long stone shed through the idyllic paths of this island, which the French government and Pan American Airways were intending to convert into a tourist resort. The shed was almost totally dark inside. Facing each other and running the length of it were two continuous platforms of wood which served as beds for the prisoners. They were tilted slightly so that the men's heads would be higher than their feet, since there were neither pillows nor mattresses.

Gouleau, our dark guardian, said: "Now that there is no more of this, it is hard to believe that it ever existed — that fifty men should have been enclosed here in darkness, with only a half hour's promenade morning and evening." His voice took on the lullaby rhythm again.

"You couldn't blame them for what happened in the darkness — fifty men spontaneously going mad and fighting like snakes in a snarl, or one man killing another by quiet strangulation. From halfway across the island you could hear them weeping, singing, orating, or the cries of the pederasts, like herons. Most of them had lovers, whose faces were unknown to them, and what must have been most horrible to the newcomer here in the dark was the touch of an assassin's hand on his throat or a lover's on his thigh. You could imagine him, trying not to cry out, and then the word blurted, echoed, tossed from wall, to wall, until those who slept slashed at their neighbors or hugged them by mistake. During the time of the Vichy administration, a corpse was dragged out almost every morning."

Gouleau beamed benignly at us. "You see the holes here and there in the bed platform? They are called the *matelas perforés*. The ones who were dying of dysentery and too weak to move were bedded there. Dubois!" he called to his convict servant. Dubois came forward promptly, smoothing his candy-cane pajamas. "Show your tattooing to our friends."

As Dubois stripped off his single layer of clothes obediently, the line of tattooing, which had seemed to be a necklace around his neck, spiraled downward and separated to twist like springs around all his extremities. And between the coils were literally hundreds of faces, designs, and phrases such as No Luck! A Woman Put Me Here! and Misery, I Am Thine! On one of his extremities, he said, the lettering fluctuated, diminishing or enlarging according to his temperature.

Without books, without diversion except what their bodies afforded them, the prisoners produced their own museums on their skins with a sharpened bamboo splinter and ink, or vegetable dyes, such as indigo. And when you saw tattooing upside down it was usually that of a man who, because of his "foolishness," had been shackled in the solitary cells and had kept his mind balanced by tattooing his dreams upon himself.

☙

Gouleau tossed his head in the direction of Dubois, who was following us at a respectful distance. He chuckled around the cigarette which was stuck to his lower lip. We were walking toward the shore. "It seems odd to me," Gouleau said, "that Dubois should still be alive, for he was always the most unpopular *bagnard* among the guardians who preceded me. That is not a comfortable honor. He's a good-looking fellow, as you see, even though my predecessors got his teeth. Ten years or so ago he was so damned pretty that the few guardians who had wives here kept him most of the time in solitary under one pretext or another. They had trouble enough usually to get a civil word for themselves from their women in this *bled*, this paradise of hell."

Gouleau paused to point out a little inlet blocked by rocks from the sea and its sharks. The convicts were permitted to bathe there as a reward for good behavior.

"On the balcony of that house above the pool there used to sit a warden's young wife while the men were swimming. She was a sun bather, an exhibitionist, a tease. You can understand that she caused more discomfort than pleasure among those poor devils, who hadn't seen the whole skin of a woman for years, but naturally they didn't dare complain."

Gouleau pried loose the butt of the cigarette with his tongue and spat it out. He replaced it with a wisp of grass. He was a simple man. "Now here's the peculiar thing. We could only guess later that, though this woman enjoyed exhibiting herself to the convicts who swam in the pool, she never stripped before her husband, whom she obviously detested. And so it was that the guardian of the men at the pool was usually the husband, who would sit quietly beneath a bush, staring, his hand on his pistol holster, probably tortured by the problem of whether he should shoot his wife or the convicts gaping at her. And naturally there was no one he could complain to either.

"Our Dubois here had troubles enough without the affliction of the woman on the balcony. One of them was his determination to escape. He had even boasted about it.

"One day he was missing; and the story goes that he slipped out of the parade from the pool to the cells, and entered the house of the woman, where he found her still upon the balcony, naked as a worm. The temptation was too great for him; he had suffered for too long the teasing sight of her; there was one thing to be done, and he did it. He upended her and put her across his knee and spanked the daylights out of her just as the sun was going down."

Gouleau shook his head deploringly. Things like this just weren't done in well-kept prisons. God knows what the world was coming to.

"Then," said Gouleau, "he borrowed a spare pistol and a clean handkerchief from the shelves of the woman's husband, and draped her spanked, bare, fainting figure over the balcony rail, and left the island quietly in a boat made of bamboo and blankets. This, of course," said Gouleau, "was a matter of embarrassment to everyone.

"Well, sir, the mainland was advised of his escape. Dutch Guiana was notified, and within a week probably every Creole and Indian along three hundred miles of coast was watching for Dubois, to get the reward money offered by the Penal Administration for his capture. The husband of the spanked wife was permitted to search for him too. He didn't like it very much, but it was a matter of honor, you understand. You can't have your wife's rosy backsides draped like a pennant across your balcony and she shouting to the treetops the whole story of it.

"Dubois and the husband met at last, somewhere south of St. Laurent on a forest trail. They came face to face around the roots of a fromager tree, and it was Dubois who had his gun out first. '*Monsieur le Surveillant,*' he said, politely enough, 'if you will sit down quietly, cross-legged, and hold that fern in your right hand and that cashew fruit — there it is, just above your head — in your left, I shall not kill you.'

"The husband was very angry, but he did as he was commanded, and he became particularly angry when he saw that Dubois was pointing his own stolen pistol at him. But, none the less, he clutched high his fern and his cashew fruit. They discussed things then.

" 'I don't like people spanking my wife,' said the husband, a little surlily. 'I won't stand for it.'

" 'There are few wives,' said Dubois, 'whom I have enjoyed spanking less. I would point out to you also that I have not shot you yet, that so far I am saving your life, and that you are deeply indebted to me.'

"The guardian-husband considered this sophistry, his hands trembling a little as he squeezed the fern and the cashew fruit which ran like blood across his fingers.

" 'Thank you, Dubois,' he said. 'As you certainly have saved my life, I can only express my appreciation by giving you your freedom. For thirty days. Is that fair enough? I shall have you then.'

"They parted with caution but amicably. The husband,

a chastened and a wiser man, returned here to the islands and hugged his wife with one arm and spanked the daylights out of her with the other.

" 'This is for Leblanc,' he said, 'and this is for Dubois,' giving a *rat-a-tat-tat* like a drummer on her pink behind, 'and here's one and another and another, my bright coquette, for Pierre and Maurice and Jean and all the others in the pool. The boat is waiting,' he said, while she hung head-downward upon his lap, limp as though across a balcony rail. Then he poured glycerin and rosewater on the bottom of her, smoothing the unguents delicately into her. 'Now I shall take the boat and find Dubois.'

"Which he did, within the thirty days, and brought him back and kept him in solitary confinement so he could reach him readily whenever he felt disgruntled. But this wasn't often now, for he and his wife got on famously. She was demure as a daisy, and he was twice the man he used to be, thanks to Dubois."

Ruth looked Dubois over with rather a jaundiced eye. He shrugged and, as he was a privileged trustee now, he felt free graciously to change the subject to Devil's Island, which lay before us across a strait about two hundred feet wide. It was very small, an oval island packed with palm trees.

"I've been here seventeen years," he said, "and do you know what I've dreamed about the last ten years? No, *mon-*

sieur, not France, but Devil's Island. That must be the paradise, *monsieur*. Figure it to yourself, there were never more than twelve men on it, political criminals of high class, talking with each other about books and things. Sometimes, like the Captain Dreyfus, they had as servants men who were my companions among the *transportés*. But not me. I was unworthy."

"Tut, tut," said I. "What's that thing there?" Beside us on the rocky shore was an iron edifice of wheels and cogs. Directly opposite on the shore of Devil's Island was a similar structure.

"There used to be a cable running between the two to take provisions across and sometimes a man who was sick. It's a hell of a piece of water for a boat. Current for one thing, and sharks if you tip over."

The job of greasing the cable, he said, was so dangerous that the convicts who volunteered to straddle it and slide back and forth along it with an oily rag were rewarded, when they didn't fall among the sharks, with two bottles of wine and three ounces of tobacco each.

"Here's our ship," said Gouleau.

A heavy-timbered whaleboat came around the tip of Royale Island, sucked quietly and rapidly toward us by the current. Six men in striped uniforms were resting on their oars. Ruth and I got aboard gingerly with our cameras wrapped in Pliofilm. The men grinned, spun us in a semicircle for the take-off, then bucked the current for half an hour until we came almost within grappling distance of Devil's

Island, where the current outmaneuvered us and sent us slithering toward Trinidad. It was a straight pull now. The water gargled like a demon against our bow as we inched, millimetered, toward the platform of stones which was the dock.

"That, I think, is a shark," said Ruth.

It was; a dark blue sickle slipping effortlessly upcurrent. As plain as teeth and tide was the fact that escape from Devil's Island was nearly impossible.

"Paradise!" said Dubois ecstatically as we bounced ashore from the heaving boat. His dream was realized. He had reached his Devil's Island.

It was pretty close to the dream of that lush, green, outlandish island you had in childhood, surrounded by the cold desks of the schoolroom and barren mathematics. Here were escape and freedom, you felt. We climbed the casual, gently winding road the convicts had built to the central ridge of the island, perhaps fifty feet above sea level, and looked the length of it across two rows of little stone prisons. They seemed more like country cottages now, with vines dangling before their open doors and the gardens of the former inmates still blooming unattended. It was a peaceful scene but for the square watchtower with its gun slots.

"That's Dreyfus's house behind you." Gouleau pointed.

"The house of the Master!" breathed Dubois, awed.

"Master!" Gouleau snorted. "Master! We called them the

prima donnas, the ones who lived over here. No criminals in all the world have been so spoiled and pampered as these nuisances on Devil's Island! You have read the books, the newspaper articles. Then look now at the terrible cell of Captain Dreyfus!"

"In its day," said Ruth, putting a filter on her lens, "it must have been a handsome villa." House hunters in Westchester, I thought, would pay a fortune for that snug little estate if it could be transplanted. A stone wall surrounded it, and within was a generous house of two rooms, one for Dreyfus and one for his personal military guardian, who amicably philosophized with him on the trials of being outcast, played chess with him, and took him on walks to the other end of the island, to sit respectfully beside him while he cut images in the rock to baffle scientists of a hundred years from now.

There was a decent privy attached to the house. The kitchen was across the garden, adjoining the chicken coops and servants' quarters. Were it not for the barred windows and the rusty bolts on the doors you would have thought it an enviable winter resort.

"They only locked him up at night," said Gouleau. "He had the run of the island during daylight, until we heard of the rescue plans."

The *cause célèbre* of Alfred Dreyfus was one of the thrillers of my youth. Over a hundred books were written about it. The Sunday supplements portrayed it in grisly, imaginative drawings, wherein the convicts of Devil's Island suffered all the tortures of the Inquisition. Zola, Clémenceau, Jaurès boldly fought against this most shameful governmental persecution of all French history.

Briefly, Captain Dreyfus, the son of a wealthy Jewish manufacturer, was holding a minor post in the French War Department in 1894. A charge of treason was brought against him because of the similarity of his handwriting to that of an intercepted letter addressed to the German military attaché in Paris. Both Church and State, anti-Semitic and anti-German, dragged Dreyfus to court, and on evidence which was scarcely even circumstantial condemned him to Devil's Island.

There he might have been forgotten, if it had not been for the industry of the Chief of Intelligence, Colonel Picquart, who dug up evidence, embarrassing to Church and State, which indicated that a certain Major Esterhazy was the traitor. Esterhazy was tried and acquitted. Picquart was booted out of the army. Then the *affaire Dreyfus* became a proper issue, with all the liberals of France on the side of the little man in his Devil's Island cell.

It was about this time that the penal establishment in French Guiana heard rumors, through its own convicts, of an attempt to be made to rescue Dreyfus. There was to be bribery, a boat in the night, and the "prima donna" was to be abducted to France to confront Esterhazy with new evidence found by his increasingly powerful supporters. So Dreyfus no longer walked in freedom above the rocks by the curling sea. He, the Lord of Devil's Island, could no longer pass the time of day and crack proverbs with the minor political recalcitrants who were his companions.

His door was locked, and he was, for a while, chained to his bed, until in 1899 he was tried again *in absentia*, found guilty still, but pardoned. It wasn't until 1906, twelve years from the beginning of his durance, that the decision condemning him was reversed.

He was rowed to Royale Island by convicts who revered him, the Master, as a symbol of police injustice; he sailed the fifty miles to Cayenne with *libéré* boa men who had cut throats in their time; and he returned to France with a boatload of unsuccessful colonists, cutthroats also, who were being transferred to prison in the metropolis.

But Alfred Dreyfus was free, and honored by all of France. He was made lieutenant general in the First World War and given the cross of the Legion of Honor; finally in 1930 the papers of the German military attaché were divulged, giving incontestable proof of Dreyfus's innocence and Esterhazy's guilt.

❧

We went on waiting in Cayenne, watching the docks, listening to the skies for planes, snatching our mail to learn how soon the rest of our equipment would arrive. The dry season was already half over, and we had the length of Guiana to travel by routes unknown to us. Only one man living had reached our destination of the Tumuc-Humac Mountains, Captain Richard of the French Army Geographic Service, but he was in France and couldn't help us. Our approach to the mountains would be different even from his.

I felt short of breath. I was racing against the rain, which would slow our progress if we had to travel in it, by swelling the rivers and the creeks. Ruth, who was to make the moving picture in color, the first ever in French Guiana, was counting suns as a miser does his pennies, ticking them off against the rainy season which should start in November, when color photography would become impossible.

Above the doubts, the depressions of such a journey as this, the niggling questions to yourself at night (Dammit, have I bitten off more than I can chew?), were the problems of keeping face with your sponsors, to whom you had prudently promised a little less than what seemed possible; and of trying to make sense to local authorities, who demanded your precise itineraries and purposes in forests which were within a few days' bird-flight from their offices, but unknown and unexplored.

It would sound silly to say, "Really, I don't know. So much depends on what we find here, on what may swivel us to over there, and if that is useless to our project, then to somewhere else." But that is how it happens.

We didn't know. Despite our most careful planning we couldn't know when our essential food would come, when we could get a boat to St. Laurent on the Maroni River, which for a while would be our highway to the dim green lands we were after. Could we find paddlers there? How far could these black paddlers take us until we reached Indian country? Would the Indians guide us, as they had guided Coudreau and Crevaux half a century ago? No one could tell us. We didn't know.

Our room in the Hôtel des Palmistes was little more than a shelter from the sun and the droppings of buzzards, the *urubu*, which swung their shadows up and down the streets. The walls were square and gray. The conveniences were a piddling shower; we had, in the garden below, a fouled outhouse of once satiny rosewood. The dining room served refreshingly cool leftovers from the table of the *patron* and his circle of political acolytes. Nonpartisan whites such as Ruth and I were fed on sufferance until the day should come when Guiana would be returned to the Guianese.

Ruth looked out of a window to a vista of waves of corrugated iron roofs rusted and besmirched by the *urubu*. I looked out of another to the pride of the town, the Place des Palmistes, a square of palms surrounded by leaden gray buildings; the Bureau of Economics at the left, the pesthouse of a hospital at the end, the convent of the Sisters of Saint Paul to the right.

We dutifully visited the convent and were repulsed by bromides spun at us softly like soggy doughnuts, pushing us out through the door. Their faces, like their yeasty thoughts, had been munched upon by whatever toothless god they worshipped. Green was their garden, a dark sea-green with no brightness in it, and narrow their gate.

We were as Christian as wandering people usually are, but our second attempt to inform ourselves on the religion of

French Guiana was as unfruitful as the first. We awakened at dawn, sweltering and nude beneath the mosquito net; I wiped the sweat from my eyes, blinked at the blue haze among the palms, and listened. Ruth sat up beside me. Near us was the sound of a carillon, a tinkling and a gonging, an arpeggio of ripe notes which seemed suddenly the only purity we knew in Cayenne.

Madame la Patronne sneered as we asked her, tucking our shirttails in, where we might find the author of this strange harmony.

"The anarchists," she said, drinking a pre-breakfast snort of orange pop. "See the Monseigneur of the Church of Saint Paul."

Carrying our Revere recorder, we hurried to the house of Monseigneur. The bell rang slowly in its depths. The door opened across the pale face of the black-gowned secretary. We were clean, we were burdened; we smiled, dreading that during the length of a smile might come the end of the exquisite music in the tower. I felt Christian as hell, half awake on an empty stomach. The slanting eyes of Ruth were moist.

"May we see Monseigneur? May we record this music from the tower?"

There was a cough in the corridor, and the door half closed, then opened slightly. The face, white and pocked as coral, said, "Monseigneur is occupied. The carillon is rung by anarchists, a whole family of them, and their cousins and their aunts. They are not Christians, you understand. They are a cross we must bear, because only they can ring the bells. They are like vermin on the ropes of them. The bells swing

[31   ]

and jerk them off their feet. The women's skirts fly up. The men dance on the ropes. But Monseigneur must employ them when babies are baptized and the parents buy the Masses."

The door began to close, across an ear, a temple, a phlegmy eye like a prune in custard. "They are evil, evil!" said two thirds of the mouth, "though the carillon this morning is for the baptism of a legitimate child; for the illegitimate, it has five notes only. . . . Go with God," he added as the door banged and from the tower came the sweet tolling of the sentimental anarchists.

This was discouraging to us, who had wished innocently enough to be informed on the status and effect of religion in French Guiana; we turned to the street with our burden of cameras and tape recorder.

"*Mon capitaine*," said a half-nude *libéré*. His shoulders were hunched forward around his beard because the woman's silk blouse he was wearing was too tight for him; it would have split if he had coughed.

"Hello, Coco." I lit a Pall Mall and gave him one.

Coco was an *exalté*, a lunatic, the King of Cayenne, who had, he said, executed a disloyal subject in France many years ago and retired here, incognito, almost. Thirty years of the *bagne* had bought him freedom now.

"Perhaps, *mon capitaine*, you would be interested to visit a group of my subjects who are more agreeable. I refer to the Sisters of Saint Joseph of Cluny. You will follow me. They have been advised."

Barefooted, he led us to the convent, I carrying the tape

recorder, of course. The convent wall was a face without features. The eyes of its windows were closed against the world. The mouth of its door was low, narrow, pursed. Coco knocked imperiously upon a panel, lifted his beard, and drew his shoulders back as far as the ragged blouse would permit.

The door to the convent was opened by a *garçon de famille*. A quiet laughter greeted us; the nuns were laughing here, and *La Mère* Javouhey, who had founded the order, smiled in bronze at us from a niche.

The doorman disappeared and we followed the fragrance of a garden through dim passages to a courtyard where the laughter was. The young Mother Superior met us, smiling, and led us from table to table where the Sisters were fashioning feathers into flowers with which they eked out their livelihood. They were of the order of Saint Joseph of Cluny, the obverse angels on the bad penny of French Guiana's past.

❧

La Mère Javouhey had brought the first of them from France in 1828, after the soldiers and the professional colonists had signally failed in the development of what is still, potentially, France's richest land overseas. This was after the renowned catastrophe of Kourou, when fifteen thousand wide-eyed settlers came out from France to what they had been told was El Dorado. They had come with their ice skates and high-heeled dancing slippers, and their imported musicians, who played terrible tunes as they, too, starved, or twisted with dysentery, or froze with fever. The fifteen thousand lay down around their silly opera house and died.

La Mère Javouhey, *le grand monsieur* as she was called, established the wilderness town of Mana, far enough up the river to be uninfluenced by the political corruption of Cayenne, and in seven years it flourished. The government gave a small subsidy to her — later to be withdrawn under pressure of Cayenne — but it was her own money that charitably bought thirty-two of the more miserable Negro slaves for forty-five thousand francs to build the town that had defeated Frenchmen and to teach men how to live on this savage land.

She was quite unorthodox; she spoiled her slaves and freed them in a few years' time; the escaped assassins from the penal settlement found sanctuary with her; the lepers were her friends. They, too, she announced to the horrified administrators, must have their private and free demesne, and so she built for them, a few miles farther in the jungle, the leper village of Acarouany. But all this required money as well as the good will of those who worked with her, and so she made money as logically and directly as any of her purposes was achieved. On what, she reasoned, would the men of French Guiana spend most money with least persuasion? On rum, of course! And why, she reasoned, should not women manufacture it? Why shouldn't the holy Sisters do so, if the monks of Europe found no sin in it at all?

So she founded and made prosper the distillery at Mana, nourished with the cane of her own plantations. The nuns pinned up their skirts and rolled up their sleeves and began the distillation of what is still the best rum in French Guiana. And they understand it as a tribute that it should be piously referred to as *Pee-pee Ma Sœur*.

The same zeal and good humor of Mother Javouhey are evident now among the Sisters of the order at Mana and St. Laurent and Cayenne. Godliness means good gaiety to them, and they tend in this spirit their convent, their paying and nonpaying schools of six hundred students, their orphanage, their distillery, their occasional theater, their commerce in feather flowers.

∽

The young Mother Superior took Ruth's hand and mine and led us from the cozy little chapel to the garden again. "There are only twenty-five of us here now, but we have to fight to keep things going. We get no money from the government. We are tolerated, *hors la loi*, beyond the law, beyond the pale."

In the courtyard we saw them swathed in black beneath a sun that was harsh and male and naked, twining feathers into exquisite flowers, patiently, to sell for the benefit of the needy they have with them always.

"Sister Ursula," said one old nun who had spent fifty-five years in the colony, "will you pass me the flamingo? That's a fine bright feather! I can't see the others very well today."

"Sister Jeanne, here's the egret for your fine centerpiece."

"Marie, my sister, can you spare me the Arras? The blue

[35]

and gold will go nicely with my pink Spatune. How could one believe that it builds its nest in mud?"

Complacently they talked together, like children talking in a secret cave of their very own. The world was far away.

The feathers of parrots, parakeets, ducks, *hoco*, the *urubu* vulture feathers as black as death, were piled in soft mountains before their small quick white hands. These feathers had been brought by Gallibee Indians, who loved the Sisters, or the Boni blacks, still pagan as their slave ancestors from the West African coast, or the penal men, the incorrigible derelicts whom they had befriended.

The plumes were washed and mounted in their flower pattern; never were they dyed. There were lights in them for the brightening of bored ladies far away, though Sister Ursula could have worn one better than most of them, as a crown upon her cowl, or Marie of the crooked nose could have worn one straight across her straight heart.

And old Sister Jeanne, who had been disciplined once when the grim flower of the vulture was discovered crumpled beneath her pillow — Sister Jeanne, whose friend the assassin had been executed shortly afterwards — looked up at us over her mountain of flowers, smiling. She ruffled the feathers sensuously against their grain, to make them straight.

"There is no help for us outside," she said, "no subsidy now; so we live on our wits, which are God's. We are island women," she said, and her voice was like wind in a ravine. The harsh male sun beat down on her. She pursed her old lips and blew a feather flower sunward. "There," she said, "go I, but for the grace of God."

❧

But for the grace of God we should already have been on our way up the Maroni River. Our provisions had not yet come — held up, it seemed, by a dock strike at Martinique — and we were not consoled by the Préfet Vignon, who had replaced Governor Peset when the territory was turned into a Department. Vignon was tall and fresh, new to colonial administration, eager to make a name in it with the changes which the colony required as it discarded its penal past. There would be showers for the schools, vegetables for the school-children grown by themselves, a huge Moorish hotel with patio, columns and swimming pool to attract tourists. Sure, and there would be roads; but not those wildcat bushways such as his predecessors had built.

The old-timers smiled at all this. They had seen every new administrator abandon the roads built by his predecessor. The glory of achievement must begin anew.

While sparkling new governors came out with magniloquent notions of cleaning things up, the Creoles in their pidgin thinking thought only of flinging the white men to the sharks. Even the *libérés* then had ideas of taking over.

There was one of them we loved, an old blind poet, who had spent half his life atoning for the murder of his publisher. Our Hercule was a reasonable man, except for the lacuna in which he had lost recollection of the act. Squatting on the sidewalk with his tattered back to the wall and his blind blue eyes turned to heaven, he would wave his cane wildly, to the danger of passers-by, and bellow ballads at them. He would get that miscreant of a publisher! He would stuff him like a goose with paper, with contracts, with unworthy advertising, with dunning letters to authors demanding that they finish writing their books on time. Then, by God, he would rip up those documents like the publisher's own skin! This was wistful, wishful thinking, of course; in actuality he had merely shot the monster.

We became fast friends. He even listened to my poetry and translated it into throbbing iambs, booming at the serious dark politicians on the hotel terrace. I never got my cut in his profit on this, but Ruth did. Whenever the take was drinkworthy he would do a bit of legerdemain with the coins until they came out to exactly thirty francs, enough for two raw taffias and a generous tip, and gallantly ask Ruth to join him in a short one, apologizing to me for circumstances which could not include me too. Then the bearded old ragamuffin would limp away on the arm of Ruth, whom he loved, to the corner pub. Hah, but he was a gay blade still, he would be thinking, as he turned to wink a blind baby-blue eye at me.

The only catch I saw in this benign cuckoldry was that the administration might get to know that I had inspired some of Hercule's songs, and confuse them with his own ringing philippics, which he hurled at the heads of the government. These had been tolerated by the police because they were really noble verse; but if they were to be attributed to me, though I should have been proud to be thought the author of them, I saw that our expedition upriver would be farther away than even now. Crime and punishment in Cayenne were too much matter of course for my liking, I thought, as I listened gingerly to Hercule howling, "When I and my miserables shall rise up and smite thee . . ."

"There's Ullmo," said Ruth, tucking her hot shirt into her slacks again. The oldest and haughtiest car of Cayenne chugged past us. Barely above its front window ledge we could see the clenched hands on the steering wheel and the face on the great mustaches of little Colonel Ullmo, once condemned to fifteen years of Devil's Island for treason. But it was not strictly treason, he explained in the mass of manuscript which he hoped we might publish for him in our just United States. He had been in love and so had become ambitious, and when a Foreign Power had rejected his offer to sell military secrets he neatly turned his treason like a stocking inside out and blackmailed the French Ministry of War with the threat of selling its secrets to the Foreign Power.

With cloak and dagger of the best Sabatini, Colonel Benjamin Ullmo slunk through the Gorges of Ollioules to his moonlit rendezvous with the French officials, flogging his courage for that *belle Hélène*, who watched his shadow until it was drowned in the flame of guns. She did not see him for twenty years, until he, like Dreyfus, was freed and returned to France. Unlike Dreyfus, he was so dispirited by France's indifference to him, who once had filled pages of its newspapers, that only once did he see the aged *belle Hélène* who had faithfully written him all these years. Then he returned to the Guiana of his penance, and took a job as accountant in a dark corner of a warehouse, rejecting society as it had rejected him.

∾

The seas around Cayenne were infested with sharks, but the shark stories of the place, like tales of teeming serpents in the jungle, were founded mostly on hearsay, and seemed to be based on two incidents only, one of a child which had its ankle nipped and one of a dog which forfeited an ear.

We swam merrily from the beach of Dr. Riberas, for the water was emollient beneath that hot sun, the sharks ignored us, and our host was a merry one. The salt soaked into us — good for you in the tropics, said the experts — and we gentled its way out again with cocktails that had been swung in coconuts. Even itinerant horses liked Dr. Riberas's cocktail parties; there was one addict with glanders and curly ears, who joined us regularly on the terrace, twostepping daintily from one table to another where there were sandwiches, helping himself to them, and breathing down our necks.

Dr. Riberas cultivated such odd pets! He had a wealth of mosquitoes on his estate — of which some were remarkable, he explained, in that they had no sting and as if in compensation flaunted a brightly colored, fanlike tail. But that wasn't all, he would say, as he took a second cocktail away from the horse; the utility of these beasts was that their larvae ate the larvae of the maleficent mosquitoes.

∾

The dances and entertainment of the Cayennese were mostly for the blacks, with the yellow Chinese and the gold *métisses*, the half-castes, sharing the fun.

There was the Skyscraper Ball, two stories up, on the outskirts of town, where the native *béguine* went larruping around a frayed veranda, and the Orientals and the Africans, smoking cigarettes as they danced, or balancing glasses of beer behind their partners' backs, made a sort of counterpoint to the rhythm of the jungly earth beneath, the fierce earth of which you were always conscious, the earth of growth and decay.

There were balls at the Town Hall — starchy, with speeches, with black folk democratically dancing with whites they held at arm's length, while the *hoi polloi* jammed around the doorway to listen to that strident band.

The Chinese, more Francophile than most French, held their serious jamborees among the tables of those playing dominoes or mah-jongg. It was their Benevolent Association, alone in Cayenne, which had declared holidays when General Leclerc, far away, had propelled us to victories.

There was a little ball on a promontory by the sea, with a gas lantern and a *libéré* who used an accordion, and four or five couples who staggered back and forth in the open kiosk, drinking crème de menthe, wandering to the rocks for quick goats' caresses, returning thin of lip and tight of eye to pirouette again.

And there was the ball of the *surveillants*, a sinister affair which you probably visited only once. The *surveillants*, with rare exceptions, were not men you would choose to grace your hearth. The question was moot as to whether the *surveillants* were brutalized by their association with inveterate thieves and murderers, or the other way around.

Like husbands and wives, these two classes, supposedly contrary, grew to resemble one another, and their faces were odd and shapeless. Ruth and I were invited to their ball one night, and promised a gift which, we were assured, would be useful to us for our lectures in America. We accepted.

"It is probably the last instrument of its kind," said our host, "now that the *bagne*, the penitentiary, is finished here. Ha! Ha!" he said. "It was the secret weapon of the *bagnard!*"

Even in the clean air outside the ball of the *surveillants*, as we walked slowly toward the only lighted building in the district, we felt uncomfortable about the music which came from it, French jazz on tunes we could recognize but which came pumping, spurting, blurbling out at us like unchecked blood. The jazz of forced convict labor, as we knew. Electricity elsewhere had been turned off at 10:10, but the gaiety of the *surveillants* must be legally illuminated. Like darkness which hides physical movement, this dazzling blaze without shadow concealed the thoughts, the memories, the lust of men dancing dazzled within it.

The making of pain was their trade and they were nourished by their product. The music of their convict band tonight was a sort of fermented derivative of pain. You could hear them thinking: "Play, you bastards! Be gay, you bastards, or we'll flog your livers loose!"

We sat at a little table with them, drinking rum punches to keep our own livers from turning over. The table was so small that our faces were in each other's way, and the sweating face of one of their wives was sometimes so close to me that it was a little out of focus, as in dancing.

I was remarking to myself that these women were even more sinister than their husbands when I saw the wry, set grin with which Ruth listens to conversations which bore or revolt her. The *surveillant* beside her was laughing like mad and scratching down the collar of his open khaki shirt.

"*Quel drôle de type!*" he said. "But the captain hasn't heard it! Landed *wham* on his head!" He leaned out of focus toward me but just within saliva range. "He was an acrobat, *mon capitaine*, one of our pupils. But yes, I must explain to you; he was a *bagnard*, a *condamné* — Hell! one of the criminals here! He was so cocky that he laughed at our prisons and showed us how he could climb any wall with his fingers and toes. He would climb up a tree like a monkey when we wanted coconuts, and then, by God, he would climb down head-foremost! You seize the point? Head-foremost he would come down!"

The wife of this *surveillant* roared with laughter on my shoulder, and I could see Ruth wondering how I felt.

"But up he went this morning and down he came, *wham!*" said the *surveillant*. "He had flung down the nuts to us, then turned himself around, and headfirst he had started to descend the tree. He was cocky, all right. He was still smiling as his ugly face came down toward us, until Ferenc over there

[43]

called out to him. A joke, you comprehend. Ferenc had read one of the letters from his mistress in France. She was a person named Thérèse. So Ferenc said, 'Thérèse is here waiting for you, dear!' And down he came, *wham!* Dead, you comprehend? Really I shouldn't laugh, because I, personally, am going to miss him."

This was too much for the *surveillant's* wife, who got up and held her convulsed belly with ten dirty fingernails and rocked with the comedy of it all. She picked up her baby, which was asleep asprawl on a bench beside her, and nuzzled its ear as though to share the story.

Worse than the *surveillants*, I thought, and worse than their glutinous wives, was the presence of these babies at the ball, for their faces too had the distrustful squinting eyes and the surly mouths of their parents.

"I'll bet they suckle blood," said Ruth in English rapidly as the mother *surveillante* bared a thing like a breast and screwed the baby's mouth to the end of it. Only the convict who played the violin paid it any attention. He looked hungry, like De Maupassant's beggar in the train, who went mad with greed before such a performance.

"Ha, ha!" I said jovially. "Your babies here stay out late and learn life early, *n'est-ce pas?*" I nodded, grinning my falsest grin. The drink, I was thinking, had a peculiar flavor of milk.

Ruth shuddered as we danced toward the windows. "This whole business," she said, "is so grim because it is so matter of fact!"

[44]

"They eat agony," said I, as an aphorism.

The music stopped and the conversation also, while everyone waited to see who was going to change partners with whom. As we walked back to our table we could hear the flying cockroaches being ground up in the electric fans.

Our host, the *surveillant* with gray gruel-colored eyes, was offering his promised gift to us, a capsule of highly polished aluminum about three inches long, smoothly pointed at both ends and joined in the middle by intermeshing threads.

"You can see," said our tutor, with one eyebrow raised far up, "that there is space inside for at least ten thousand-franc notes, folded small. It is a contrivance, *monsieur*, which fits readily into an orifice of the human form. It is called the 'plan.' It is the bank of the criminals who have no other place of security for their treasures, surrounded as they are by the world's most expert thieves. Freedom may be locked in this capsule if one can escape with it, but if we catch him — ha! ha! it is the drollest — you would not say that we were ungenerous with the castor oil!"

This was the night life of Cayenne.

❧

The young Préfet Vignon leaned back in the cool somber room of the "Palace," brushed cigarette ashes from his shiny white jacket, and said with a smile, "The roads shall be completed. There will be showers in the schools, and the children will eat vegetables which they must learn to grow themselves."

We spoke of the market, while the shadow of a convict gardener passed back and forth across the windows. Eggs were twenty-five francs, or the same in cents, apiece. Celery, an eighth of an inch thick, was five francs for three sprigs. Onions were no bigger than shallots and cost five francs per wisp. We would still be puzzled, seven months later when we left French Guiana, as to how the people lived at all, for gardening was beneath them. They had seen the white convicts beaten to the earth and grubbing with bleeding nails to make vegetables grow. And vegetables grew mightily in the fertile soil of French Guiana, with a mixture of sweat and tears, a cruel laboring which the Creoles would not emulate though they starved with their pride.

We reminded the *préfet* that the rainy season would be upon us in several months, and that our food from the good sponsors in America, Borden's and Dorset, must come soon to be of use to us. We should have to leave without it otherwise, without stocks at all, we said to the *préfet*, since Cayenne had nothing to furnish us. Then, for the first time, our *préfet* showed that he had, after all, the makings of a colonial administrator. He yawned, flapped a hand on our pile of credentials, glanced at their signatures, didn't bother to read them, and passed them to me with a sigh, as who should say, "Stout fellow! You see? All you have to do is leave!"

The busy man stood obviously up, in dismissal of us.

"But look," I said, "don't you care to read? . . . Doesn't it interest you that . . ." The letters which the French ministers in France had written about our respectability had impressed me, and their interest in our examining their wilderness had made me hopeful of some similar enthusiasm here. But no; the impression growing on us was that we were interlopers, suspect, maybe spies, and that the local administration would be happy to see the sterns of our canoes.

❧

That next Tuesday was an exciting day, what with the bad butterflies swarming. The bad butterflies gave us the itch as swarms of them flew over Cayenne, dropping the barbed fuzz of their wings into our every pore. But we scarcely noticed it. Our food from Borden's had arrived — pure coffee, powdered milk, Hemo, powdered lemon juice, enough to supplement the native diet we should have to live on upriver. And beside the Borden's boat in the harbor lay a cocky contrived sort of vessel which would take us, deck passage, to St. Laurent. It was a two-masted Brazilian affair of rotted wood.

St. Laurent was on the Maroni River, the frontier between French and Dutch Guiana, our base for the long journey upriver by canoe to the mountains.

And these were terribly far away, we thought that afternoon as we packed our baggage stiffly, keeping a balance with the dysentery which beset us, and walking sedately, mincing, to the hospital for our shots of emetine and opium. Dysentery is too long a word to be chalked on public walls, but it is meaner than many another.

It was complicated that hot Tuesday afternoon by the heads in the hospital cupboard, which we must photograph even though our boat would be leaving within the hour. The heads had been mummified some fifty years ago when the guillotining of them was still more sport than therapy, and as they were balanced by the intern's thumb up their gullets and brought from shadow into sunlight we filmed the relics of those old murderers compassionately — until we were swarmed upon by current murderers, sent by the Prefecture to see that our baggage should be transported and we conducted to the Brazilian boat.

The anarchist sexton rang a bell for an illegitimate birth, or it may have been for us. The butterflies doused us with their itching plumes; and with all our goods we hurried cautiously to that contrivance which the Brazilians called a boat.

Up the seas we went, and down into them — banging our bottom, tossing the sails, racing and easing the auxiliary motor, flinging baggage and passengers along the deck. When you put a cigarette to your mouth you had to clamp your teeth behind it lest it plunge down your throat, hand and all. All but four of us on deck were deck passengers, and those four were Creole ladies of means whose pre-emption of the two cabins we decided not to dispute. The hold was no better. A hundred natives lay crisscrossed in it, each with his chamber pot beside him, and they and the chamber pots pitched with the boat.

Ruth and I set up our camp cots on the deck in a space near the middle, where the tossing was not so bad and the air fresh though moist. Proud as I was to feel that no reasonable luxury had been neglected on our expedition, we had not brought chamber pots, and there were of course no other facilities aboard for a shy young couple gallivanting with dysentery on a honeymoon. The seas came up and walloped you when you sat on the deck rail in broad daylight with dozens of speculative eyes upon you. It was fine training in self-denial, gymnastics, and nonchalance.

As the wind howled at the ancient boat, and the great billows juggled us, we lay flat on our bellies clutching the edges of our cots, and Ruth would say, "Whee!" and I would say, "Whoo!" as the cots half lifted clear of the deck, remained suspended in midair, and banged down again. There were no stars that Wednesday night, nor could we have seen them anyway as, side by side, synchronized, face to the deck, we were fascinated by this miracle of levitation.

I was curious about Ruth, who had done nothing of this sort before and had ahead of her a six months' journey by canoe into quite unknown and hostile lands; but even this she loved, and I was wakeful with the great pleasantness of having her there.

Between bumps I mentioned to her that somewhere among the knots of deck passengers I had seen Mohammed, our Arab convict-cook. Ruth declined comment as the great murderer himself, leering with yellow teeth through a dark stubble beard, stooped close to us and yelled, "Cargo of pigs!

[49   ]

Cargo of pigs down there! We'll see some fun in the morning! Pigs and Creole bastards!"

Definitely we were not taking to Mohammed as one should to a retainer with whom one has to spend six months in the jungle.

"Look here, Mohammed," I said, turning on my back and looking up into his teeth, "you are going to work hard, you understand? You are going to carry baggage. You are not going to drink even native wines. I'm responsible for you, and if you try to escape I am going to shoot you. Can you cook?"

He leered at me as though this might be a joke between us.

"Like this, like that. But just wait for morning. I'll have fun with that cargo of pigs who think a murderer isn't good enough for them!"

I rolled over when he was gone again, just as the boat was rising to a swell, and nearly broke a tooth kissing Ruth's knuckle good-night.

When I turned my flashlight on my wrist watch it said half-past three, and the boat was lying quietly beside the shadow that was Royale Island. Ruth wakened. We sat up, unwrinkled the shirts in our pants, took a drink from the canteen, and looked down through the rail at the stone dock where several convicts in striped garments were receiving their provisions from the boat. The searchlight threw their shadows far behind them, twisting up the cliff. One shadow contracted quickly as its owner approached the boat.

"*Le capitaine Davis?*" the grave shadow asked beside me. "*Moi-même.*"

It was Duluc, condemned for life, keeper of the lighthouse on Royale Island, who had befriended us when we wandered in confusion among the grim relics of Royale on our previous trips, and who curiously felt indebted to us. He slung from his shoulders a great stalk of bananas and a knot of young coconuts.

"Take them!" he whispered, clutching my shoulders with the lean sensitive hands that had once closed the windpipe of a colleague. "Quick, Captain! These are from Mann and me. We'll remember you in the cells."

Ruth touched those two devices of murder on my shoulders and they loosened as if sprung. "Bless you, Pierre," she said.

"Bless you and get out of here fast," I said, pushing a chest like an anvil. "They'll miss you. Quick!"

Over the rail he went and down the side of the ship like a vampire. I was pleased with having secretly slipped my flask into the pocket of that old professional, until Ruth said, "Nice flask too," and from the dock came Duluc's voice, roaring, "Eh! *Merci!*" The pink spot of him found its shadow again, and it stretched quickly across the dock and bent up the cliffs, drawing the caught body of the man to the greater shadow of his lost world.

❧

We were wakened by a roar and a pounding and then the

terrific impact of something crashing into our cots. We scrambled up from the deck and narrowly missed the second charge of a five-hundred-pound cartridge of carbon dioxide which had broken loose from its moorings and gone berserk with the pitching of the boat. It poised in the center of a well-cleared deck. The passengers were on the rails or in the rigging. The tube teetered, rocked with the sea, paused, aimed, came roaring toward us again, crashing against the iron feet of our Komfort Kots. We pounced on the cots and wedged the thing between them, while the passengers cheered, and the crew put a bridle on it.

It was only then that we and the passengers in the rigging noticed that the halyards of the ship, the cords from rail to mast-tip, had something odd about them. And when the hatches were flung back and the steerage folk came forth, furious, we saw clearly that against the pearly sky of dawn were strung a couple of dozen chamber pots, evenly spaced like pennants along the halyards.

"Soup, *madame*?" said Mohammed sweetly, offering us a steaming bowl.

Opposite each other on the Maroni River lay the towns of Albina and St. Laurent, respectively Dutch and French. Both were flat and sprawling, tiny places. On the Dutch side the houses were sanitary and sparkling white, arranged precisely; on the French side there was a casual congeries of winding, tree-shaded dusty roads, dotted irregularly with moderately modern buildings and patioed antiques such as the Dutch would never tolerate. The French side was colorful, picturesque; the Dutch was functional. There was the meagerest food for even the rich in St. Laurent, and not even a contraband cigarette; whereas the shops of Albina were amply laden with Dutch and American treasures to lead us down garden paths and through back entrances to seek and slaver over our illegal purchases. Dutch Guiana, like British Guiana to the west, was explored and exploited and profitable; French Guiana still buckled at the knees beneath the burden of her old penal administration; she was geographically *demi-vierge*, with most of her rich interior still unknown.

Seated on the balcony of our government apartment in St. Laurent, our feet on the rail, our knees askirted with maps which were distinctive by their empty spaces, marked *Region Inexplorée*, I realized how hard it would be for even a publicity expert to make our expedition seem re- markable, though it might turn out to be, for unexplored spots of jungle were within twenty miles of us now. It could be justly said that no white man had ever put his foot there — and there. And even if we should reach the Tumuc-Humac Mountains, our El Dorado — what was such a journey, after all, but a bit of sport through the rapids and fine scenery and a mere three hundred miles? It was the distance from New York to Boston when you took the country roads.

The heat rolled up from the street and over our balcony. It wasn't insupportable, but it was uncheering. How could I explain to anyone, I wondered, that most true explorers never called themselves this? They were geographers or anthropologists or bug hunters, say; "explorer" was an untidy term with vagueness around the edges. But there were many like me who had to accept it, because of wanderings into little-known or unknown places, with a smattering of ethnology, an awareness of directions, an unusual appetite for fresh air and, above all, an insatiable curiosity to look around corners and over ridges and horizons and through the chinks in curtained windows.

This is what we should be doing, if we could find paddlers willing to undertake our little journey; but the few we met held the flattering view (1) that our destination was a terribly long way off, (2) that it was dangerous, (3) that whatever was in that area was unhealthy to know about.

Mohammed had just brought us a rum punch in glasses decorated with the fine Algerian whorls and arabesques which were his thumbprints, when a booming and a puffing sounded from the steps below, and up came Gougis, one of the two most prosperous merchants of St. Laurent.

"I shall have Boni paddlers for you in a fortnight," said he, tossing half his drink without a swallow straight into his throat and down.

"Not Boschs?" These were cousins of the Bonis on the Dutch side of the river, more tractable because they were still more savage.

He ignored that. He had no room in his mouth to answer it with the mouthful of words already there. There was no stopping him. Ruth asked about his wife and he kept on constantly, jumping up to lean over the balcony and shake the sweat from his broad forehead, yelling an order to Mohammed, and continuing with his opinion of what should be done about French Guiana. For the first time we heard not only a statement of positive belief that the country could be recuperated, but positive programs, a dozen of them, constructive even though they were fantastic, of what should be done, and fast.

"For example," he said. His example matched his girth — "This, for example," he said with a lunge toward us, swinging from his pocket a nugget of solid gold that was about seven inches long by two inches thick.

Ruth took it from him. It was rich orange gold. "So that's the *Pépite* of Fanfan?"

Gougis took it back quickly, as though she might make away with it, his seven pounds of treasure. He told us then the curious story of Fanfan, a Creole prospector, who dreamed one night of a woman whose face he could not see. There was only a voice where the face should be, and it told him to go to a certain spot on the Petit-Inini River, which he recognized as a site which had been worked and abandoned a century ago. The woman held the nugget out to him, and her voice told him he should find it there.

But Fanfan ignored her. How could he find at least three men to help him follow a dream to a mining prospect that was known to be fruitless? But he had the dream again — the woman was angry now — and finally in terror of her he persuaded three friends to accompany him, up the Maroni and into the far branch of it called Petit-Inini, and down a creek of that until they came to the ruins of the ancient camp. There they panned the alluvial sands and dredged them by hand.

There was nothing, not a grain of gold, and Fanfan's companions were furious with him and threatened to leave him the morning after they ran out of provisions. But that night in the dreams of each of them the headless woman appeared, standing before a tree which in each dream was different, but the voice which came from the space where her mouth should be told each man what she thought of him in the same terms she used to the three others.

When in the morning they had brewed a little coffee from yesterday's grounds, and discussed the dreams of the night before, they went trembling to their respective trees, which they easily recognized. Then they spread vines diagonally from corner to corner of the square they formed, and where the vines crossed in the center they dug.

When they told the story later they agreed that at first each had touched something like a face beneath the mud; they could feel the features of it, but it seemed to slip from the fingers of Fanfan's partners. Fanfan then reached it, closed his hand upon it, and felt it stiffen as in death. When he drew it up it was the great gold nugget, "*la Grande Pépite.*"

Gougis stroked his nugget as though it were the face of a woman he loved.

❧

The Bonis were coming, Gougis said, but there was no hurrying them, though the rains were coming, too. Meanwhile at the *cercle*, the central club of St. Laurent, we met the notables of the town and most of their families, down to their barest babes, who were trundled in perambulators up the stairs and rocked with one hand while m'ma played bridge or drank rum punches with the other.

The new *sous-préfet* and his wife were usually here, playing bridge in rare good humor; and Roger Raoust, lean and drawn with too many years of successful gold mining; and Maurice Demougeot, who was turning to account the precious Guiana woods; and Monsieur Cuisinier, whose gentle practice as Chief of Customs made him beloved by all but the smugglers, to whom his very lisp was fearsome.

And for a time there was also Michel, the barman, a trusty prisoner who had murdered very little, said he, and very long ago. Michel was sleek, good-looking in the vulpine way we had noticed in his colleagues before, and immaculately dressed in white. He would serve you a drink respectfully, with a bow, as if it were no less than a vintage poison, blended by a master brewer. He pushed perambulators up and down the bar when their passengers got restless, smiling down at them with the love of a man who hadn't seen young veal in quite a time. He stirred Martinis with a polished ivory pestle, artfully made to resemble a human bone, he had said, until the new doctor discovered that it *was* a human bone.

Everybody loved Michel, and he made a fortune in tips, for we all knew about his mother, buried by mistake in

Potter's Field, whose bones would be disinterred, thanks to our largesse, and reburied decently by the little white church where she had caroled as a child. There were cads among us who spoke wonderingly of the Martini mixing rod, but there were many others of the notables who sent petitions to the administration demanding that Michel be pardoned.

It was a certainty that he would be. We would slap him on the back and say, "Good old Michel, practically a free man, eh?" and he would say, "Yes," with the gravity of a good citizen.

Michel aroused our displeasure but once, on that evening when he did not show up for work. And thereafter he never turned up for work again. He had *évadé*, he had "done *La Belle*" — he had escaped in a little boat which he had deftly made from a backhouse which he also had made and so arranged that with a dozen screws and a little caulking it could be quickly and silently converted into a seaworthy craft.

Our disappointment in Michel was still tempered with a certain pride in him when he wote the *cercle* from Venezuela, enclosing a valuable antique hatpin belonging to Madame Rousseau, with a note to the effect that he felt honor-bound to return this, as he wouldn't be wheeling perambulators any more.

We went to the market hopefully each morning, for one day there might be food in it, and we frequented the grassy banks of the Maroni where the canoes came in from upriver, bringing naked black Bonis and secret cargoes of gold to smuggle through the Chinese village which lay decaying along the shore. The canoes took on merchandise for the Boni villages, only a quarter of the way we must go, but they wouldn't take us even that far.

So we would return to town past the fairy-tale dilapidation called a "wood-turning house" by the three *libérés* who owned it, and when we could find ice and taffia, and fruit juices, our gay old cutthroats would put a handspun wooden cocktail shaker on the lathe and spin it until the froth bubbled through the seams; or we would visit the penitentiary with a warden — who shall be nameless here, because we saw a telegram from France stating that Hassoldt Davis should not be permitted to film this Camp de la Transportation, somewhat of a blow to us who had hoped truthfully to show that conditions in the penal settlement were less gruesome than imagined.

Again, as in Cayenne, our vitals were gnawed with wondering what we had done wrong to incur the displeasure of the bureaucrats, considering that four ministries had officially wished us well on our enterprise. But we went none the less to the famous Camp de la Transportation and, with permission of the *sous-préfet*, filmed a Mass in the tiny chapel, dramatic in that the windows of the chapel were closely barred and an armed guard kept an eye on those lean men in prison stripes as they genuflected or told their beads. Something of them, perhaps, might escape to God. And we returned with them to their cells, which were immaculate small whitewashed cubicles, where a strip of canvas was stretched taut for a bed and the walls were usually covered with cheap magazine cheese-cake; no man here had known a woman in many years. One cell had a ship model in it, carved of turtle shell, and one had a cat which shared its owner's scanty meals, and one had a sign hung on its heavy door: *La marmite de la cuisine vous attends. Vous êtes Chocolat!* This meant that his turn had come to serve as waiter in that corridor.

The Director of Prisons was an old man whose gentleness deceived us, and we sympathized with him for having reached the years when he must lose his job. "But what can I do?" he asked, spreading white fat hands before us. "This is all I know." It was when we asked him about one or another convict who had appealed to us as servants that we saw shadows behind his adipose sweetness and light. "Ah, that one," he would say, "he committed a *bêtise*. Stubborn too. For a while we had to tickle him from time to time. You know, coax him. He was such a tease!"

While waiting for the Director to meet and guide us through the prison, an antiseptic tour, I had my hair cut by an inmate who was as eager as most of them to tell me the story of his innocence and ask me to intercede.

"It was no more than you would have done, *monsieur*, if you had been a good husband and a professional barber." Snip-snip went his shears. I felt his hot breath down my neck as he exploded, "Caught the bastard *in flagrante delictu*, as we say, with my old woman, though he didn't know I was near. Guy had the nerve to ask me for a haircut next day. Nobody

THE DAMNED

but him and me in the shop, you see. Sometimes I wish I had a witness to prove it wasn't murder." Snip-snip went the shears by my ears. "So first I clopped him on the head with the Guyen's Cream Lotion, just to make him sleepy, see? Then I gave him a harelip with the shears, then I pulled his top eyelids out and snipped half-moons in them, then I notched his ears and made an ornament of his ugly nose." Snip-snip went the shears. "Then I hove him into the street as you would have done, *monsieur*, or any decent man, but how could I know that the bastard was a bleeder? The *flics* jumped me just as I was applying the alum to save his bloody life!"

From the courtyard I heard the whistling of Ruth, who had been worried about my operation, and the voice of the director.

೭•๑

Misdirection is a great art among magicians, but it was out of practice here. Our guides might have said, "Pick a card" for "pick a cell," and there would be a clatter in the prison block to the left of us, so we picked the forced card, the cell, which was a fine example of penal humanity. The whole show was a little naïve, for we had no slightest doubt by now that the so-called Devil's Island colony had been grossly libeled in the Sunday supplements, that horror and torture were no worse here than in the jails of Cambridge, Massachusetts, after the sophomores, including me, had dropped — for some reason which escapes me now — water-filled

[61   ]

balloons or whatnot on the heads of passing policemen.

We sought no evil here. We hoped only to prove by personal inspection and the cold eyewitness of film that the romantic legend of Devil's Island was done with, and that French Guiana could finally plant its own hot fertile feet into the same earth as Dutch and British Guiana and, perhaps, flourish equally. The sure, the encouraging thing was that the pathetic weeds of convicts were being transplanted to France as rapidly as the government and the Salvation Army could manage it, leaving the old good earth free for the new venture of settling displaced persons from Europe.

There was an embarrassing few minutes during our tour of the camp when we passed through the grassy lane of the solitary confinement cells. The grass grew nicely here; there were few feet to tread on it. There was quiet in the cells, not a cheep from them, and I thought of the men asleep in them, or holding their breaths to hear our footsteps across the soft grasses, or shaking with such terror as was impotent to cry out, or mad and mute and sufficient to themselves in their dark wombs, or quite possibly forgotten and dead.

If a convict, working on the roads or the gardens or in private employ, were to be absent from camp more than twelve hours beyond the hour when his return was due, he was considered an *évadé*, and sentenced to from six months to a year of solitary confinement for attempted escape. This was the system originated by those who had thought to found a colony by penal labor. The independent and assured type of convict with the courage and imagination to attempt escape, the energetic convict, was confined uselessly for six months to a year, without benefit either to the colony or himself, while his complacent weaker colleagues diddled along the roads. It was no wonder that French Guiana lagged far behind its neighbors to the west.

Guided by the director, by the Chief of Camp, and by the head guardian, Ruth and I went through the terrible aisle of disciplinary cells. Our guides cluck-clucked at the shame of it all; they spoke sadly to each other, prefacing their phrases for us alone, off the record, with *"Vraiment!* But really! . . . "

There was, meanwhile, a hunchbacked convict who carried the cameras we were forbidden to use and whose hump the director kept slyly stroking for good luck. And he whispered, "Bureau, the fat, lived for a year in there, in the darkness. We used to push lizards and frogs through the grid of his door. He kept alive by eating them — raw, of course. Christ, the vampires were terrible here! When Bureau came out with scarcely enough skin to clothe his skeleton, he told us of how he managed to live in spite of them."

He spoke to Ruth. "May I have a private word with the captain, please?"

We walked slowly behind the others. "The vampires settle on your feet," he said, "and you don't feel them. They don't suck much blood, but the wound doesn't heal when they leave you, so Bureau told the guardian he had dysentery and put the bed pan under his feet at night. In the morning it

would have from a pint to a quart of blood in it, and Bureau
drank it for breakfast."

"Geraniums," said Ruth.

"What? What?" said the director.

"Geraniums." Ruth marched trimly ahead of us, pointing
with a switch at one weed and another, frowning. "Waste!
Waste!" she added blithely.

ﾟ◎∾๏

We were shown the advantages of life in prison. The
kitchen had a fine green soup, tasty too, and light and fluffy
unpolished rice, and twice as much corned beef per daily
ration as the free civilian was permitted to buy. We tried
this twice. And in the dusty commissary the occasional freed
convict would be equipped with straw hat, shirt, pants, and
leather-soled shoes, made of beautiful leather too, and too
big for us.

Our little hunchbacked convict guide came seething forward. *"Pardon, monsieur le directeur!"* he cried. The *directeur* kept on talking of the fish on Fridays which the prisoners
enjoyed, ignoring the man and yet helpless to send him away
before us.

"Monsieur le directeur," he said, "will you stop a moment
that the American can see this place of the guillotine? After
all, *monsieur le directeur*, it is I who last made it to function,
no?"

Between the rows of cells where we were standing were
five stone pedestals upon which the guillotine was last erected

in the 1930's. The grass and Ruth's weird geraniums leaned over them now. "This was the athenaeum, the coliseum," said our guide, striding quickly from one pedestal to another, holding out his hand, palm up, for approval. "It was here I stood" — and he indicated the air ten feet above him — "and through those air vents above the doors of the cells the eyes of everyone were looking here, right here. They hung by their fingers to the air vent with their bare feet spraddled on the walls. I could see their eyes when the sun was right. I would not have you think they were looking at me. They were watching the head of my client. Every one of them was watching for the slice of the blade."

Our officials were uncomfortable. We were, too, imagining the day's end when we should be gone and our wide-eyed, outspoken little fellow would have his accounting to make in the stark stone jury room we had seen in an isolated place.

He wouldn't be quieted. "There, right there," he shouted, pointing to a whitewashed door like any other. "We have a specimen there. Is it not true, *monsieur le directeur*, that Abdullah, the murderer from Algiers, will be the last to be guillotined?"

"Would you like to see him?" The Chief of Camp turned to us, closed his eyes, puckered them. "He has been there eight months, awaiting execution. He will not be executed, since the new regime. He will be pardoned like most of these other *misérables*. We tell him so, but we have no papers to prove it, nor to remove him from the solitary cell. He has tried to kill himself by jabbing pins toward his heart. They don't quite reach, so he has pounded others in on top of the first, trying to hit the head of it, but he has no luck, so we pull them out occasionally."

"He'll make a fine houseboy, when he's freed," said the director. "ABDULLAH!" he shouted. Then he turned to Ruth. "You would like to see him, I presume?"

We said no, but the guardian was already at the mahogany door, swinging a key around his finger. In the darkness beyond the door as it swung open stood the tall, straight, lean figure of an Arab, dressed immaculately in white shorts and shirt. He moved forward two paces and slipped his heels together. He stood straight and addressed us so quietly that I couldn't fully understand him. It was terrible to look at him, who would be closed in darkness again when the door again was closed.

He had been humbled to a subjection which made my muscles twitch, remembering a time in my teens when I, a reporter, had been swept into jail with the mob whose rioting I had been quite unsympathetically reporting. My tongue slid to the place where a tooth had been beaten out by the police while two of them held me against a wall. And now I went blind for a moment with the darkness of the cell where I squirmed for three days among the twelve others who fought blindly for the comfortable corners. And I remembered my shameful humility when I was interrogated at last by the police with raw, pink, visible faces; terrible pink engines they were, cruelly destructive, but they were visible and moved in set directions, and I was shamefully grateful to them, while the blood still dripped down my chin, for not being any longer the shadows of fellow convicts in the cell who had punished me all that while, convolved and thrusting at me in my corner. I remembered how in sudden daylight the rancor died in me, and the pride, and I spoke as if my lips were just on the level of the sea which in a moment might again submerge them.

Everyone *tchk-tchked* at Abdullah's plea that his case be reviewed, and he was officially assured that it wouldn't be long now; his freedom, not his death, was imminent. He went back quietly into his cell, probably wondering if he had two pins left among his treasures which might match, point to head, in the direction of his heart.

"It is true, he will be freed," said the director as we followed within the sharp cool shadow cast by the cells. "But in his case it's absurd. His second and third murder took place here in the colony, after he had been paroled to work as houseboy for one of the *surveillants*. He fell in love with a young Creole widow, who grew tired of him, so he slashed her and the baby in her arms with a razor as she came out of the gate one day."

The striped hysteric who was opening sesames for us halted before a double door with two padlocks, and pointed at it. The director shrugged. The Chief of Camp found two fat keys and spread the doors like wings to reveal the fearsome breast of darkness within, and the implements against it. This was the house of the guillotines; there were three of them, glittering royally with golden hinges which were heavy brass. The wooden standards stood upright like undertakers, surrounded by coffins in which the finer mechanisms were stored. There was a clean click as each oiled latch was opened. We looked at the great blades, greased and comfortable in dirty satin, tapered for quick diagonal slicing like a fish's ventral fin. There was a big basket, brightly polished, lined with tin, to catch the body, and a small one to catch the severed head.

I tried to be objective about these accessories to reciprocal murder, to smile or frown understandingly, but it was difficult. I kept seeing the five stones of the courtyard and the lean monument upon them, and the eyes of the condemned watching through the narrow transoms.

But in the interest of documentation I asked our hunch-backed executioner about his trade, once the door was closed and we were heading for the gate. Instead of responding, he told me a tale of murder.

ᏋᏇᎧ

Once upon a time, and not very long ago, there was a little lighthouse, and it was called in French Enfant Perdu, Lost Child. It stood far out to sea in a stretch of violent water, about halfway between Cayenne and Devil's Island.

Among the murderers were certain incorrigibles, and they were sent to the lighthouse to tend it and be tended by it in a manner as certain as the guillotine. They were always sent in pairs, for that way they died more quickly, and it is of such a pair that this tale tells.

[68   ]

They had been friends in that sinister twilight district of Marseilles, called the Vieux Port, which none but the gendarmes visited, and they in bands of four. Their troubles had separated them for a while, but the kinship of murder brought them together again in the same bleak house at Cayenne. And when they were deposited by the authorities on the lighthouse island called Enfant Perdu it was no time at all before the Lost Child had made them enemies.

Confined together by the waste of space and sea around them, with only themselves to depend upon for any diversion, they sat on the rocks at night and talked beneath the revolving beam of their charge, the lighthouse. They polished the mirrors of the light and talked to the reflections of themselves. They walked in opposite directions around their lonely acre, and talked, and suddenly aware of each other in passing each would be angry that the other was paying him no attention, and they would start shouting.

"Thou plain bastard!" one would yell across the islet. "What the hell didst thou do anyway? Murdered four women? I poisoned eight bankers, and they at their soup!"

"Don't cross me, Marius!" the other would bellow through the wind and the spray. "Thou plain poisoner! Would'st thou have the guts to cut up a woman into little pieces?"

All they had left now was this memory of murder. They sat on the steps of the lighthouse and boasted of it, of its quality, its technique, its art.

"Piddler! Puke! She might even have been thy mistress

if I hadn't saved thee from her! God damn it, would'st thou have had the guts . . . "

"And where, my son," the other would say in an unctuous voice, "did thy — thy — patrimony go? The bankers?"

You could imagine them, in their pale, striped convict pajamas, sleeping one above the other in the bunks which were squeezed into the thin cylinder of the lighthouse, and the one in the bunk above leaning over its side and snarling at the other who was asleep, "You sissy, was it you who stood behind them, correct and attentive as a waiter should be, when they fell forward, plop-plop-plop, into their soups, and did you disembarrass them of their sixty-three thousand, seven hundred and forty-two francs?"

There would be a silence. The man in the upper bunk would bellow so the long tube of the lighthouse echoed him: "Answer me, pig, or I'll put my foot in your face!"

And in the morning the man in the bunk below would be changing lamps in the head of the beacon, so that cautious people might avoid such rocks as he lived on, and below him, trying to hook a free fish from the surf, would be his cut-throat companion. "Yah, you *espèce de relégué*," he would yowl at him through the tunnels of the wind, "you bugger of banks, was it you who was so favored as to laugh at the ladies then and have them thank you for it, while you carved small pieces slowly from them, and they said, 'Yes, my little one, no, my little one, yes, my little one,' and you gave them a drink again, and 'No, my little one,' they'd say — Caress me here'?"

This led to inimical relations, this loose talk and jousting and bravura between men who were colleagues, after all. It grew worse, as the long season of the rains was slowly tipped, like a boxful of vipers, over French Guiana.

Normally a boat with provisions should have stopped at the lighthouse at the end of each month, but one month passed and the next and there was nothing but corned beef and beans to eat. The rain was incessant. It clattered against the narrow window which lighted the men on opposite sides of the table, telling themselves what great murderers they were. The seas were so great that fishing was impossible, but once they had a bit of luck as a small fish was hurled to the rocks. They ate entrails and all. They radioed to Cayenne for help, and as the third month was passing and they were reduced to dried beans only, a cutter came bounding toward Enfant Perdu, but it went away again with a short blast of its foghorn, for landing was impossible.

By now they were bleeding at the nostrils with scurvy; their spongy gums were shrunken so that their teeth wobbled when they talked; their bodies were spotted with sores.

It was on the night when they ran out of charcoal for the brazier that one of them said, eating beans half cooked over a fire made of furniture and the rags they had wrapped their ulcers with, "Sweetheart, I am tired of thy boasts. I am bored with the look of thee. The stink of thy ulcers is so offensive I can even distinguish it from my own."

"My little rabbit," said the other, scraping his drool from the table and eating it again, "we are reduced to beans for living. Let us live by the code of beans. The foulness of thee discourages what little appetite I have left. Ourselves, we have no arms. The bean needs no knife at all. Let us throw out our knives now, and divide the forks between us, and one of us will pierce the other suddenly."

Then began a pretty play of table manners, the guarded thrust of the fork to the beans and its quick withdrawal into the fists of these mad murderers. The furniture diminished to feed the brazier. The ankles of chairs were cut off, and then the knees. The table was lowered proportionately with them. And each man hid his forks in a secret place.

One of them, climbing the ladder to the light, would say, shouting down through the tube of the lighthouse: "Peacock, the ghosts of thy women abhor thee. The tine of thy fork is of lead."

And the other would shout up at him, "There will be a boat. The boat will come, with mushrooms and truffles and lobster *à l'Armoricaine*. There will be no gravy in thee then."

Such conversations became so unpleasant to them both that when a boat did arrive in a calmer sea, when their furniture had been cut to its barest knuckles and the beans were eaten nearly raw, they rushed from different sides of the Lost Child's acre to plunge into the sea, their batteries of forks in their belts like daggers, and swam to the bobbing package which had been set adrift for them.

Neither swam well, said those watching from the boat, which stood off at a safe distance from the rocks. They must have been half blinded by their illness, or blinded by their hatred of each other or their lust for the package. Evidently they didn't see the gray half-crescent of fin which circled them, nor the others which came after it when they were less than halfway to the package.

They kept fumbling against each other and striking at each other's faces, tangled in the billows of the sea as they might have been in bedclothes of a hostile bed. They may have seen the sharks eventually, for then they were swimming with metal in their hands, and the crescent fins were nearly on them.

The captain took a chance, turned the cutter toward them, and swung out the boom of the derrick with the cargo net. The package bobbed gaily along. The fins moved evenly in their tightening spiral. The men thrust at each other for swimming room, stabbed at each other with the metal things as the great net sank beneath them and twitched them suddenly into the air. The net stretched long and tightened around them, squeezing them together, tumbling them about like fish.

The boom of the derrick lifted the length of the lighthouse, and swung its catch across the deck and the heads of the watching seamen. There the winch stopped and the net was suspended motionless for a time, as the men were caught by their flailing arms and legs through the meshes of the net. Their gasping rose above the wind. Both of them held fistfuls of forks in their hands, jabbing at their entangled bodies, and gobbets of blood dripped onto the deck.

"You womb of a sausage!" screamed one of them. The

winch caught, loosened, lowered the net a little, caught again. "Moss of urinals!" yelled the other as the winch snapped them apart and flung them into each other's arms again.

"Christ, my hat!" said a sailor, spilling blood from it.

"Never mind your bloody hat!" the captain bellowed. "Get onto that net and get the forks from them!"

The wind, whistling around the Lost Child of a lighthouse, settled in a hot, exhausted, quiet lump upon the boat. No one and nothing moved except the snarl of flesh in the net; you could hear the forks as they struck on bone.

The net spun slowly to the right, contracting upon the murderers in it, and unwound slowly to the left again. Blood dripped into the mate's cup of coffee on the main hatch, and he kicked it overboard. A fork tumbled and stood stiff in a halyard. The winch snarled, choked, and dropped its cargo suddenly. There were bits of pink-and-white-striped convict pajamas shredded like excelsior around the pink-and-white carcasses in the net.

When we were not frequenting the market, the shops, and the deeper dives of St. Laurent, exploring for simple viands to eat, when we were not cozening murderers, lepers, and politicians to beguile an egg from them or a cigarette, our days were active despite a sub-equatorial climate nearly as bad as that of New York in July.

We encountered a famous man, Brestine, who had somewhat the freedom of the town though he still was serving his reiterating sentence and wore his sharply pressed, striped convict clothes. He was an artist and probably the finest counterfeiter in the world, with, he claimed, nearly nine hundred practically faultless bills to his credit. He had no samples, he said; the prison wardens had taken his memory book. They were collectors' items, said Brestine, quite truthfully.

Brestine had been liberated year after year, for he counterfeited culture wonderfully, too, but before he could collect enough money to buy his passage to France, he would generously give a self-made bill to some false friend and so earn ten years' more imprisonment. No one, really, wanted him to leave, for he painted very good religious murals and gay canvases for clubs of the *surveillants*.

We met him first in the dark house of Monsieur Manœuvre — a fence, dispenser of stolen goods — where we had come to seek eggs. Manœuvre introduced us to him, a luminous lean face wearing a straw hat in the shadows.

Bright eyes he had, for he said quickly, spotting the pips on my French officer's shirt, "*Mon capitaine*, send me back to the cell if you like, but I am unable to help you. I have traded in Madonnas, I have traded in pornography, but I am innocent of the trade in eggs."

"Eggs?" asked a small voice behind him, and out stepped the champion butterfly catcher of the penitentiary, a dwindled man with one arm only. He made a few sweeps with his lonely hand, and, presto, there was an egg.

"Beautiful!" said Ruth. "Do it again!"

"Hah, *madame*, tomorrow. I had once a reputation as an ambidextrous magician until I married a certain person who shall be nameless here. She was an acrobat, one of those who come sliding from incredible heights along a cable suspended only by her teeth. They were strong, her teeth, the pale yellow kind, the strongest as dentists say. During our courtship I had been so far exalted as to write verse to them. But we had tiffs, we had quarrels. She could produce no eggs like me, I said, and she riposted that the only way I could chew a steak was to take my teeth in my two hands, which was indelicate, *monsieur*, and led to ruder words exchanged until the day came when she bit me in the biceps."

"My," said Ruth, drawing back a bit. "She went that far?"

"Though she had been swinging by her teeth all day, *madame*, she had the envy to bite me in the biceps. I swung her off her feet; it was no good. She clung to me and was chewing on me — *oui, monsieur*, chewing — until I lifted her through the window and suspended her at some distance above the pavement. Mind you, I meant her no bodily harm; it probably was I who was the more surprised when she finally let go and I was left with only an ear in my right hand . . . this one . . . Would you care to see it, *monsieur?*

Ruth made a sound of deprecation.

"*Madame*, the wound in my biceps festered while I was in jail and truly grieving for her. It became gangrenous. They cut it off. I have few pleasant memories of this period at all."

⊘≈⊘

With one or another of these strange people as guides we did what little touring there was to do inside the area limited by the towns of Mana and St. Laurent. The *préfet* wanted photos of the abandoned penal camp called St. Jean, so we went there by *pousse*, or pusher, since the miniature train no longer functioned. We saw the train, though, a lean pathetic thing, rusting and tarnishing with jungle rot. It had run for a little while, under the care of a condemned murderer with a particularly surgical bent. But one day he had run it to the end of the line, in the woods beyond St. Jean, and set out afoot for freedom from there. The little train then, like a faithful dog whose heart is broken, lay down and died.

So we took the *pousse* along the narrow-gauge rails, nineteen kilometers to the camp of St. Jean. The *pousse* was of the size and form of a hand car, though it had a wooden park bench as a seat upon it and was propelled by two convicts who actually pushed it along with bamboo poles. And it went at a hell of a lick. We whizzed past the abandoned Tiger Camp, which had been devoted to murderers only, and saw that the jungle had already returned to its very windows. Our polesmen pushed in perfect unison along the continuing road which had been hacked through the trees. The green woods broke open like a wound again as we went past the "new camp," abolished in 1942, and again we were deep in our clean trees which committed neither murder nor punishment.

At the nineteenth kilometer we emerged into a spacious farmland at the edge of the Maroni River. The ghost town of

St. Jean, once the abode of thieves considered incorrigible, lay around us on pastured hilltops, and though it had been abandoned in 1943 the jungle had not yet dared to mate with the proud and cultured daughters of its vast vegetable gardens, the decayed gentility of flowering onions, cabbage, and asparagus such as one found no longer in the towns. St. Jean, to the Creole population of the colony, was not an example of what might be done with the rich earth they had, but a reminder that the culpable man could be enslaved to onions, cabbage, and asparagus.

There were only thirty-one thieves and murderers left here now under the kindly guidance of the wardens Santini and N'Zila, who offered us such a sausage with a red wine chaser as couldn't be found this side of Budapest, yet these convicts had filled gardens and nurtured sixty-five head of cattle in preparation for the arrival of Europe's displaced persons. There had once been three thousand criminals in this jungle jail. Now, said Santini, the camp could lodge fifteen hundred European refugees in the administrative buildings alone, even before the cells were converted; one hundred families could find immediate asylum here. It was a project upon which I was to work with the Freeland League when I returned to New York.

We wandered through the old prison blocks and over the walls of them, looking down, as the jailers did, into the horse-shoe-shaped series of cells, roofed with bars only so that the obstreperous could be easily seen and quickly quelled.

We visited the dispensary to have my tropical ulcers

dressed by a convict veterinarian; returning to the grassy street I had a contretemps with a previous patient, a bull, which was aware, though I had forgotten it, that I was wearing the vermilion trench cap of my French regiment. As I leaped over the rail of a veranda Ruth was winding her Filmo and cursing because she had missed the scene. The thirty-one gardener convicts, who were making a heyday of our visit, were more sympathetic — for most of them, they said, had at one time "evaded" in an attempt to join our troups of De Gaulle in Africa.

That was a fine patriotic twist to the *évasion* alibi, for few were the *bagnards* who had not tried their luck with *La Belle* at least once. There were many in the jungle still, and it was because of them that the thousands of empty cells were padlocked, lest they sneak back to pass the night safe from jaguars, and reorganize. But the jaguars were less fierce than they; and the Indians were less hostile to the small groups going upriver. These lost men, seeking the darkest way to Venezuela, without firearms, had frequently murdered parties of whites for their possessions.

I spent a bit of thought on this, considering the long journey ahead, with Ruth as my only dependable companion.

❦

We walked in the dusk that evening, over the gentle slopes of what once had been the cruelest village in the world, walled against the sunset by the padlocked empty cells.

There was a convict named Plomb (lead) who was attached to us, and we turned to him when the strange moaning from the jungle was noticed by us both; it was a funereal ebb and flow of sound, something between a whistle and a soprano voice.

"It is what the natives call the singing serpent," he said, "the anaconda. And you will find this is no legend; it is known to science. But I do not like it while evading. It seems to sing to the right of you, just there in that tree! But you are not sure. Look, *madame*, is it not before you also, at the foot of the wall? There! There!"

Damned if it wasn't there also, and Ruth and I took to the crown of the road.

Mr. Plomb tossed up his head and the laughter ratcheted from the unscarred side of his mouth. "But my next evasion, hah! You know where that will be? To Florida, *mon capitaine*, to Miami, *madame*, where the Americans love such acts of heroism. You know that old René Belbenoit, who twice escaped, has now become an American citizen by Act of Congress? I shall do better. I shall write a better book. I shall make a film so moving, so touching, so humanitarian they shall use it in the schools."

We were on our way to dinner at the warden's house, so Mr. Plomb talked fast, hopping about in front of us. "It is said that René evaded the second time with the help of Americans. Personally I shall sell myself as shares, *mon capitaine*, heh? You can invest in me right now for a thousand francs! Think of the film, the book! Fifty-fifty, heh?"

Carefully draped over the shoulder of Mr. Plomb, giving

THE DAMNED

him the appearance of a Persian rug peddler, was his blanket.

"Tell you what," said I, "if you're short of funds, I'll buy that blanket from you." We had often and vainly tried to buy one.

Mr. Plomb gave a leap and came down weeping.

"*Capitaine*, you are without a heart! You would buy my own mother from me! You who don't need one! This!" he cried. "This!" He snapped open the blanket and swung it around him. "This is the only mother I have!"

I had found this blanket-worship fairly common among the old *bagnards*. Every convict received a blanket when he entered the penitentiary, a huge and handsome thing striped red and green and gray, which felt to me as if it had been woven of the pelts of young porcupines. The newcomers sold them or swapped them for tobacco and rum; not so the old-timers, to whom they were portable homes, portable names, refuge from the sun and rain.

Psychologically it was equally curious that the veteran convict had no fear of solitary confinement. The novice feared its tightness, its darkness, its vampire bats, but to the old-timer the *cellule* was Nirvana; there was no work there and no further punishment; it was cosy; you could die at your ease; it was back to the womb.

I apologized to Mr. Plomb for wanting to buy his mama. He refolded her carefully.

"Anything else I would sell you gladly, ha-ha!" he laughed. "Even the tattooing off my back."

[81]

Furious with frustration at finding no paddlers, we left word with Gougis to accept the first thing in the shape of a boat paddled by man, woman, or child while we went up the Mana River in the launch of Maurice Demougeot. Demougeot managed one profitable wood industry in a country where, literally, the myopic colonists had been unable to see the wood for the trees. And at the gray little town of Mana there were cane plantations and reasonable facsimiles of gardens tended by the Sisters of the Order of Saint Joseph of Cluny. It was depressing to learn that in all French Guiana, totaling nearly thirty-five thousand square miles, there were less than fifteen square miles under cultivation.

Mostly by the sweat of his own brow Demougeot was making his sawmill and export business pay, shipping out a noble wood, the Angélique, which may one day serve instead of the dying North American oak. His chief problems were labor, which was nearly unobtainable among even the half-nourished natives, and dollars for the purchase of machinery from the United States.

"But let us see those less fortunate than I," said he, launching us upriver again to the leprosarium of Acarouany. We climbed the many clay steps to the plateau, following an aged convict leper who bore a yoke on his back from which hung two five-gallon petrol tins of river water. We passed beneath the black arms of a wooden cross to enter an immaculate village where at first nothing seemed to move, though we could see figures standing, lying, sitting, in the blistering shade. Then they moved, as in slow-motion photography, around us. They were terrible cartoons of men and women, for some had no noses and some no ears. One Annamite boy danced crazily ahead of us, striking the stylized boxing postures which his Khmer ancestors had commemorated on the walls of Angkor Wat. Like most of the others he had been sent as a convict to French Guiana, and had paid for his crime doubly by contracting leprosy here, but his spirit was unbroken; he punched fists without fingers at the bare sky that was a thin blue like an acetylene flame, and he pranced on feet without toes. An old, old man crawled on his elbows and knees from his hut's doorway and spoke in thick words like bubbling porridge to the missionary, Father Izart. When he had had enough fingers to carve with, he had whittled a sign for his dwelling: 1916 — *Pour La Vie*.

Ruth walked with Mother Genevieve and three of the extraordinary young nuns who were devoting their lives to the lepers here. There had been a fourth, but she had recently contracted the disease and lived in a leper hut like her charges.

They had insufficient drugs. Chaulmoogra oil from Siam had been unobtainable since the beginning of the war, and their small quantity of American Leprolin caused fever and so was refused by the patients, though they knew it to be good.

The obstinacy of the human spirit, I had thought, was imbecile. The attitude of never admitting unquestionable defeat was a burden greater to those who served the hopelessly afflicted than their suffering was to themselves. But humbly I recanted at Acarouany, seeing the individual gardens behind the huts, hearing a phonograph, visiting the barbershop run by a fairly whole leper, who encouraged a healthy vanity among his clientele. And there was a multiple murderer returning from the hunt with a deer which he would share with all the village. The cornea of his eye was like a tiny cesspool leaking from a rotted brain, and his nostrils were like a baboon's, uptilted, one of the most evident signs of leprosy, which is now politely called Hansen's disease. And there was the gay old lady with cheeks rouged by some vegetable dye, but without hands, who graciously shook her head in refusal of the flowers I picked for her, saying cryptically, "Thank you, *monsieur*, but I am still in flower."

This seemed to us wonderful when we first met the lepers, but when we returned to them a second time and a third, to film them as discreetly as possible for the leper foundations of the United States and France, we found ourselves being accepted and trusted by them, and they would shake what once were forefingers under our noses and tell us of the sinister things beneath their levity. And Father Botro and young Mother Genevieve confirmed these disclosures in the bare dining room where, after washing our hands with potassium permanganate, we sat wearily before small glasses of rum.

൦∾෧

There was revolution here. A week before in the moonlight Mother Genevieve and Father Botro had finished their rounds and were returning to their beds, when the revolutionaries came slowly swarming behind them to semicircle them into the dispensary. They stood tight against the far wall, while the lepers cried that Father Botro was a crook, that he had defrauded them: that 350,000 francs had been given him to purchase film and a projector for the colony; that he had pocketed it. And Father Botro, standing before Mother Genevieve, had held his shoulders back, his beard up, and replied that it took a long time to get things from France even to Cayenne, and as long as that again to St. Laurent and Acarouany. And Mother Genevieve tried not to tremble, for she knew how these hysterical lepers had often threatened their nuns.

"My children, be patient," said Father Botro. "Your ills and your grievances are my own."

But they came closer to the wall where the two were standing, and one of them shouted, "Give us each a thousand francs of the money that was sent to us!"

Father Botro raised his hands up and took from the wall the crucifix which this community had made for the worship of those too ill to attend the chapel. The Christ on it was a terrible image. His eyes bulged. He had six fingers. His nose was hooked and generous. His skin was smooth and glistening. He was heroic, with one hand ripped loose from the nail and a foot extended to descend from the cross.

"Children of God," said Father Botro, "here is the Christ of your creation. You, Pierre, cut the rosewood for his flesh, and you, Marius, made an ingenious blade and carved his crucifix, and you, Louis, made the body of him, and you, Bartholomew, gave him the face of God's own son."

"I did," said Pierre.

"I did," said Louis.

Father Botro walked into the midst of the lepers, holding the crucifix high. "Pierre, will you take this crucifix and hang it by your bed and in the morning accuse me of treachery, when the sun can lighten your poor old eyes? Can you, Louis, put your sick hand on the clean body you carved for him, and call out the lie that none of you believe?"

When Mother Genevieve felt the wall behind her again and opened her eyes she saw that little Father Botro had alone lifted Louis to the surgical table, for the other lepers were no longer there.

"He's breathing," said Father Botro, "but it's that old embolus again. Hold him now, while I . . ."

ా

I was rather embarrassed before Ruth because I hadn't yet produced a going expedition to confirm my bold talk of a venturesome past. The explorer discovers a great deal to be lived up to on his honeymoon. Here were the great cases packed high on the veranda beside us. The shotgun — the pistol — the Holderness Underwater Aqua-Gun — all were clean and oiled, though probably disappointing as armament to one accustomed to movie expeditions. Nor were there pith helmets or high boots, those encumbrances to exploration in the last century. These particular heresies were dimly viewed by Dr. François, a local entomologist whom we had invited to accompany us.

François was a quiet, studious Frenchman, devoted to his laboratory research, who none the less had made journeys into central Guiana. He was devoted to the hard, the Spartan, way of life in the bush, and was already bolstering his burdened morale by starting to grow a beard. Already, too, he was living with us. We objected to his hobnailed boots echoing through the termite-hollowed timbers while we took our siesta in the heat of the day, and he found frivolous the sounds of typewriters and ice against glass at a hot three o'clock in the morning.

At last we had good news from Gougis that some distance up the river there were canoes approaching — Boni canoes with paddlers he knew, who, mysteriously, by the rumors of the river, had learned that we needed them. And on the same day we received our provisions from Borden's Milk Products and Dorset Foods, destined for jungle testing but wonderfully acceptable now. We drank cold milk made of Klim (— a pinch of salt) and Borden's Instant Coffee, iced (— a dash of rum), and treated the more deserving of our friends, including lepers, to Dorset's meat stews.

Our spirits were so lifted again, with the assumption that we should soon be leaving St. Laurent, that we found quaint now many of its customs that had been abhorrent and downright diabolical before. Now we only smiled when we were wakened by the frantic church at the corner, knocking us out of bed with its insistent bells from 5:30 to six in the morning. It was no invitation to worship. It was furious, commanding, threatening hell to the sluggard — me — in bed. It was like a Chinese water torture, but these bell notes were of molten brass. And when the energetic padre next door marched his Boy Scouts back and forth before our house during our siesta, instructing them in the bitterer uses of the bugle, we just said philosophically, "Ah, but we'll be up the river soon. . . ."

We could not, however, condone the activities in the parochial school yard across the road. Our second-story balcony had a fine view of the sinister goings-on within — of the little French urchins, white and black, marching by threes around the yard, shrieking something about *La Fillette* (the Little Girl) . . . "La fillett-*ah*, la fillett-*ah*, la fillett-*ah*, ha-ha-*hey!*" until I took to moaning it in the night. But the sinister thing was that as they marched — these starched babies crunched by sun helmets three sizes too large for them — the good Sisters, similarly helmeted, swooped like crows up and down their column, giving great whacks to the loiterers. On their fourth turn about the yard, suddenly they were shepherded into a black, windowless shed, where probably they were eaten. We never saw them emerge from it, though we watched every evening and saw only their replacements next day, shrieking as they marched to doom.

It would have been useless to try to call to them above their own sweet childish shrieks, and I had no slingshot, so the next best thing was my bubble-blowing material from Woolworth's, which later endeared us to savage children along the river.

The wind was on my side and wafted the bubbles, danc-

ing, scintillating, across the school yard. This usually broke
the death march to the shed, while the sisters screamed and
the tots jumped high, joggling their helmets off, to catch the
bubbles of beauty before the very door to which they were
being beguiled. In this way I probably saved many lives.

⤬

But the most curious life we saved, according to the owner
of it, was that of the prison doctor. In the gloomy general
store of Tanon, filled with casks as high as my shoulder, I saw
this little fellow bustling like a gnome, popping up behind a
barrel, leaping for a rusty tin on a high shelf. When he caught
sight of me his face grew suffused with excitement.

"*Mon capitaine,*" he spluttered, "perhaps you are my savior!"

I did not deny that I was flattered, and I frowned at
Tanon's grin.

The good doctor's whole head was shaking. "May I come
to see you? May I tell you about it?"

"Why, of course," I replied benignly, "I shall do what I
can. Come to the house at six!" — and with another dirty
look at Tanon's grin I turned to the door, followed by a sigh
from the doctor — "But it will be so long!" Damn Tanon,
couldn't he recognize a savior when he saw one? Was it
every day that he was asked to save a soul?

I had quite forgotten about the doctor by six that evening,
for on the way home I had been caught up with by one of
Gougis's sons, whose bicycle came to a churning stop beside

me, braked by the boy's bare heels against the stony road. He saluted like a veteran and announced that the paddlers had come, or almost come: they had been seen at Isle Portal and should make St. Laurent tomorrow.

Ruth and I were merrily drinking a Hennessy and water, happy with the thought of those black jewels of paddlers, when there was a crunching of gravel below, then Mohammed's voice announcing, "*Monsieur le capitaine docteur des prisons!*"

"Forgot to tell you . . ." I hastily began, too late, for he was suddenly with us, clicking heels, helmet in armpit, snapping a kiss at Ruth's hand.

"Feel my hands," said he; "my heart! I am so nervous I must sit down, folding myself everywhere to keep the trembles in!"

"By all means! Have a drink?"

"Ah, yes."

Simple, I thought. Plain alcoholic. Out of funds till pay day. Sure enough, he had crossed his knees, his arms, folding himself everywhere.

Ruth said, "Doctor, I'm glad you're here. You can straighten us out on so many things. . . ."

The doctor was managing his glass with both hands. "Pardon, *madame*, if I interrupt. You will notice that I am quaking. I cannot sleep. I writhe. My surgery suffers. And I, a fiancé!"

"Have you tried Vitamin B$_1$?" Ruth too was trying to be helpful. "We have fresh bromides, sleeping pills, fresh vitamins from A to F, a tremendous stock of drugs which Ciba and Burroughs Wellcome gave us generously for you people here."

"What I would suggest," said I tenaciously, "is ten milligrams of B_1 at bedtime, two plain aspirin, and a cup of warm milk; we've got some Klim. But who are we, *monsieur le docteur*, to suggest to you . . ."

Down came a flash of white past our Primus lantern, banging against the table and covering the doctor's drink in a fold of gauze. It was our entomologist's butterfly net.

"Forgive me," said François, removing the net and with it the glass of Hennessy, like a conjurer. "This is an unusual Culex."

The doctor remained suspended, like a Culex in amber, not a jitter in him. "Let me explain," he said measuredly, "before catastrophe occurs. . . . No one but you, perhaps, can help me. You are Americans. Maybe, since you have the freedom of the customs here . . ."

Ruth's eyes switched toward me. Drugs? Doctor of the camp?

He leaned forward, folding himself again. "Have you any . . . Quakair?"

"Pardon?"

"Quakair, *mon capitaine*, *les Quakair*. Quakair Wats!"

"You mean Quaker Oats?" My hand too was trembling as I poured him a fresh drink. Ruth and I downed ours at a gulp.

"But of course, the Quakair Wats! I am hopeless without

them! My memory decays! My articulation ceases! But *mon capitaine*" — his voice was throbbing — "My ulcers! My fiancée!"

Ruth found a can promptly in her neatly ordered kitchen baggage. The gift of the Holy Grail could have been no sweeter to him. "A Mass should be said for you," said he, as he went quietly down the stairs, his lust in his arms.

11
The Bonis

ON THE NIGHT of our liberation from the penal colony, dogs howled at the moon, arbitrary cocks began crowing at 3:00 A.M., and the alarm of the church bells exploded when we still lay wet and dreamless and panting in the dark. We wakened to awareness of feet trampling past us like the marchers in Reading Gaol. Through the mosquito netting we saw the diffused images of dozens of pink-striped convicts wearing wide straw hats, industriously piling our baggage on the backs of their smaller fellows.

I got out of bed exhausted and immediately began to drip at every pore like an old radiator. Ruth hobbled out the other side. We were not surprised to find our entomologist, already booted and helmeted, plucking impatiently at a quarter inch of beard.

Added fuel had been flung yesterday on François's pale fire, when I went to see my paddlers and their canoes. Both were sound, but I had made changes in the *pomekaris*, the small, thatched sun shelters at the stern of them, heightening them a little to take our folding duraluminum chairs.

"Chairs!" exclaimed François, in a voice windy with shock. "*Chairs* on an expedition in canoes?"

"Of course, my old one! Look at them! You can fold them,

swing them round your finger, so light they are, yet they'll stretch flat enough for you to sleep in."

François shuddered. This was carrying comfort too far.

"Damn it, François, we are having every comfort we can afford on this expedition, the only condition being that it be portable, durable, and inexpensive. We are making this expedition and a film in color on half a shoestring or less, but, by golly, if I reach the Tumac-Humacs and find a Ritz Hotel, I'm going to stay there and not in the woods."

"You haven't brought a tent with you too?" he asked.

"No, François, we haven't brought a tent. A thatched shelter is cooler and healthier than a tent in the jungle. A tent," I added meanly, because I was getting fed up with his strictures, "is only another encumbrance of Hollywood expeditions, like boots and helmets and beards."

So on this sweltering morning the three of us marched somewhat grumpily ahead of our column of convict-drawn carts laden with what still looked like mountains of equipment for the five and a half months we were to spend in the bush. Three months of these were to be without contact even with the upriver traders, since there was a huge gap between the last Negro Boni village and the true wilderness where the nomadic Indians might or might not be. We should have and send no mail. We should have no radio, as ours had not arrived in time. The world couldn't reach us, nor could we reach it, as we meandered, by intention, blithely, up the river which had killed at least one man of every expedition which had gone even two thirds of the way toward our goal.

The thought of this seemed melodramatic even to me, but it was quite factual, and I watched Ruth walk straight down to the fierce Maroni River, superintending her half of the convict porters and their baggage carts. She was good to watch.

The last of the thatched Chinese shops on stilts gave us tea, which we took standing while we looked over our crew of half-nude blacks distributing the baggage in the canoes, shifting it back and fourth until the weights were even; the bow of the canoe should rise fractionally when the crew and passengers were aboard. We had three dugouts about twenty-seven feet long, one for Ruth, one for me, one for François and Mohammed. Each had two paddlers, a bowman, called "bossman," and a sternman, called *patron*.

I had accepted the advice of old-timers in the colony to let the Bonis dispose of the baggage as they pleased and in general to let them decide on matters of river policy, on when and where to make camp, but we were to discover that this would have to be adjudicated on its merits later on.

The baggage was covered first with palm fronds, then army ponchos, and fastened securely with vines in preference to my nylon cord. We were tipping our jolly band of convict porters when our Boni headman, Afokati, came up gently to me, straightening his loincloth. He spoke a little French, as most of them did from trading on the lower reaches of the river, and it was with great dignity that he said, "*Capitaine*, do we have a uniform for the canoe?"

I got off to a good start immediately by guessing that this

meant a flag, and with some ceremony unfurled from its cardboard tube the flag of the Explorers' Club, number 127, which I too was very proud to fly. Afokati was enraptured by the size of it — which was about twenty by thirty inches — for it would be the biggest flag on the river, and was red, white, and blue, which would represent French Guiana, Dutch Guiana, and the United States. The initials, EC, and the dingus in the middle, which represented a compass, might also bring us luck.

He plugged the flag into gunwale holes just in front of my *pomekari*. He took off his paper helmet — for town wear only — and with it gestured Ruth to the seat in her canoe, François and Mohammed to the seats in theirs, and me to mine.

I could scarcely believe it but we were off, "into the unknown," as "intrepid" fellows are wont to say. The Chinese traders watched us go impassively. Our gay convicts raised a mighty roar. "Ho! said Afokati, who stood behind me, the *patron*. I stood up, leaning my back against the *pomekari*. "Down, *capitaine!*" I ignored this and turned to see that Ruth's canoe was well balanced, and that of François following hers. I gave an order quickly, my first, for traveling in the jungle with any natives depends on the sort of authority which I detest — yet I had to establish it now.

"Stop!" I said.

Afokati paused but briefly with his paddling. "What?"

"Afokati, stop!"

He did stop. Ruth's canoe drew level with mine and I

tossed her the only posy I had been able to find on shore, a sort of dandelion.

"Let us go," I said; and we went, to my great relief.

❧

Sitting back in my own *pomekari* at last, with my cameras and miniature armament suspended by leather thongs from the thatched walls beside me, and my notebooks, cigarettes, and charts caught between the fronds, I squinted at this river — which I wasn't at all sure I was going to like. We had no choice. It was the only western route leading to the extreme interior of French Guiana. It was the only route with a fair assurance of native populations near the Tumuc-Humacs, and these people were my primary concern.

Half a mile away to the right lay the Dutch shore, as flat as ours, hemmed with palms, and between was slick water that glistened and wavered with oyster-colored lights. This was still the estuary; the sea was pushing us on an incoming tide, so our boys paddled hard to make the most of it. We passed the tiny island of St. Louis, counted twenty-three small huts upon it, and four lonely men; they were convict lepers, waving to us, knee-deep in the water. We watched the current, and floated cans of food, quinine, Vioform, and tobacco to them, for we had no time to stop; the sun would soon be plummeting through the equatorial horizon.

We got to know these four old lepers later. They had leprosy of the nerves, a torturing thing but without skin lesions. They had their gardens of eggplant, squash, tobacco, to supplement the penal diet. They were congenial, wove and bartered with each other intricate hats made of bandages; escaped occasionally and went roistering into St. Laurent, spreading good will to their fellows and probably their disease. One had been cook at La Grande Chaumière, and one a cameraman who had murdered his director. One trained little birds, and the little last man was so awed by his companions' exploits that he gaped all the time in wonderment, which made everybody happy. It was an idyllic island.

We passed close enough to them for them to retrieve our packages easily, and one of them, the great cook, flung a bottle into my canoe. We waved good-by and paddled harder, for the tide was about to turn. I sloshed water on the bottle to purify it, took out the slip of paper, doused it in antiseptic cognac and read: "Recipe: Soak bread in crêpe Suzette batter with few granules of cheese and fry."

That was as nice a going-away present as one could wish.

❧

At Isle Portal in the sunset we were hospitably received by Tanon's men, who ran the distillery and the sawmill there. We were given an empty bungalow where we could set up our cots and kitchen, and offered cocktails made of the first run of rum, the *cœur de chauffe*, the "heart of the heat," and there we discovered that Mohammed, too, had a taste for rum, and none whatever for cooking. He sprawled, plastered, by his charcoal stove, surrounded by his panting four dogs which we had agreed he could take along, being assured by the prison authorities that he was a mighty hunter with only his dogs and a knife; his past precluded firearms. Sleepily he counted his mongrels again and again: Bobi, Bato, Dienne, Taio; while we cooked our own dinner — and excellent it was — of bread soaked in crêpes Suzette batter with a few granules of cheese, and fried. François said it should be baked, not fried.

The rhythm of river travel slid us from our cots to the canoes next morning, scarcely conscious of the change except for hunger, which we quelled with avocados, and my angry wondering as to what should be done with this fraud of a cook.

For hours there would be no movement but ourselves on the river, and no sound but the occasional melodic voices of the paddlers. We were sliding through jungles, already uninhabited, sloping toward us from balata trees to *palutivier* to *moko-moko*, an erect plant with inverted heart-shaped leaves which grows in the water, in many ways similar to papyrus, for its stems could be beaten into paper, if the whim was on you; but it also provided fine fishing ground, for the fish nibbled at its roots.

Asa, my bowman — the best hunter, the best savage of them all — would lift his fifteen-foot pole from the water, turn his face which was still smeared with the sacred clay, the *pemba doti*, to frighten the demons of St. Laurent, and whisper like a challenge to me, *"Fissy-fissy,"* which meant fish; and so solid was the forested shore that the echo would return, *"Fissy-fissy. . . ."*

And I, being firm, would say "No." They were testing us, these first few days, to find out how pliable we were and how much they could get away with for their own fun on the river. And as with all other primitive servants, the best politics at the beginning of a trip, which would inevitably end by their being your masters, was to get at least the first week's hard work out of them by consistently saying "No." You would of course give in at last and be lenient, because you had grown to like them and they truly seemed to be all you had in the world. You would kick yourself for an ass who couldn't learn from past experience — but there was the temptation of wanting to be liked by your men; and once you said "Yes" they had you.

The balance of the relationship between Boni and *bakra* — ourselves — was difficult to maintain so that both might work efficiently. François overdid it, and was disliked by them — for he didn't just say "No," he said "Never." Ruth began by giving them orders, which were not acceptable from a woman (it was only the leader and a male who could command them), but she gained their respect quickly afterward by swimming better than they, by having larger and certainly more shapely calves than theirs, which were attentuated by a lifetime of disuse in canoes, and by the sublety with which she managed their leader, me.

Their sensitivity, their gentleness, was amazing. Afokati knew few words of French, but when he had to pass close in front of us on shore he remembered the phrase which he must have elicited with difficulty from the Creoles of St.

Laurent: *"Excuse-moi."* And because I brought flowers, which are rare in the jungle, to Ruth, he did so also until our more serious troubles began.

Quietly a canoe from upriver would come upon us, with children paddling it and an old black woman sitting limp in the middle. Afokati would chant *"O dio!"* — but gently, so as not to disturb the drowsy passer-by — and the response would come dulcet to us, *"Fai di ba!"*

Afokati was a gallant gentleman, too fine to attempt to boss the band of brigands which was his crew, and which in the wilderness ahead was to boss Afokati.

I stood up uncertainly in my teetery dugout canoe, trying to appear sure of movement, casual. Ruth's canoe moved sleekly fifty yards away, her men plunging down their poles in perfect harmony, lifting them, reversing them in a spangled arc of dripping water, thrusting them through the current again, like knives through tissue. Ruth was standing, leaning back against her *pomekari*, filming with what is called "French film" (no film at all) in her camera — simply letting the shutter spin, pointing the camera at one and another of our paddlers to accustom them to it.

During the first week they were too unsure of themselves and of us to protest; during the second they grumbled but kept paddling none the less, for they wouldn't be paid otherwise; and quickly then, after obvious discussions of the matter, and no harm done, they ignored our toys.

"Bobi," I shouted sternly, "sit down!" The champion dog of Mohammed's stable slunk past me and sat down in my chair. I looked for the other dogs. Ruth's Dienne was eagerly posing for pictures, and Bato and Taio, in the canoe with François and Mohammed, were trying to get away from them to the peril of the canoe, for François had discovered that they were rich in Vers Macaque, an agile worm, which he was trying to collect.

"Got one!" he shouted. "Beel, got the worm!" I could have guessed it, for Taio had dived overboard and was swimming for my canoe. Our conversations boomed across the river, rich and resonant, from wall to wall of the massive forest. We had to use short sentences, so they wouldn't echo back and overlap before we had finished.

"Cocovenens!" François called. "Co-co-ven-ens . . ."

"Sorry," I replied as Taio showered me, "you were saying?"

François said something deprecating about explorers who should have stuck to their damfool mystical poetry. He was trying, he said, to teach them the ways of the jungle, and the best way to begin was with the bacillus.

"For example, the Cocovenens," he shouted. "You wouldn't know anything about it, would you?"

"No," I said. "Sorry."

"Rare," he said. "Catch it from coconuts."

"What's that?"

"From coconuts, my friend. Fever. Nausea. Same as mushroom poisoning. Do you know anything about it? *I* do. I shall present Cocovenens to the world on an *argent* platter like a sacred but evil head."

[104   ]

"Good! Good!"

But François wasn't listening. He had put me in my place, and was busy again charting the Maroni River, which had been charted nine times in the last seventy years. Forgetting the lapse when he had been chasing Taio's Vers Macaque, he continued making survey notes at three-minute intervals, drawing the river bends, marking the presence of huts and other landmarks.

"Beel, how many huts do you see there, seven or eight?"

"Eight," I would say, "but there may be others in the bush."

He would write down "Seven" categorically, and lean back exhausted on the chair he had hewn from a box, un-planed, unsanded; an explorer's tackle or a masochist's. He was exhausted because he had had no siesta — unlike us dilet-tantes — being busy with his three-minute survey; and so meticulous was he, between worms and landmarks, that he saw nothing of the river, the sky, the parrots flying.

Ruth said maliciously, when our canoes had drawn to-gether, "That concrete marker, François, just before the last village . . . Could that have been one of Richard's?" (The French Captain Richard who had plotted the river in 1938.)

" . . . fifty-eight . . . fifty-nine . . . sixty." François counted, and made a point on his map. "What's that, *madame?* Marker? Richard? Didn't notice. I was plotting the village."

This was the detachment of the scientist, I supposed, and his unilateral logic. The river to me was infinitely various even in these lower reaches. There were lilies to be noted and the serpentine roots of fromager trees, so like sleeping boa constrictors that the Bonis would never cut one lest it be an image of the boa, one of their animistic gods. And in the shallow water we found the same tropical fish which I had paid great money for at home: the guppies, the Danios, the Tetras. Golden butterflies, which were invisible against the sparkling water, materialized in beautiful contrast against the black skins of our paddlers, disappeared, reappeared on the shore to bejewel the old lean trees dressed in vines like ladies whose laces were decaying in the House of Usher.

❦

"François! Hey! That must be the falls called *Dédéyou!*"

"Yo!" sang Asa at my bow. "Yo-oo-oo-oo!" chanted the others.

We had been traveling close to the Dutch shore and now rounded a point to find a wall of white water, not very high but very earnest-looking, extended from shore to shore and buttressed in the middle by islands. Standing up I could see over it to the roiling acres beyond.

"Dédéyou?" I asked Afokati, as François wasn't speaking to me again. But the Bonis weren't either, and I remembered, from that excellent book *Djuka* by Dr. Morton Kahn, that they would never name a falls before passing it, for fear that its special god would be angry.

Our three canoes were in line, close together, but no one said a word while Afokati studied the rocks strewn through the cataract, the curve of the spurting waves, the slick shallow places, superimposing them, as you do with a split-field view finder, upon the carefully charted image of them which he remembered from his last journey.

"Yo!" he sang quietly, poling my boat to the lead. We edged toward the falls between rocks which were invisible to me but which the boys detected by the movement of water above and around them. The bossmen of the other two canoes jumped out and waded up to their armpits to steady and push my canoe. They strained and groaned. The stern went under and water in gallons swirled forward toward the baggage. I swung my neat Knox hat into service as a bailing tool, sitting cross-legged in the bilge for steadiness. Up went the bow to meet the falls, and the gunwales which were on the level of my ears roared as the hot white blood of the god pounded past them. I looked over the edge and was smacked by water in the eye for my impertinence. Asa was chanting "Yo! Yo! Yo!" each time he plunged down his enormous pole, and as I looked at him through the spray I said, "It's true, all right; the damned 'living statues' of travel writers do exist." Glistening with sweat and fume, his muscles jerking as though electrified, he was a noble machine.

With a great heave we were over and into the shallow rapids, where Afokati held us while the others returned for Ruth's canoe and then that of François. Ruth wasn't bailing; she was sitting to her waist in water and blithely filming it all.

"Easy on the film, darling. We have over eighty more of these to get through before we even see the mountains."

"Good," she said, slowly panning down to a close-up of the water.

The rest of the afternoon was an unremitting dogged battle with the rapids. Our boys' pink tongues were sticking out like candies, and the twined spikes of their hair, though oily enough to be nearly waterproof, were beginning to droop. They wouldn't last long, for they were village coiffures contrived by adoring wives, and on this celibate expedition it would soon be expedient to shave off such folderol. All but Asa's, the intransigeant's. Savagely he would make no compromise with water, man, or the vanity brokers. To hell with his hair, let it grow horns; which it did.

Big and little dugout canoes passed us steadily down-river and with each of them there was the same crooning exchange. *"O Dio. . . ." "Miti baka. . . ." "Fai di ba. . . ." "O Dio va yoo tam. . . ." "Eeyah. . . ." "Unnnh. . . ."* Salutations and friendly queries about health and relatives. . . . And, we thought in our innocence, how friendly it was on the river; everyone loved everyone. And so they did, 'way down here.

On the edge of darkness we arrived at La Forestière about 6:30, when in these latitudes the sun, invisible for the last hour behind the tall trees, gives a visible sigh, like an expended workman, and plunges over the brim of the world to what might be oblivion, nescience, Nirvana for suns.

La Forestière had once been a penitentiary of Annamites, and once a sawmill for a reckless and unremembered company of Americans. All that was left of it now was a two-storied and double-balconied mansion with outhouses, fit for phantoms only. Wild chickens took proud, proprietary steps through the empty rooms and easily dodged the arrows of our Bonis with a little feint and a chortle. There were gigantic frogs, a foot long and six inches in diameter, to welcome us like butlers on every staircase, monstrous creatures, immobile, haughty, chins up, in the moons our flashlights flipped at them.

Installed on the balcony — Ruth's and my cots together beneath the simple cubic house of nylon netting which was to be our joy on the expedition, with François's hammock slung beside us — we settled down to supper lit by that wonder among lamps, the Totelite, a portable fluorescent light, smaller than a typewriter, which spread a brilliant illumination, the color of morning moonlight, for twenty feet around us. Among the many products given us for testing under equatorial jungle conditions, the Totelite was among the most useful. No other camp light can compare with it for luminescence and simplicity and reliability.

But Mohammed brought us soup, and another product failed the test, and its sponsor will, I hope, understand our dual disappointment in receiving from Mohammed a soup made of corned beef in which had been placed our plastic spoons and forks. Corned-beef soup is no viand for those who have crossed Dédéyou falls; a can of one of Dorset's broths would have been the thing, heavily laced with sherry. Corned-beef soup, we thought, was no proper food at all, particularly when you tried to eat it with a spoon which the heat had dissolved halfway up the bowl, so that it looked like a baby's pusher, and a fork whose tines had disintegrated like decayed teeth.

We ate corned-beef plastic soup, raking it and hoeing it, to our benefit possibly, and slid into our cots to talk for a while of the immense and shining day we had accomplished. François tossed pettishly in his hammock; he was fighting hard for sleep so that he could be up before us. We had no intention of getting up before seven or eleven or eternity, so long as the night was pleasant with us now.

The little ache in the back of my arm, which reached to Ruth's shoulder across the wooden framework of our cots, was diminishing with sleep when suddenly the dark globe above me cracked with a thunderous racket, and we sat up together, listening.

I had lived in many an Asian and African and Polynesian jungle before, and loved the things that growled or squeaked or went boomp in the night. So long as you could hear them you had nothing to worry about. They were company after the loneliness of daylight when jungle life was torpid beneath the sun. But this sound came roaring across the whole western horizon, roaring slowly but fortified in counterpoint by echoes and the echo of echoes. It was like the rumbling of boulders in immense tin cans, like the gurgle of thick water going down a cosmic drain, and like nothing earthly.

François pretended to snore, and the snore was smug, for he had us, of course. The fancy explorers were sitting bolt upright, baffled.

"François, my old one, would you care to explain what makes this noise?" I asked pleasantly.

"Huh? Huh? Why can't you let people sleep? Noise? That? Howling monkeys, my poor Beel." And he added, "What did you expect here, chimes?"

Howling monkeys of such dimensions I had not reckoned on. I lay back and listened, marveling. There were two tones to the hullabaloo now, a baritone and a contralto.

"Is this an argument?" Ruth asked.

"My dear *madame*, you have nothing to worry about. It is one old monkey only. He talks to himself. He is a ventriloquist. He has two voices. Good night, *madame*."

In the canoe next morning, at the compromise hour of nine, I scanned my neat little library shelf for information on the howling baboon, or red howler, or *Mycetes seniculus*. Afokati, poling at the stern behind my thatched *pomekari* and so unable to keep tabs on me, asked Asa in the bow what the *bakra* was doing. "*Bookoo!*" said Asa respectfully, of the magic sheets I held in my hands, to interpret the signs and omens of them.

Quelch wrote: "When full-grown the howlers are about the size of a large dog, but the throat and neck are immensely swollen out in the males owing to the extreme development of the hyoid portion of the larynx to form a deep and wide bony sac, which enables them to produce the astonishingly loud noises that far exceed anything that any other animal can bring forth."

Sir Crossley Rayner, writing of British Guiana, noted:

[111]

"Before breakfast I was awakened by a frightful noise which sounded like the death agony of some animal caught by an alligator, but which I was told was only the howling of a baboon in the forest"; and Vincent Roth, a hardened old-timer, wrote that: " . . . the howling, or to be more accurate, the roaring, groaning, gargling of the Howler is indeed a fearsome sound . . . " and went on to tell the Indian legend of how the Howler got his vivid coat.

In olden days (it was said) the Baboon was black all over and he was very proud of his terrifying voice. Indeed so vain of it did he become that one day he even challenged Thunder to a competition as to which could make the more terrible noise. Thunder agreed, but on condition that Baboon open the tourney. So Baboon got up into the top of a high tree and gave vent to his far-reaching roar. 'Is that all you can do?' asked Thunder who, with that, made one terrific crash, so loud that fire (lightning) came from his mouth and singeing Baboon's coat knocked him off his high perch to the ground. Baboon was so afraid that ever after he only made use of his voice in the fastness of the forest when Thunder was nowhere near.

Actually one never does hear Baboon howling during thundery weather. We were to miss this old orator when we returned down-river during the rains.

We never could see more than a hundred yards ahead on our glistening road. Where the river curved, the two shores seemed to merge in an unbroken wall of forest, as they did a hundred yards behind us, so that one had the impression of traveling on a narrow lake, but a lake elastic, endless, stretching forever before us and contracting behind. Only the sides occasionally closed in on us and again expanded as we rounded a bend. But for our efforts in our three lonely units, the canoes, and the tearing, swilling waters, it was hard to believe that we were moving.

Hours went by without a distinctive landmark. The sun, like a good toaster, toasted us evenly on both sides and turned itself off when we were cooked enough. We came in twilight to the village of Apatou at the foot of the sparkling falls.

Our Bonis, they said, had to stop at last because "these same shoulders" were tired; there was "deepy-sleepy" in them. It was obvious that they didn't want to stop at Apatou, although it was a village of their own people, but the "deepy-sleepy" was stronger than they.

I looked up the steep clay steps past the beak-nosed wooden idol which protected the village. A committee of women, and no men, was waiting for us beyond it.

As our canoes dawdled back and forth before the landing I remembered that Apatou was one of the matriarchal villages, still fairly common among the Bonis. These matriarchates were respected and hated equally by the itinerant Boni males, proud stout fellows who lived by their legends dating over two centuries back to the era of "blackbirding," when some thirty thousand slaves were dragged from Africa to the New World.

Many escaped from the plantations of the three Guianas and the Caribbean Islands. At home in the bush, which was almost identical with their African homeland, they waged war successfully against the Dutch, freeing their fellow slaves and exhorting others to join them, until in the latter part of the eighteenth century the white men sued for peace. The treaty, which is still effective, was dictated by the blacks — or Djukas, as they called themselves — giving them freedom from all colonial laws, a sovereign country of their own in the forest, and a substantial annual monetary tribute from the Dutch forever after. Dr. Morton Kahn has pointed out that this reversal of white exploitation is probably unique in the world today.

Our Bonis of French Guiana were almost exclusively rivermen, and sociologically inferior to their Djuka cousins across the river in Dutch Guiana. There was little heart in them, and no ambition. Their art was narrowed to the intricate braiding of hair, the exterior decoration of their huts, and the fine phallic engraving on the interior of their womblike calabashes. Their music was paltry tom-tom, too tired even for the discipline of rhythm.

During that afternoon I had felt that there was something wrong with Eimo, Ruth's bow paddler. There was a certain look in his eye and he was sweating more than normally and brandishing his long pole rather than swinging it with the balance of efficiency. And from time to time he had thrown out his chest, bared his teeth to the sun, and chattered, "Zig-azig-azig! Zig-azig-azig! Zig-azig-azig!" a tuning up of his one-man orchestra for a feat of song which should have made the baboon quail.

In his happy moments he was devoted to us, to Ruth particularly, but on the bad days, when his own god Massa Gaddu, and not I, was in the ascendancy, he became *kitta* — exalted, entranced in lunacy, which often is dangerous, but in Eimo's case was expended in song. We could understand enough of the Boni language by now to know that his lyric was not complimentary to the black man's burden — which was Ruth and François and I.

Now at the landing of Apatou he bared his white teeth and screamed, "Eiiiiiiiiiii-mo!" announcing his male presence, and we drew into the clay steps of the river bank and climbed them, ducking beneath the fringe of palm fronds, called Azang Pau which was suspended over the path to brush the demons from us. We looked boldly up the long wooden nose and into the eyes of the Aflamu idol, which was there to intimidate the likes of just such as us — and these were the same eyes, undercut, cavernous, that I had seen in many West African fetishes.

❦

It was pure Africa we were entering in South America, even purer than the Africa of today, which has changed in many ways under Arab and European influences. The decadent Bonis, never refreshed by evolving cultures outside their inbred group, still built huts which were duplicates of those of their ancestors on the Ivory Coast. The amulets, or *gri-gris,* hung in little sacks from their necks, were straight survivals, and the tattooing by irritated cicatrization, particularly the nubile tattooing on the belly, was the same as that affected by the Gold Coast slaves who were once called Coromantis after the Dutch fort in the Indies from which they escaped.

"Coromanti" is still in use as the name of a ghost which is seen in the forest, among the flange-like roots of the fromager trees. It resembles a bubble about three feet across, and explodes around anyone who touches it, driving him mad.

It had by now begun to seem to us that if you weren't mad on this Maroni River, there must be something wrong with you.

❧

Moima, the Matriarch or woman chief of Apatou, greeted Ruth warmly and was rather cool to me and François and the mere Boni males. She was a champion old suffragette with close-cropped gray hair, and a grin like the handshake of a solid man. As in other matriarchal villages, we noticed that hers was remarkable for its cleanliness, its gardens or *abbatis,* and the architecture of its thatched wooden huts which were invariably of two windowless rooms sealed by hand-sawn boards against the demons, and further protected by food offerings at the door and bottles of foul fluids which might tempt them to stay outside.

In such a matriarchate of the Bonis the women do rule the roost, and usually better than the men in the patriarchal villages. The woman chief has her corps of female councilors, and matters of general policy are decided by them with the complacent seconding of the men, who also serve as accessory functionaries in the production of children and the crops of the *abbatis*. Warriors have not been needed for many years.

As among other members of the race generically called Djuka, descent is traced through the female line, not through the husband, the nominal father of the mother's children, since paternity is always doubtful. Inheritance is matrilinear, through the mother's oldest male relative. Thus the head of her own father or even grandfather, while her husband may be the eldest male relative of some other married woman and therefore the ruler of her brood.

Mohammed, our cook, became the meagerest of us males when he had finished a bottle of my rum and had started testing the demon bottles around the matriarchs' doorsteps. The goblins would get him, these wise women said. They had done so already and long ago.

On one side of us the women were pressing out the poison of manioc, pure prussic acid, by squeezing it through wicker tubes, then soaking the pulp and drying it to make *cassava*, *cuac*, and tapioca. Youngsters were carrying younger youngsters on their backs, in the African way, not on their hips as the Indians do. Old men were thinking together and snuffing a liquid snuff brewed of rum, tobacco, and pepper. Young men stood upon a rock patient as a frieze, their bows and arrows poised over the dark river where the *coumalu* swam.

An old woman was bent far down to the little broom with

which she swept the village immaculate, and another matriarch, in a slot of the jungle behind our hut, in a mottled shaft
of sunset, was putting clay heads upon the bamboo platform of an altar beside a pot of ruddy liquid fenced with
blood-red spears. This boded no good for her enemies, probably male. But there was a third woman following her,
black and beautiful, not a matriarch yet, still wearing her
nakedness haughtily beyond the deadline where G-strings,
the *calambés*, should cover their maturity; she had come to
the sacred grove to suspend her dream boats, hollow crescents
of clay wherein her dreams might voyage to the dreams of
her beloved.

François went early to bed that he might rise and growl
at the dawn for its tardiness, but Ruth and I sat quietly before
the hut and made friends with the children — way past their
bedtime too — and talked as well as we could with their
very self-sufficient, nearly parthenogenetic mothers. They
brought gifts to us, pot stirrers of wood called *kabu*, and the
lavender necklaces called *nyoké*, to ward off illness, which
surely were strung with the same seeds as those of the Middle
East. And when we had returned gifts of cloth and nails
and cologne to them, they shyly showed us their sicknesses.

Ulcers were common among them, and leprosy, and *boboni*,
which is dysentery. Many of them said that their *boudins*,
their sausages, were sick, and it required some explanation to
realize that the French *boudin* meant meat tied in the in-
testines of pigs, or sausages; it had been converted to mean
Boni constipation.

We treated them as well as we could with the sulfa drugs, penicillin, bicarbonate of soda, aspirin, and ointments, and gave salt tablets to the grinning malingerers. Water, we said, and the juice of green limes, was good for most of their ailments.

The babies were piled like ripe fruit on both sides of us, against our knees, reaching to touch the fire-lamp which was fluorescent and cold. "*Citalsi,*" one said, pointing with the six fingers of one hand (polydactylism is fairly common), meaning the stars; and an older girl gave a hoist of her breasts to the sky, pointing with them to *manti*, the moon.

The swathe of the lamp fell across the murderer Mohammed, playing with the babies. And other babies laughed and wriggled beneath their elder sisters' fingers, which crawled like spiders through their hair, looking for vermin. There wasn't a man about the house.

We sprayed the little heads with Aerosol and became magicians immediately, a doubtful honor as the rest of the village now swarmed to us for treatment. Ruth took a salt tablet to show that it was good, and washed it down with lime juice and Three Star Hennessy, which was good also.

"*Dingi aboon*" they said, which meant that the *dingi*, drink, must be *aboon*, good. "Deepy-talkie" was the language commonly used among themselves. "Talkie-talkie," which was spoken by ourselves and by children, was a relic of their British slave masters many generations ago. Though most of their ancestors had passed through Surinam, the Dutch gutturals had been so unpalatable that few had been assimilated. Talkie-talkie was an imitative, phonetic language, not hard to interpret as it was explained to us by the little brown leper girl named Lobbie Sweetie (Love Is Sweet).

For Ruth, whom they called "Papa," as they called the queen Matriarch "Granman," they danced a gentlewomen's dance, sitting on their tiny individual stools, flicking palm to elbow and elbow to palm rhythmically with rich clopping sounds, tossing for inflection their bakelite bosoms, chanting:

> *Aboon be ai, kana kong kong!*
> *Mosi arigo, kana kong kong!*

(How good it is to be with thee!)

The song stopped short, truncated. We could hear the insects metallically singing like music boxes. Then the children muttered:

> *Goni . . . donfoobi . . . seebi. . . .*

(Gone is thy spirit within me. . . .)

The red howler monkeys broke that pause in a rising roar across the horizon, as our young matrons whispered:

> *Gaddu gimmi sonni . . .*
> *Gaddu gimmi . . .*
> *Sonni. . . .*

(God, thou must give me thy sons. . . .)

The chorus to this was known to our patriarchal Boni paddlers, and the sound went up:

> *Oh-oy-oy-oy-oo-oo-oo-oo . . .*

Eimo, slung in his hammock beside our hut, came awake with *kitta* again. His voice rose, steaming and jerking, as though his river, the male Maroni, were tumbling backward up the falls.

The matriarchs of Apatou picked up their benches, slung their babies, and walked sedately away, with merely a nod to Papa Ruth, while Eimo howled like an ape at God, Gaddu, who had inflicted him with women such as these.

The voice of Afokati came from the forest near by, and then Toma's and Asa's and Abbibal's, sleepily at first but shearing through the night, contrapuntal to Eimo's lusting melody. We knew the *kitta* was dangerous; the proud dark women knew it, and we heard the simulated closing of their unlatched doors.

Eimo's was the last word, a noise in the night with no love in it, and his echo suddenly was a whisper of hammocks swinging empty in a rainy wind.

◦≈◦

For days now we poled along stretches of the river which were thorny with rapids, walled with immaculate timber, but quasi-civilized. Canoes spurted past us and the naked Bonis or Boschs in them would salute us with tremendous cardboard helmets which they had painted and silvered in the same deviously phallic designs which made all their wood carving remarkable. And women and children alone would scoot suddenly over a wave and past us, in minute canoes, steering with token paddles.

"*O Dio,*" said our boys.

"*Fai di ba. . . .*"

Sometimes they would pause, listening to my typewriter, and ask our Bonis if that music made sense. The babies stood up on born sea legs. Their bellies were swollen over malarial spleens and their navels protruded in bumps. They were already canny rivermen, equipped with little bows and arrows with which they did shoot fish, and once a canoe came paddling back to us, hard, against the current, holding out an arrow on which was impaled a clear rubber tube.

"Is that good to eat?" they asked, and we said no. It was one of the hundreds of prophylactics in which we encased our film against humidity. We heard later that a party of Dutchmen following us over this part of the river had commented unfavorably on the business of the Davis expedition. But not so Pekein, our twelve-year-old mascot, nephew of Afokati, who collected a few film casings from the many we flung overboard, blew them into balloons, and rubbed them with a fingernail-on-blackboard screech against his oily chest. We finally took to drowning them with rocks, probably to the disappointment of the Dutch expedition, which judged that our honeymoon had petered out.

We were soon to learn that our Bonis, though they spoke no English and no proper French, were intuitive to the tenor of our conversations, and usually, even when hating us later and hating themselves for it, would adapt their moods to what they felt our talk implied. This was a discovery which was more than disquieting; it stopped free speech after that morning when, according to François, they took their cue from us and discussed their family lives with some abandon, and generously decided to reserve judgment on ours.

The rapids were called in Boni the *sauts*, the jumps, and they were incessant, for there were little rapids between the eighty large ones which we should have to pass. We went through Saut Peti Tabaki and rested at the Creole village of three huts, where we bought bananas from an old woman whose fingers, swollen with elephantiasis, were as thick as the bananas. She lifted her long skirt to show us her feet which were the size of sofa cushions and strapped to boards. Our boys called her Mama, and she was very old, and frightened of the rains which would come in November, when her hands and feet were sure to ache terribly. I gave her a stock of aspirin.

"And for my son?" she asked.

Around the hut staggered a man of forty with the lines of eighty in his face. Looped over his shoulders was a child's hammock. His loincloth — or *cache-sexe* as the French call it — could not hide the monstrous deformity of his disease, for the hammock supported his testicles, which must have measured two feet in diameter. We gave him, too, a supply of little incongruous pills to tide him over the rainy season. Nothing but surgery could help him now.

The gratitude rushed out of him in a flood of talkie-talkie. He waddled to the hut and out again with mangoes, and when we last saw him from the canoes he seemed to be flicking the pills in series into his mouth.

[123]

"Is there much of that?" I asked François when he looked up from his stop watch.

"All through the three Guianas, but not much of it and not nearly such a danger as the other tropical diseases: malaria, leprosy, dysentery, old-fashioned tropical ulcers like what you've got on your feet now," said he with a certain hauteur. "And chigres."

"And leprosy?"

"Six to eighteen per cent of the population. I do not commit myself."

Chigres we had always with us on the Bonis' feet. The chigre is a microscopic beastie which burrows beneath your toenails and lays eggs in a sac which swells with their growth until the pressure of it is very painful. Then sedulously you cut around it, take it out, and throw it away. If the sac is punctured, blood poisoning results quickly and you are likely to lose the toe, the leg, or the whole of you.

François told us of one of his colleagues in Cayenne who developed a magnificient sac of chigre babies. He wouldn't touch it, excruciatingly painful though it was, and tending it carefully he took the first boat to Paris with it to present it to the medical societies. It was their misfortune that he died on the boat.

"Don't move, Beel!" said François, staring. "Hold your left arm still! Approach your boat to mine!"

Flurried with excitement as our canoes drew together, he fumbled through his kit, dropped his watch into the bilge, then his butterfly net into the Maroni, from which it was retrieved by the mascot, Pekein. By the time he finally had clapped a test tube over the Anopheles mosquito which was trying to find a tasty way through the insect repellent on my arm, I might have been a martyr to malaria, though my chronic malaria of twenty years' lineage, set in its ways, and resentful of intruders, would probably have staved off these new, primitive germs.

I got along fairly well with the old-timers within me. We understood each other. They were of the family-retainer type, and always would announce trouble in advance, though I too would feel it coming nearly every year. It was never severe any more, and I accepted it tolerantly, discreetly quelling it with small chidings of quinine.

"Yo!" sang Asa, as we headed for other rapids. Conversation was becoming rich with yo's. Eimo's voice replied from his canoe, "One-one . . . one-one . . . ," thus advising that we take the canoes through in single file. We wound among stony little islands, each of them with its pair of butterflies doing a lonely fandango above it. The rocks were furred with moss and lichen, and slippery as we pushed the canoes against the frothing, furious curds and whey which beset us. I was in the water too, straining what little was left of my city fat, trying to keep my face with a semblance of dignity above the spume as the Bonis did. But I kept dropping into holes and disappearing, and Ruth's photographic report-age of this was one depicting strained pink hands clutching above the water for a canoe while a fine Knox hat swirled **downstream.**

François had his triumph then, and convinced me that I should sit stern and patient, the white master, and let the Bonis do it. This was an uneasy role for me. It wasn't long before I was disappearing again.

Apparently the passings of what our boys called mountains was not the same as the traverse of *sauts*. It did no harm to name a mountain when you met it, and these ahead of us, several hundred feet high, were Mount Creole to the east of the river, on the French side, and the last lump of the Paramaca chain on the west, in Dutch Guiana.

We too spoke respectfully of them, fine mountains, good, solid, lots of trees on them.

"Photo!" said Afokati tersely. His attitude was changed and he was going to see to it that we worked. I clicked my thumbnail on the camera to simulate a shutter's click, and wound up the French film.

Now we rarely knew whether we were on the French or the Dutch side of the river, or whether we were following a shore at all, due to the many islands here and the *bistouri* (channels) we had to take to avoid the impossible water of the main current. The village of Loca Loca was on the Dutch shore, and venally welcomed us, offering us eggs at ten francs apiece and an old gray duck at five hundred.

Loca Loca was Dutch and prosperous, and its population entirely black. The few wooden shops were newly painted and the African huts were cleanly thatched. The *abbatis* (hillside gardens) swept up in green and yellow masses of manioc, bananas, gourds, papaya, almond, pineapple, and cashew.

The cashew is cultivated only for its fruit, and not for the little appendix-like tail which protrudes from it and is the nut we eat. The body is pink and resembles that of a pepper in shape and size. It is tasty, but we passed it by to pick up the nuts, which had been cast away. Roasted slowly over a grill to permit the oil to leak through, and hulled when cold, they harmonized wonderfully that night with roast plantain and the fish called *coumalu*.

The cashew was further useful, said Mohammed, in that its oils, when a convict rubbed it on his skin, would make spots which were quite similar to those of leprosy and might get the man hospitalized. He could thus avoid work for months at a time, if he had a sufficient provision of cashews, and might fairly easily arrange *La Belle*.

❧

Our after-dinner ceremonies had been established by now. First our paddlers would appear, carrying their precious paddles and tiny wooden stools which were barely big enough to fit their *gogos*, their behinds (it was unfitting to put the raw *gogo* on the raw earth). Ruth and I would be sitting side by side on our magnificent Duralumin chairs. The Bonis would sit in a semicircle before us. Ruth would pass me the glasses. I would hold them while Mohammed apportioned the shot of young rum, or *sopi*, as the natives called it.

The boys would raise their glasses together — an acquired characteristic — and Afokati would say, "*Si Dieu voulait . . .*" "If God wills it . . ." Then all of us would spill a drop of rum on the ground for Massa Gaddu to drink of first, and down our portions at a gulp.

Then I would reach for my Burroughs Wellcome and Ciba kits, undo their many latches, exposing the pharmaceutical magics within, and our boys would sigh with ecstasy. Here were magics of two kinds: the negative, which alleviated pain; and the positive, which tied your guts in knots or burned the evil out of your open sores. And in that silvery box was the needle, the hypodermic which they always begged for. On François's advice we used it rarely, remembering several incidents which had occurred when other travelers had obligingly given injections to the Bonis, and the patients had died, though the needle was in no way responsible. The needle had been like God's finger, capricious, and those who had guided it had been punished by the patient's relatives.

We treated our Bonis first, then the infinite queue of village natives.

Afokati would rise stiff-legged when we had finished. The others followed him. "*Merci*," they would say, then with a shrug, "*Mo k'aller dormir*," which meant they were going to sleep, ticking like new again with taffia and salts. And usually there would be left one old couple, holding hands, holding each other's hearts, who would say sadly, shyly as schoolchildren, "*Bakra*, we are old but still in love. Will you give us, please, the means of love again?"

☙

The sun rose over the cemetery of Loca Loca, which we had not noticed the night before when we were choosing an empty hut. We took our coffee with us and moved around it, refreshed by this sweet bright air, savoring it in anticipation of the heat which would stifle us a few hours from now. There was one sentimental grave, from a man to his wife, which was framed with a wooden bedstead, and another enlaced with empty, half-buried bottles so that the wind went *Whoo-oo-oo* across their mouths and scared the demons away. Even the rodents, the agoutis, were frightened of eating the grave plants here.

François waited for us by the canoes, chronometer in hand, and off we went again, to the French shore of Antonia, where we filmed a spider crab, climbing over the nude thigh of a Chinese lady on a poster which had probably been flung away because she was rotted in spots. This was a tremendous beast, seven inches from opposite toe to toe, which François caught with a chloroform sponge; breaking a leg of it, he became irritable for the rest of the day.

As the rising sun drew down its veil of shadow from one hut's doorway and another, revealing bottles, statuettes, desiccated fruits placed as offerings around them, as the shadow pealed the night's dark magic from them, I remarked simply that the Lares and Penates of the Negroes, here as in Africa, seemed sometimes to be ignored in daylight and frequently profaned by the contents of the coconut chamber pot. This gave François fits. He screamed that Lares and Penates were *"Termes inexacts! Termes poétiques!"* — unworthy of scien-

tists, especially those doubtful ones who already seemed to
have received the *coup de bambou*, or sunstroke, as a result
of not wearing cork helmets. (Ruth at the moment was
changing film beneath her thin felt hat, and mine was full of
sliced coconut. We were feeling very well indeed, but unsure
that François was the right companion for us.) And Mohammed, François's canoe mate, wearing a cotton cap and squatting between François's blistered knees, turned around and
leered at us. Obviously the expedition was still going badly,
and it worried me.

An expedition leaving civilization is a delicate thing, a
machine which, to function properly, must be perfectly balanced, in work, relaxation, nourishment, diversion, and in
co-operation in all of these. The crotchets of one man can
throw the whole machine out of alignment, and in the jungle
you can find no spare parts. I remember that seasoned traveler, Armand Denis, saying that he had interviewed several
hundred men before selecting a mechanic and a photographer
to accompany his five-man Asiatic Expedition. And he preferred that these should not want to play cards or talk politics. Those he chose were perhaps a little less expert than some
he rejected, but they were better capable of integration in the
expeditionary unit.

When François had quieted, a six-corner conversation
broke out among our paddlers, obviously regarding the rights
and wrongs of the white men's argument. We were constantly to note with wonder their acute perceptions. Our
slightest movements, the raising or lowering of a voice, our

very silences were discussed and interpreted. This took time out from paddling and was to be discouraged.

"*Allons! Allons!*" I protested. "Too much talkie-talkie!" We were passing the village of Bonaparte, a golden village beneath giant fromager trees with thick rounded tops like Fijian coiffures. Here we were to see the last of the *awara* palm, which bleeds a fine cooking oil and whose pericarp makes a tasty soup, similar to the almond soup of the Balearic Isles.

❧

I could taste this almond flavor still, as on a midday at Al-cudia Puerto — which is a cove of smugglers at Majorca's tip — where I had assembled five carloads of the prettiest prosti-tutes in five towns. I was to make a film there with André Roosevelt. I had come ahead to select actors and actresses and locations for our scenario. The actresses had been impossible to find, for there was no stage talent to draw upon, and the respectable pretty girls were closed behind the traditional barred windows — with wilted roses ready to clutch in their teeth — or dragged by the rubber hide of their virtue close behind their chaperones.

I had the actors, the locations, the collaboration of the Majorcan Government but not one actress. André wired cryptically BORDELLOS. This annulled my government spon-sorship when it was noted that with more and more of a harassed look I was visiting four and sometimes five brothels a day. It was costly to pay for pleasure unachieved, for

merely a line-up of tired women where there might be a film
star lurking. It was due to the one-track mind that is the
single genius of explorers that I finally rounded up the five
carloads of them and conducted them, singing like parrots,
over the mountains and swiftly past the monasteries and
down to the plain of Alcudia where I had virtually stumbled
into the very cave the scenario required.

I remembered this as one of the weird spots of the earth.
It was a hole in the ground, perhaps thirty feet across by
fifty deep, and bulging to a width of fifty or more at the
bottom. A flight of old, well-hewn stone steps led into it to a
floor strewn with fallen rock. Three passages led from it
straight to hell, and between two of them stood a great rock
carving, a monumental bas relief depicting Saint George and
the dragon.

("Dragon?" said Ruth. "Sorry to interrupt, but Eimo says
we are now hunting a dragon lizard for dinner, an iguana. . . .
So what then?")

Then all my ladies trooped tittering down the stairs and
made a play of putting tiny handkerchiefs over the rocks for
them to sit upon, for I had thought it a great idea for us to
have a picnic here, on location, and have each heroine try out
her part before the audience of the others.

The bowls of almond soup were coming down the stairs,
when one of them said, "This is a bad place. It is haunted, I
know, because I was born right over there," and she pointed
diagonally at the sky. "They say this cave was used as a
church when the Romans were persecuting the Christian

martyrs. The Romans finally found them here. Those tunnels are full of bones."

A ripple of pre-prandial indigestion went through my cast.

"María," I said, "now I want you to be a Christian martyr. You stand by the tunnel here."

"You look into it first, *señor!*"

With a match for guidance I stepped into the tunnel boldly and followed it for about twenty feet until the flame diminished and there was unmistakably the smell of sulphur. A fresh match burned bright for an instant and suddenly died away. The fumes of the place caught at my lungs, and I staggered coughing back to my picnic of movie stars.

"Nothing there but a bad smell," said I gaily.

"Bones," said María.

Steaming in the midst of us was the iron kettle of *sopa de almendras*, the spume of it redolent with almonds, chicken, basil, cream. Antonina was cutting the peasant bread, chipping garlic on it, folding it over golden slices of saffron-flavored *sobresada* sausage. Saint George and the dragon were menacing each other through the rising steam of the soup and I was on the way to becoming a motion-picture producer, when the mouth of the cave above us darkened with a cloud like a cork, and a clap of thunder deafened us.

My dainty ladies screamed, staggered among the shards. There was an answering rumble in all three tunnels branching from our central cave. Grit fell from the walls. I flung my hat over the soup tureen, calling to the girls to be calm. Then a sound like "whoosh" came from the tunnels and with it such a Stygian stench as to propel the girls screaming up the stairs and into the rain which was lavender-lit by lightning.

I followed cautiously with the hot pot of almond soup swinging against my leg. A shard fell and chipped a piece from Saint George's knee. I crawled out to the field where the high grasses were racing like horsemen, but swifter than they were my movie stars, their shoes in their hands, racing to the automobiles.

I am not one to abandon ever an almond soup, and this one so encumbered me that all the cars had sped away from that cave of hell before I reached the road. Exhausted, embittered, and hungry I sat down in the whipping grass, watching my first expedition return through the mountains to the brothels which had borne it.

I burned my hand fishing my hat from the depths of the almond soup, strained the soup through the hat — a tropically perforated Knox it was — and ate the almonds sadly.

❧

It was with a jerk that I returned to the finite, the actual Maroni River. The canoes had come to a sudden stop when the poling against the rapids ceased. Our boys poised, listening, staring fixedly at a tree. They were frozen still.

"Dragon!" said Ruth.

"Where? Do you see it?"

She pointed in an offhand way and turned her Ansco toward the mass of inscrutable greenery. Nothing moved there;

nothing, apparently, was different in color or size from the branches and leaves. I was to become used to this but never less annoyed that the Bonis, probably half of whom would have worn glasses in New York, could clearly see birds or animals in trees, or fish beneath the roiling waters, which my perfectly normal sight couldn't detect at all.

Abbibal, who had seen the prey, was indicating it to the others in a manner which further confounded me, as it always would. There wasn't a straight line in him, or in his directions. Bent over his pole with which he held the canoe against the rapids, his right arm was limply half raised and crooked at the elbow, horizontal. His forefinger was crooked vertically and waggled up and down. "Ahhh . . ." said the other paddlers quietly. He had practically put his finger on the prey, and no one cared that the eyes of us poor white trash were aching.

Asa took the same stance as Abbibal, with horizontal and vertical bends of his elbow and forefinger so as not to lose his place, which left Abbibal free to place an unfeathered crooked arrow in his bow. I looked up and down the tree, to the right of it where was a horny, red-podded Roucou bush which we were later to see pressed for the skin-dye of the Indians, and to the left where Rosailles flowers were growing on their shrub. (They had red, carnal buds and slick flowers the color of margarine which closed with a smug little smirk at night.) I still saw no dragons.

Then there was a whish of Abbibal's arrow — I couldn't see the flight of that thing either — and a scramble among the branches, the twigs bending down and snapping up again as the invisible body fell through them until there was a splash in the river. The Bonis howled. Our bowmen plunged overboard leaving our *patrons* to keep us head-on to the current. The water churned in blue and silver; the boys were down for an unconscionable length of time until I was certain that all their gullets had been slashed by the iguana, but they came up jumping half out of the water with the iguana transfixed upon three of their arrows.

He was unlovely, a node of scaly ugliness about four feet long, with wattles like a turkey cock's and a well-spiked spine. Before he was dead the boys chopped him apart at the base of his tail, flinging his body overboard. The tail was their delicacy. Had it been a female they would have performed a brutal Caesarian for the eggs.

There was no time on the river. It may have been that night or another that we cooked the iguana's stinking tail, and relished every inch of it. The cool evening raised our spirits a bit from the slough of persistent argument with François. The mist in the eastern sky was like that on a frosted glass, and I thought of Calvados sipped long ago beneath Brittany's apple trees.

❧

The natives sat close around us, Mohammed alone by his pale fire, for he was stingy with the country's munificent wood, mumbling his perpetual explanation of the murder which had sent him here. "Corporal," he said; "I was corporal, and there was this soldier, the thief. We had the argument, you understand. . . . I did the manly thing, and we both regretted it afterward."

And the boys said they had seen the spoor of a *bofu*, which was a huge donkeylike animal, the like of which I could in no wise place, and they told tales of the peccary, the wild pig, swimming in hundreds across the river, and suddenly there was an explosion of a splash quite near us, as though a tree had toppled over. This was a *couleuvre*, an anaconda, dropping from a branch. They were amphibious, as we were later at closer quarters to learn.

The spot where we had camped had once been a village, but the thatch had fallen long ago, and only the altars remained, little platforms on stilts with their pennants of leaves still flying. And there were crucifixes which had nothing to do with Christianity, draped in mildewed white cloth. The Bonis turned their backs to them, eating their usual dinner of dried manioc, *cuac*, mixing it with water and hastily chasing it down with smoked fish and sugar cane. For this record I noted that the fish, of the barbel family, were called *comata* and *gancoi*.

The whining, tinny sound of a music box was all around us, the chorus of insects with their blended metallic scream, while a bird said, "We ain't curious . . . we ain't curious . . . we . . ."

Inside our large square house of nylon netting Ruth and I sat quietly on our cots, listening. We had put out the lantern. The sparks of our cigarettes moved in odd patterns. The two kinds of fireflies examined us through our cage, the orange one panting to keep his light aglow, and the thin green little fellow, who never settled, flogging his pulse as if he knew the tenure of life depended on it.

We were thoughtful before them, and sat waiting impatiently now for our old red howlers to chant their vital bravado to the skies.

∽

In the morning we perceived that nothing on this river ever changed, neither life nor death; it was a fusion of them. The hush of its pools and the roar of its rapids mingled together, as sleep and waking did. You could neither hear nor ignore the yawn of it: not quite sound, not quite silence.

The butterflies flew uncertainly. At night the old monkeys howled, but their voices had the quaver of frustrates howling beneath the sheet of leaves pulled tight above their heads, their harems indifferent to them. The sun was never hot enough to make you sweat with gusto. The bugs were languid. Nothing was absolute in French Guiana.

This was bad river, the boys said, but they said it on shore, with their backs to it, lest the water god, the serpent, should hear them.

"And farther along?" I asked, as the canoes edged into the white waves.

"*Anaboon!*" they said cheerfully. (That was "bad" too.) My rough map of the country confirmed it; there was a *saut* or rapids every quarter inch for the next two feet of map.

Slowly the long *takari*, the poles of the bowmen, made arcs over their heads and led us through secret paths of foam. The sound of a Pan American plane, so high as to be invisible, shuddered in the sky. The passengers, I thought as I examined my toes for chigger bites, were probably being served their prefabricated luncheons now, by natty little hostesses in high-heeled shoes. And I leaned back contentedly, for a moment between *sauts*, and blessed my great uncomfortable world.

We rounded the bend before the Saut Singa Teté, a brute of a falls, unloaded the canoes, and hauled them by immense vines across the spurting rocks. The men with the baggage waded through like tightrope walkers. We moved on to the fuming milky breasts of Mama Saut, and blinded by their brightness turned into a *bistouri*, a by-pass arcaded and curtained with vines and vegetable parasites. The sunlight caught us like a golden fist again and tore us from our smooth water to the rapids above the falls, where we saw what is called a mountain in those parts, Mount Lebidoti, about a thousand feet high. The Bonis cheered, for this was true Boni country at last, no matriarchs in it.

You could feel, at this hour, the tiring of the boys, and knew it to be almost exactly four o'clock, whether or not the day's march had been harder than usual. In their business of transporting traders along the river, particularly the Dutch, they were accustomed to business hours, from six to four, and we were therefore unsettling in that we liked to work later than four to get the opaline twilight shots; to sit up late at night, reading or discussing what a fine thing anything was; and to get up only when there was no more sleep in us at all.

Afokati would sigh a sigh to produce an echo and gently urge his companions to bear with the *bakra* until we found a village toward the setting of the sun. He was a patrician with a finer tolerance of other people's caprices or convictions than any of the *bakra* he bore to their destinations of woods, just woods, like any other woods. He was a sterling gentleman, and I was often ashamed before him.

Ruth called across the space separating our canoes, in her rich voice — "*Zumba-Zumba*, Afokati," — asking him to go slowly here, for she had her camera against her cheek.

"*Pardonnez-moi! Madame! Excusez-moi!*" It was continually startling to discover that the choice of French phrases he had learned had been those of courtesy and gallantry, among perhaps a hundred words which were his entire vocabulary.

This evening there was an ancient paddler in a boy's teetery canoe, who kept passing us, veering into the moko-moko plants in quest of fish, and passing us again. He was shaped like an old brown shmoo.

"*Fai di, Papa,*" he said to me each time he passed, and "*Fai di, Papa,*" he would say to Ruth equitably. And Afokati replied always with such patience and gentleness as to dissolve the gravel of my concerns, "*O Dio, fai di ba.*"

The ancient shmoo held up a coconut. François tapped it, shook it, passed it back.

"Five francs," said the old fisherman.

"No," said I; I was going to set no precedent for purchases on the river until I learned their value.

"Bill," said Ruth, "I'd like it."

Then it was too late for me. Afokati scratched five francs in centimes from the folds of his calambé, bought the coconut, and dropped it casually into Ruth's canoe.

I stood up in the canoe at the wrong moment then, for we were entering the Saut Bona Songa. The anger of my embarrassment faded quickly in the realization that I was learning to my profit the manners of a Boni gentlman.

In quick succession the *sauts* came at us now. We hadn't finished bailing the boats after Bona Songa when the cry went up again, "*Saut! Saut!*" and there ahead of us flashed the dreaded *saut* called Laissez-Dédé (Leave Him Dead). We negotiated this by a *bistouri* which, though calmer, did leave me not much alive, for I was still being pretty intrepid about bounding overboard and giving a heave and a ho through the rough spots, the self-made Boni who could work twice as hard as his help. This was false philosophy, as I had always suspected it might be, for the boys were happy to have me work twice as hard as they.

I got no plaudits from Ruth. "You'll bash your silly head in," she yelled, "and I've run out of film!"

I grabbed her canoe as it reached mine and staggered along with it, my nose underwater while she patted my head the while as she might a dumb but faithful dog. That put an end to my heroics for quite a time.

Sitting in the canoe again my hands shook with fatigue as

I examined my cameras in their pliofilm bags. I was putting a haze filter on the Ansco when the dirge began, "*Saut! Saut!*" And true enough there was a handsome *saut*, if you like *sauts*, called Apounu Soungu, or something similar for all I cared. I got a little satisfaction in stopping it dead on film at a five-hundredth of a second.

"One-one!" shouted Abracadabra who was in the lead. The canoes were to follow one by one. "*Saffi-saffi*," crooned Toma. (Softly, softly; let us gently take this passage between the rocks.)

Ahead of us on the Dutch shore was a sandy spit of land with three huts on it, unkempt, disheveled dwellings. I looked at them with love. "*Finis*, Afokati. We'll camp here."

We paddled ashore with all our Bonis staring at us, not at the shore.

"This is Gandel-Natianingi!" Eimo said.

"Fine," I said. "What was it you said?" I wrote it down.

Eimo's huge shoulders hunched in a shrug. We landed with the last of daylight.

"Toma's father lives here," added Eimo, meaningly.

"Good," I said, picking up my musette. "Where is he?"

I lent a shoulder to Ruth as she hopped from her canoe to the sand. "It looks deserted, Billo."

François and Mohammed came gloomily ashore, annoyed that I had kept the boys paddling this late. François's nose, through preoccupation with disease no doubt in the laboratory, detected something which only an intuitive quiver in me felt.

[142   ]

"Bill, it stinks."

It was abruptly dark enough to turn on the Totelite, and the shock of its cold light brought the residents of Gandel-Natianingi from their huts. A few came on all fours. Some limped. The dozen or so who lived in the huts were all emaciated. These were people I had known everywhere in the tropics. There was no mistaking them: the twisted, silent, whimpering mouth, the voice without palate, the nose turned up because there was no bridge to it any more, the sudden squat with thin knees reaching just to the eyes, like fence pickets. These were lepers.

François, of course, was furious, but not Ruth. "Now's the time to try the hammocks," she said, walking through our hosts to a likely tree and testing a limb of it.

"Darling, do you know these are lepers?"

She was busy now with the unloading of the canoes, and with no hesitation found the United States Army hammocks in the depths of baggage, which always bewildered me.

This was the only time on the expedition that hammocks were to be used at all, for my hatred of them was ingrained by now and my fury at the folly of them, anywhere else than on a boat or in a garden, was such as had made generals stroke my arm pacifically and coo, "Now don't you worry, Davis. We won't use the dirty word again."

The hammock may be fine for the Indian who is migratory, or the soldier on long marches when he must carry his furniture with him. Even so a bed of limbs and leaves is better. The Latin American in his stifling country house keeps a brass bed for show (as he keeps the electric refrigerator in the living room) and conforms himself lengthwise to the crescent of his hammock, or sleeps crosswise on the width of it, which is wider than those we know; and the Nordic explorers of his jungles affect this torture on the presumption — a frequent fallacy — that natives know what is best for them.

While I hitched the beautiful Nylon cords of the army booby trap and pried open the green labia of its many folds, I spoke my piece on the subject.

Our entomologist chuckled throatily. "What's good enough for the Indians . . ."

" . . . Isn't, damn it, half good enough for us. François, my old one, if you sleep in it lengthwise, on your back, you're bent in the middle, you get cramps; you can't sleep on your side or your belly. If you sleep on it crosswise, no matter how stiff you spread it, by morning when the dews come on you are sunk in a canvas valley. You're enfolded and hot, whatever you do, and if you happen to be obliged to get up quickly as in war or exploration among the long-eared Indians upriver, you're sunk. You'll flounder and teeter until they have the head from you."

The pragmatic chuckle of François was his response as he climbed into the strait jacket he had slung above the pile of clay pots which our lepers had made for trade down river. He had spread some of these in a circle around him to warn him of a leper attack, and over his head he had suspended his simple kerosene lantern.

Ruth and I finally got our hammocks hung, the ropes straightened, the mosquito netting raised, the zippers loosened by force from their false teeth. Around us squatted the lepers, their knees in their eyes. Ruth gave them chocolate.

"Are these men all there are in the village?" I asked Afokati. Ruth's hammock jittered as she got into it backward. "Where," she asked, "is the father of Toma?" and disappeared into the green petals of her thing. I thought of the man-eating plants of Madagascar.

"Where is Toma's father?" I repeated.

The circle of lepers thrust their chins forward in unison toward the largest hut.

"Toma!" I called.

I moved my light around us. The Bonis had gone.

This was uncomfortable. Taking my light with me I looked through the doors of the other huts. They were empty. The strange people followed me, approaching and receding like a tide, and when I came to the large limp hut of the father of Toma, the tide was before me. The lepers squatted there, making their little animal sounds of both pity and menace. The stench of the father of Toma came out, but the corrupt, kindly guardians of him made it plain to me that I was not to go in. I wasn't to see a respected man who was rotted and alive.

Sometime in the night I was wakened from the half sleep that a hammock induces. There was a crash of crockery as François's hammock came down amidst the clay pots, and while I fought my way from the enormous womb of my own army hammock, through netting and zipper to land asprawl on spread knees, the pots burst into flame from François's lantern, which had fallen too, cracked its glass, and spread burning kerosene across the pathetic labor of our exile hosts.

Ruth was the trim shadow working beside me to reattach the hammock to stronger branches, while François kicked the bits of pottery around.

"Have you another lamp chimney, François?"

"I have not. Is it your affair?"

"You have a flashlight, surely," I said with malice.

"I have not. I am not a Boy Scoot!"

We made no slightest criticism of him, the bearded, the helmeted, the fallen explorer, but while we were putting his house in order for him, placating his Lares and Penates, he stood far from us. My Totelite on the ground showed only his bristly, knobby knees until suddenly he came into full view like something catapulted, and we saw that inching beside him were the knees of our hosts and their feet with no toes on them.

"Let's forget it now, François. We'll pay these people in the morning for their pottery, won't we?"

"I will not be involved in this," he said loudly. "They might have told me the limb was decayed."

"François," said Ruth softly. "François."

"*Peste!*" said he, lighting his broken lantern. The wind whipped its flame through the shattered glass. "I must relieve myself. *Merde!*" He turned to the woods and I hurried after him, trying to offer him my flashlight. "I am not a Boy Scoot!" he snarled at me.

Lonely as an old hated bug he went away, into pure darkness when his lantern guttered out, and I with my unkindness was lonelier still.

What the hell, I thought, is the sense in this? Let him go, and bless him; he wants no part of us. I returned to my hammock, unzipped its machinery, bent the spine to conform and stared at the moon, the color of brass, through the green nylon netting.

"Darling, good night," said I to Ruth. The taste of brass was on my tongue.

∽

As we approached the confluence of our River Maroni with the Tapanahoni on the Dutch shore and the Abounami on the French, the rapids charged like white wolves at us from every side, and our cook Mohammed remarked that he was getting tired of them. Seated almost between François's knees in their canoe with his charcoal stove before him brewing eternal tea, Mohammed slyly drank my taffia and defied Allah to witness. The Mohammedan religion forbids alcohol, even in tea.

It was only when Mohammed coughed so quickly and violently after a gulp and spat a mouthful upon the stove, where it flamed, that I moved the taffia to my canoe, replacing it with Quaker Oats. Perhaps his lust for them could be excited to equal that of the little doctor at St. Laurent.

Up we went through the Saut Como Tabiki, catching the huge fish *coumalu* with bow and arrow and scarcely a pause, and delicately our canoes minueted between the mossy pedestals where lavender flowers waved at us. These were called *coumalu nyan-nyan*, after the fish which seemed to love the purple shadow they cast on the lee side of their rocks. They smelled of ozone, of electric sparks.

We passed Cottica, a Boni village which smelled of latrines, because of the manioc which was being soaked, dried, baked, spread flat on the thatched rooftops against the sun. And we did a strange thing then. We spun suddenly and raced down-river again, through the same purple paths between the *coumalu nyan-nyan*. There had been no talk among the boatmen; apparently there was no order given. I had learned by now not to object to what might seem their whimsies, unless they involved actual malingering, and so it was no surprise to see a little canoe approaching us, paddled by a monkey-faced woman wearing a sarong of pure white. Only then did Afokati explain that this was Eimo's wife.

Even before we could turn again toward Cottica she had passed us, with never a glance at our flotilla or at her husband, who probably had, as she suspected, spent the last month wenching at St. Laurent. Nor did Eimo say a word. We spun in our tracks and pursued her. Eimo kept spitting to show his nonchalance, as most natives do, but the muscles knotted across his shoulders with the swifter swing of his pole. The wife stood up in her small lady's canoe, shoving her paddle expertly first on one side then on the other, glancing impassively at Eimo as we drew level with her.

Eimo made a winsome growl, a wife-call. She paddled so hard then that she slapped up water into his tense sweating face. And as we landed at the village, her canoe slipped neatly backward to moor a hundred feet down-river.

François would not come ashore. There was no time for sentiment on his expeditions. The rest of us wandered casually among the villagers, asking how their rice was, their corn, their *fato*, which was a taro mush the color of *nyan-nyan* shadows. I spilled a bit of rum from a flask on the usual pagan crucifix draped with tattered cloth, while a downy pubescent girl, still nude, held Ruth's hand.

This was an odd and miraculous experience for me, who had lived, legally celibate, for so many years in the dark countries where girls like this infested your house with an embarrassment of beauty, where nothing more than friendship and an hour's understanding was demanded of you. They had been tender and clean as shadows, and like shadows evanescent, thinning quickly and gently in your interest as you did in theirs, until the need for shadow love was upon you both again.

Ruth divined something of this, and I in bewilderment knew that what I was thinking now, that what was aching in me, was arithmetic: camera stop, f6.3; speed 100; 620 film, Super XX; an 8 times red filter — to bring my dusky downy girl alive to my audience, here exquisitely dead to me.

"O-ho!" said Ruth — she had learned this from the Bonis

[149   ]

—as my camera swung back to my hip and my hand reached for hers. "Bill, there's a commotion down there."

At the end of the village was Eimo, sprawling like an old sultan on a little stool, his legs apart in the dust, his toes taut with the pleasure of having his hair combed by a village vestal. There was no smile on him. Eimo, the great voyager, returned from St. Laurent, was being lordly, indulgent. He squinted in quizzical condescension when his handmaid dragged the big rake of a comb through his three inches of wiry snarls. She needed two hands for this, and a knee at the nape of his neck.

He bellowed at her suddenly, holding up his wrist on which he wore a bracelet of his own hair tightly woven, and the girl quickly gave him every hair she had collected in her sarong, which she had tucked to catch it around the belt of his *calambé*. He was taking no chances that his curls be used in magic against him. These, like the others, would be woven into bracelets for him, so that they should not be lost.

The belief that a man may be harmed through parts of his body which have been separated from him, such as hair, nails, teeth, even spittle, is curiously worldwide and most potent in sympathetic magic. People as diverse as Polynesians, Incas, and backward Europeans dispose of cut hair either by burying it or by placing it in a sacred place. The Australian aborigines have a nice habit of getting rid of superfluous wives by stealing locks of their hair at night and burning it bit by bit until their souls wither and waste away, and in Europe today there are women who believe that their migraines are caused by mice or birds having collected their hair combings and made nests of them.

Eimo was being prudent. Now he lolled against the fat knees of the vestal and pretended not to notice that three of our canoemen were charging through the village with the violent burden of his wife in their arms. She yowled like a banshee. Her legs flailed. Her sarong had come loose and stood out stiff in the wind as our Bonis rushed her to Eimo and propelled her upon his innocent hairdresser, whom she demolished with a straight left and a right hook which swiped the sarong from her with what sacred hairs they might contain.

Eimo said nothing, lolling. He shrugged, tilted up his chin, and leaned his head back upon the heaving belly of his wife, who had seized the huge wooden comb and was applying it with vigor. She gouged his scalp and Eimo howled. She slapped him with incredible caress. He wiggled his head a little, feeling the prop beneath it, and turned to it with his big eyes wide. He put his hand upon her belly and tested it as he would a melon for ripeness.

"Bananas!" he roared. They were brought to him. Without looking at them he plucked three and flung them together over his shoulder toward where the moon was rising. Then he lay back blissfully upon the proud belly of his wife.

❧

We came to Wacapou on a rainy evening, approaching it where the river widened and pressed its currents taut against Wacapou on the French shore and Benzdorp on the Dutch. The unusual space between them was so wide that the canoes drew together suddenly and eagerly, took a bold swerve toward Benzdorp so that we might admire the immaculate façade of houses along the riverbank, and jerked us back again.

Ruth, in her canoe just beside me, shook her hair and the dark curls of sleep from her eyes.

"I am not," said she, "speaking to anyone this afternoon. Or only in baby talk. Soul's gone. Up toward the bow, I think. Waddles like a duck."

"Hey? Hey?" said François. I translated.

"Mad as the moon!" he stated.

We had thought that the large company of dressed-up natives on the shore were assembled to welcome us, waving branches of mauve and scarlet bougainvillea and chanting something very like a hymn, but another canoe was approaching from upriver, bearing a white-frocked missionary and his immense straw Annamite hat, big as a parasol.

We were scarcely noticed in the excitement of his coming. The crowd separated to make a path for him up the riverbank. The children waved flowers, the men sliced at the air with machetes as symbol of the food they would fell, the women swept the air with brooms, sweeping the evil from it. And the old missionary, smiling like a goblin, stepped ashore on his yearly visit to Wacapou.

He was French, of course, and of the order of Secularists. For a year and a half he had been paddling with his two choirboys up and down the rapids of the Maroni and into the jungle creeks where his savage flock was hidden in isolated huts. He had practically no baggage but a tin trunk in which he stored the paraphernalia for improvising jungle altars. He ate with the natives and lived in their huts of leaves and spread God's word most humbly.

Wacapou was a single line of houses and ramshackle shops wandering along the footpath at the edge of the riverbank. Their walls were of hand-sawed boards and their roofs of thatch or corrugated iron, which had fortunately skipped the Boni villages below but was indispensable here where the people called themselves Creoles and must dress their dwellings in civilized fashion as they ludicrously did themselves.

The only available lodging space was occupied by two gendarmes and their convict cook, but as their quarters were more than large enough we accepted their invitation and moved into a part of the house which had once been a store. This was excellently practical, as our Bonis, our paddlers, were leaving us here, and we might be in Wacapou some time. How we were to get transportation to the unknown country above this last village, we didn't know, and I found it pleasant that we didn't know. Wacapou was the jumping-off place — virtually the southern end of French Guiana in so far as it was mentioned at all at the club in St. Laurent, though beyond it still lay over half the length of the colony.

Standing on the steps of our dilapidated shack we shook hands with our bright black Bonis and said good-by to them, giving each his chit for payment by Gougis, and to Afokati a note to the "Granman" asking that other rivermen and solid new canoes be sent to pick us up. In this note François had insisted upon enclosing a live bullet, borrowed from one of the gendarmes, which might have been our undoing. François had read in books that the early explorers of South America sent bullets for purposes of identification when communicating with native chiefs. Our Granman, having read no books about his or our ancestors' customs, spent a week of panic, waiting for us to shoot him.

This knowledgeable gesture, and the doubt of its accuracy which must have assailed François, could have been responsible for his querulousness during the two days following. We spoke of a *sanglier* once, the French word for wild boar, and François shouted that he was a scientist and the *sanglier* was not of the pig family at all. And that argument was ended only when Ruth mentioned hypnosis for some reason, and François shouted that it was *inexistant*, no one ever had been hypnotized, and that he would go back downriver tomorrow rather than associate with such persons as us.

And he did. We tucked him into Afokati's canoe, supplied him with provisions, and watched his shadow lessen against the sun.

☙

It was at that very moment, as though by arrangement with various gods, that a medley of music rose around us. We stood on the cliff above the river, not watching the canoes any longer, but gazing south along the blue water, tranquil here, which led finally to the mountains which we must reach before the rains came on. On one side of us was the sound of tom-toms and instruments which might resemble banjos, and women screaming and doors being banged. On the other was a soulful dissonant chanting, arisen from the Christian part of the populace parading toward the chapel they had built of bamboo during the absence of the missionary.

We followed them for a little while, as they marched with their torches in the twilight; they were pleased to have us with them, and we slunk guiltily away from them to the other end of the village where the hullabaloo was. The hullabaloo was caused by the Tululu, a sort of pagan Mardi Gras enjoyed exclusively by masked male dancers who roamed around the huts in bands, snatching anyone they could, beating him with flour sacks and making him dance within the monstrous circle of the Tululu demons.

As we stood watching this, filming it, a heavy hand was laid upon my shoulder with the sort of touch which even the innocent can recognize as the hand of the law. It was Ferdinand, one of the gendarmes, our hosts — a square spare lad, clad in khaki shorts, muscle-fitting shirt, and pith helmet pulled low over the brows. It didn't quite conceal his pale blue eyes which gave you the impression of mean oysters.

"Quick," said he, "you have quinine, yes?"

I moved him politely out of the way of Ruth's camera, saying, "Yes."

"It is Jacques, my companion, the other gendarme. Malaria, and I think blackwater fever now. The black bloody urine is all over his bed."

Ruth finished shooting just as one of the masked Tululu had grown cocky enough to take a swipe at her Filmo with the flour sack.

In the brown darkness of one of the inner rooms of our rambling shack lay the captain who had led young Ferdinand upriver in search of escaped convicts. He was emaciated. His bed was drenched with red-black fluid. We turned him over, shot him full of quinine, and stumbled over the legs of the moaning figure on the floor.

This was Raphael, faithful servitor of the moment, escaped convict and cook, whom they had brought back with them from the village of Mademoiselle Victoire, a little farther south, where he had been preparing a grand *évasion* to the Dutch shore. When the sick gendarme groaned, he groaned too, and Ruth and I were touched by his sympathy. We looked at each other and understood each other without words: could we induce the gendarmes to take Mohammed back to the prisons, exchanging him for Raphael, who should cook for us and be devoted to us?

"Hah!" said Ferdinand, as we sat at the raw wood table outside the sick man's door. "It is agreed. You may have him. You may bring him back alive, or shoot the pig." We had a drink out of dirty tumblers, of Mohammed's washing.

"Raphael!" yelled Ferdinand. A groan was the answer.

[156]

"Sacred name of a dog!" The gendarme flung his tumbler smack into the man's face. "Will you get us dinner now or will you have the club?" The cook crawled to his feet, slithered along the wall to the cook shack, and began a piteous conversation with himself, from which we could catch frequent references to his mother.

"Scum!" said Ferdinand reminiscently. "Slime!" He tilted his chair against the window and his helmet back against the stars, and talked with relish of his work. The convicts were beneath contempt, beneath pity, he said, and there was no way of controlling them but with a *trompe* (a wallop), or a "boom-boom-boom," (three of the same). Most of his conversation during the instructive days we lived beside him was to consist of *trompes* and boom-boom-booms.

Ruth wasn't liking this much, nor was I, but we had a chance here to live intimately with a pure and flawless jewel of a gendarme, a rare chance unless you were a convict, so we swallowed our bile and listened. Ferdinand had ground the bastards' teeth out beneath his heel when he discovered them selling their gold fillings to procure the means of escape. He had flogged them. He had invented a means of extorting confessions.

Ruth didn't want her rum at this point, but she drank it. Her slanted eyes snapped shut and open, biting off the view of this monstrous young man.

The recipe for confession was simple. Look, you opened your condensed-milk cans with an old-fashioned can opener that left jagged edges. You saved them and replaced them in their box, twelve to the box, and when at last you had the box full you looked for a troublesome *bagnard* who might be improved by confession.

"Yes?" said Ruth, tossing her bright hair from what of her eyes was visible. "What do you do then, Ferdinand?"

Then you take his pants off and make him kneel on the jagged cans, and keep him there with a medium whip till he confesses. It was as simple as that. It should be patented.

❧

"Come in! Come in!" called Ferdinand to a gentle tapping at our open door.

The long white gown of the missionary passed through the kitchen, paused while Father Bessac complimented Raphael on the smell of his fried onions, and moved into the light of our kerosene lanterns. From nose to forehead, his mischievous face floated above his shoulders; the rest of it was concealed by the apparently vacant shadow of his beard.

"*Je m'excuse,*" he said. "Children, I impose upon you."

"But no, my Father!" Ferdinand swung to his feet; and rather awkwardly, without the help of clubs, tin cans, or whips, got the good padre to sit down. He blessed us. He would like to talk seriously to us, and he talked of the jungle world which was all the world to him since he had renounced society seventeen years ago. We listened attentively to him, drinking rum in cadence with his small drinks, mopping our faces, drying our sweated fingers so that our cigarettes should taste less salty.

We probably knew what we were up to, he said, but he was concerned about Ruth. *Poof* for the jungle down-river! It was beginning in earnest now, the jungle, and the beings in it. The Indians to the south were pagan fellows and undependable in that they were constantly changing villages, or rather exchanging them, so that like as not you would run into a tribe which had never seen white men before. These were suspicious and difficult to deal with. On the other hand, if you encountered a tribe which had met any of the few European explorers, your welcome might be even less cordial.

The earlier missionaries, he said, had tried to get the Indians to call them *bons blancs* "the good white men," but when he himself arrived at one of their villages he found that they had picked up another French word from the Boni traders. No sooner did he put foot ashore than the red-hued rascals yelled, *"Mal blanc! Mal blanc!"* and laid their arrows end to end in a circle around him. Then they danced around the circle for half the night, making foul gestures at the proud old man who stood alone in his white cassock amidst them, and he knew that if he should step across an arrow it wouldn't be long before they would be swinging his head by its beard, in no sense of vengeance toward him personally, mind you, but in remembrance of the other white men several generations back who had dealt with them and their women dishonestly.

"Their women!" said the padre. "Ugh!" They caused more trouble! Once, for example, in an Indian village he had seen an empty hut which looked like a good place to hang his hammock, but he sheared off just at the doorway, for he had noticed the signs there: this was the hut reserved for women menstruating, and a man might be killed for entering it. But many of their customs were odd and some abnormal. Among the Roucouyennes (the tribe we hoped to find) a man was forbidden to sleep with his wife for two years after childbirth or until nursing was finished, which was sometimes longer than that. We were to see youngsters of three and four still suckling at the breast. The result of this preposterous ban was that infidelity and promiscuity were of course very common.

This informative monologue was brought abruptly to an end by sky-shattering howls of an animal in pain followed by a wailing as of Arabs at the fete of Ramadan. The resemblance was in part correct. Wailing and literally gnashing his yellow teeth, Mohammed tumbled up the stairs of the kitchen and sprawled against Raphael's legs, sending a potful of rice flying like confetti all over the room and into ours.

"Dear, dear!" said the padre, plucking hot rice from his beard.

"Son of swine!" yelled Raphael. He bent the empty pot on Mohammed's head.

"*Assez!*" yelled Ferdinand. "Enough!"

The padre bowed hurriedly to Ruth. "I excuse myself, *madame*. I am *de trop*, superfluous."

As Ferdinand bounded to the kitchen, Mohammed was already outside the door and wailing through the cracks of it that a tiger had taken one of his dogs, O Allah, O Allah!

[160]

The lamb of his heart the tiger had taken, his Bobi, his best hunting dog!

The tiger, or *tigre*, in South America is the jaguar, the sort that Sacha Seymel spears; although much smaller than his Indian cousin, he is no beast to provoke. The natives dread him mainly because his cunning is superior to theirs, and therefore supernatural.

Mohammed's loss of the dog was abysmal to him, a property loss of at least ten thousand francs, which is a lot of francs for a poor murderer who spends most of his time nonproductively in a cell, but Ferdinand's boot cared nothing about this as it swung up like a ballet dancer's and smashed Mohammed's nose.

It was Raphael who was wailing now, for his rice was ruined. He had been preparing it for his poor sick captain, the malarial man in the inner room, who suddenly was shouting, "*Merde!* Give me a drink and another quinine! Ferdinand, hey my old one! Beat the tripes out of that howling pig!"

Ferdinand had already started, with a nod over his shoulder at Ruth and me. The first blow sounded like the *trompe;* the others were surely the boom-boom-boom. Pots were falling with our dinner all over the kitchen when I got there, and Raphael was sobbing that he was born of a mother like Ferdinand, which infuriated Ferdinand. *Trompe!*

"I'll descend you like a rabbit!" he howled. "That you should mention my mother's name with yours?" Boom! He didn't even feel my hands on his shoulders. He spat and stepped on the spittle. Boom-boom! "Less than that you are, the spit beneath my heel, and your sacred mother!" Boom-boom-boom!

"*Assez*, Ferdinand, *assez!*" It was my turn now. I moved him gently away from Raphael and toward the stove, which burned him to greater wrath so that he got another clout at Raphael before I could get between them.

Ruth's cigarette stuck straight out from between her lips as she made notes on these matters. "I have still to determine," she remarked, "which is the jungle and which is the penal colony here."

❧

We waited at Wacapou impatiently for canoe replacements from down-river. It was frustrating because there was no means of communication with Afokati's village. At Benzdorp, on the Dutch shore opposite, we made the jovial acquaintance of Mynheer Hermans, the administrator, and were no more than physically consoled by him, for he could influence none of the Bosch Negroes to leave with us for a journey into blank dark space. Their last village was right here.

Hermans returned from the wonderful icebox with another pitcher of cold punch and talked about the early explorers, Coudreau and Crevaux and Patrice. Patrice, he said, was probably responsible for the legend of the pale-skinned Indians, for when he made his journey of exploration in the latter part of the nineteenth century he had anticipated mine by taking a woman with him too who he explained was his *dactylo*, his stenographer. He returned without her, saying she had died of malaria, but the tale leaked out through other members of the expedition. Patrice had simply grown tired of her brand of stenography; as she had no other talents, he abandoned her to a young Indian of good family, gave her a dowry of beans and rice and fishhooks, and went on his way.

Thus, there being a law of genetics to the effect that the offspring of miscegenation is never darker than the darker partner, and as many of these Indians were quite light anyway, it was reasonable to infer that Patrice's *dactylo*, by assiduous exercise of her brand of stenography, might have considerably brightened the race.

Ruth was counting on her fingers. "I can also cook, take photographs, swim on my back, sculpt, and ski. . . ."

"There's a jungle wife!" Hermans slapped his fat thigh. "But I'm worried about these Bonis of yours. They are less dependable than *madame*, less even than our Boschs over here, whom we have spoiled perhaps less than the French have the Bonis."

I judged by one of Ruth's eyebrows that she was thinking of the tribute which the Dutch still paid their Boschs.

"If your Bonis have returned to their village you may never see them again. If they didn't like you they will send no one to replace them. If they should take you upriver they may turn back when it pleases them, or just leave you on the shore. You never can count on what they'll do."

He wiped his gray hair and pink face, and chuckled for a

while before he said, "You can't count on them. They have made fools of us, the Dutch. You remember their revolt against us was originally led by Captain Boni? We sued for peace, and when the treaty was drawn, Boni led some of his troops with their women across the Maroni (or Marowyne, as we call it) to French territory, but skirmishes still went on. During one of these we did take Captain Boni himself, and cut off his head immediately, for we knew the unpredictable fellow that he was. It is said that his wife seized his sword and slashed off the head of our own captain with a pretty blow, then plunged into the river and disappeared.

"Our men started home in their canoes, bringing Captain Boni's head in the stern of one of them. You remember the falls called Laissez-Dédé? They were passing just above it when one of the men screamed and the others turned to look, and in the stern of the canoe they saw Captain Boni's head rise from the thwarts, dripping blood, and plunge into the wake. That's what I mean when I say the Bonis are unpredictable."

"Extraordinary! They never saw the head again?"

"Never again, though they did see another head, the head of Boni's wife, swirling to the edge of the falls and over it. Evidently she had hidden under the canoe until our men pushed off, then hung onto it in the shadow of the stern. Down over the falls she went with the remains of her husband, and has never been heard of since. Can't count on such people," said Mynheer Hermans with a sniff. "Your paddlers may come back for you and again they may not."

He reached for the refrigerator handle without getting up, and it opened with that wondrous cool clank which I should dream about.

"Now here's what I'd suggest. You stay here with me for a while. I'll give you a pan for washing gold. I'll buy all you get at an honest price and guarantee you'll make money."

"Is there so much of it that even an amateur can pan it?"

"Why do you suppose the French *bricoleurs* and the Dutch *porknockers* keep coming back for more?" These were the unlicensed prospectors, mostly Creoles and *libérés*, who indeed did themselves well when they visited the towns. "The *porknockers* won't bother washing dirt that doesn't bring them in at least five or six grams per day, at a guilder and a half per gram, which is a decent living hereabouts. The law is, of course, that the gold of both Guianas must be sold only to the governments at established prices, but there are contrabanders all over the place. There goes one now. Hold on, I'll get him to paddle you home."

Untying the painter of his lean canoe was an elderly Bosch, who looked up with a start when Mynheer hailed him.

"Notice that thick roll at the top of his loincloth? . . . Asman!" said Hermans to him. "You are the light of my life, my most faithful diversion, and I regret to see that you are smuggling no gold today!"

Old Asman simpered, flicked up sand with his toes, and couldn't stop his hands from adjusting the ragged *calambé*.

Hermans steadied the canoe while Ruth and I got cautiously

into it, spinning and teetering for balance like drunken dancers.

"So," said Mynheer to Asman, "you may take the captain and *madame* back to Wacapou, and I shall forget that you are wearing your *calambé* indecently high."

❧

The traveler in strange countries is usually and gradually so accustomed to strangeness that it becomes a matter of course; by small inoculations his perception is blunted; he is habituated to surprise and immunized to the shock of it. This is particularly true of countries like India where the culture is complex, while in the simple wilderness of French

Guiana any oddity is isolated and remarkable. Because startling things don't happen there, because there is no phantasy, you are inclined to exaggerate the novelty of even little things.

I was therefore delighted at Wacapou to find that black rubbed on white produced a dazzlingly whiter white when the natives brushed their teeth with frayed twigs powdered with charcoal. And Ruth's discovery of a leaf which tasted like spinach and slid on the tongue like okra provoked us to seek the plant in the forest and identify it as *klagoon* or *macoco* or *gogo mongo*, which was small help to the New York Botanical Gardens which had entrusted to us a pressing frame for exotic plants.

The late Bob Ripley, fellow of the Explorers' Club, would have glamorized a bird named *agami*, of which there were several respected specimens at Wacapou, gainfully employed. The *agami* is a pedestrian bird and travels in troupes through the woods. It is a sentimental bird, which mourns the death of any one of its kind and will let itself be captured rather than leave the corpse. This is the common way of catching it. In captivity it is inconsolable and it is allowed to languish for a while until its Boni captor knows that soon it will die of loneliness.

Then the bereaved *agami* is put in the chicken coop, where again it is just touch and go with death, but this time through an excess of joy and loving-kindness. It sings all the time in its cracked voice, adoring the hens and the cocks alike, and eventually becomes the shepherd of them. During the day they are allowed their freedom to peck in the woods under the guidance of the good *agami;* and a weird fact is that, in his great benignity, he stops the fowls from fighting. He separates them with a few choice quacks, as he preaches to them; then at nightfall he rounds them up, every one, and leads them safely to their coop.

Such small wonders at Wacapou passed our time too quickly. The rains were inexorably coming and still we had neither paddlers nor cook. Mohammed was by now truly hopeless with strong liquors, and Raphael, as we got to know him, began to display those fits of quite unfounded querulousness that had made the gendarmes willing to exchange him even for Mohammed. Our third choice was Bella, who pleased us very much.

We were on our way to Mass in the padre's little chapel

when we saw Bella twisting like a dervish in slow motion before her tiny hut of thatch. She was an enormous handsome girl, an Amazon dressed in a man's white shorts, starched and pressed, and a jersey shirt that was stretched near to bursting across her conical breasts. She was holding a glass filled with water and golden objects against her forehead and studying it in a triangle of broken mirror.

"Good morning, Bella," we said in the rather smug hushed tones used by those who walk righteously to an early Mass.

"Good morning," said she, "but it is the devil of a headache." She moved the glass to another spot in her thick black hair.

"Are you perhaps going crazy?" I asked.

"No doubt of it," she replied, "if I can't find the worm."

"What worm?" Ruth asked. "You will miss Mass, you know."

"I would not take the worm to Mass, *madame*. It is evil. Is it bubbling?" She peered in the mirror and pirouetted.

Ruth and I stood on tiptoe, for Bella was tall, but there were no worms bubbling in the glass, only rather dirty water and several bits of crude gold jewelry.

Bella gave a sudden spin with one brawny leg straight out before her. It caught me on the knee. "There it goes! See it now!" she cried. "See it bubbling?"

Sure enough there were bubbles in the glass, probably brewed by the volcanic activity of Bella. But no, she explained, that was not it at all. She had located the worm with the glass, as with a Geiger counter, and the glassful of *piail*, magic, had killed the worm and cured the headache.

"Headache gone?"

Of course, it was gone, and weren't we the peculiar people not to know how to find and kill the headache worm? Were there no headaches in America? Pooh, they could not amount to much.

By this time other Creoles on their way to Mass had gathered round to bear Bella out. Her cure was common practice, they said. You put any old bangles — though gold wedding rings were better — into a glass of water, inverted it carefully on your head, and moved it from spot to spot until the water bubbled; that's where the worm was working and you killed it straight away.

"Now," said Bella, revived, "am I coming up the river with you or am I not?"

Ruth hedged. "Ah, Bella, I have told you that you must have your husband's permission. He would be angry, wouldn't he, if we should take you and you were cut up by the Indians, or maybe raped by our paddlers?"

"My husband!" said Bella scornfully. "He's gone to Cottica to see his wife. Married to her," she added.

As we continued in our serious little parade to the chapel, we sighed and decided definitely that Bella wouldn't do as cook on the journey ahead. There was too much of her, and too much of her was woman, the master woman. Bounding in her shorts around the bamboo schoolroom in the daytime, she beat a reasonable facsimile of the three R's into the quivering young, and a night, with her mandolin, she went serenading in no uncertain fashion the village bucks. Alone in the jungle with our six pulsing Boni paddlers she would probably not be the pacific neutral that a good cook should be, and what with her belligerent views on medicine I saw myself some day sick and trussed like a fowl and subjected to ignominies inappropriate to the courageous leader of expeditions. No, not Bella.

The Mass at the little chapel was the inauguration of it, and we entered to dedicate it to Our Lady of Lourdes and the Miraculous Medallion. It could scarcely have been more than twenty by twenty feet, but it was a generous offering from the padre's tiny flock, neatly made of hand-adzed boards of the wood called *golotee*, with fine doors of *bijoudou* and *waipa* combined — sound timber to hold the worship of the unknown god.

The inauguration would have been pathetic without the grandeur of improvisation on the part of both priest and villagers. He was a flaming sight in his homemade white cassock upon which had been stuck great cruciform orange ribbons; his acolyte children wore cloaks of bleached flour bags upon undervestments of red trade cloth. There were paper flowers everywhere, these being holier than the common jungle ones.

The chapel was jammed. The windows were trelliced with the black arms, legs, and ripe fruit-like heads of Bonis who held sticks upright in their fists, imitating the altar boys with their candles. The congregation was so crowded along the benches that overlapping straw hats made a crackling like

[170]

surf over pebbles, and it was hard to hear the padre, who took his business seriously.

The wearing of hats was obligatory, of course; there was a moment's to-do just before the Mass began, when one of the acolytes spied a baby of indeterminate sex, because of the long dress, wearing no hat. Clinical examination, which delayed Mass for five minutes, proved the child to be a girl, and she was ejected. Another few minutes later, we were startled to see what looked like a helmet walking; it was our errant babe returning beneath her father's hat.

The priest had just opened his mouth to intone, when a ragged white man sprang to his feet from the front bench and said: "Excuse me, *mon père*, may I make an announcement? Tonight, at eight o'clock," he shouted, "there will be a *séance* of ipnotism in the store of Monsieur Fougeot! I shall ipnotize a man and send him to the brink of the grave. . . ." He was silenced by popular protest, but not before he had wakened the babies. The Creole next to me whispered, "The man is an *évadé*; there is a price on his head; if you and I, *mon capitaine*. . . ."

The priest's hands, raised on high, settled on the altar of packing cases, and through the din of crackling straw hats and babies squalling I caught the word " . . . *vobiscum.*" He raised his hands again and they were clenched in fists; his beard, as if hinged, swung up and straight toward us. "Silence!" he roared. "This is what I call a drollness of a comedy! Are you not ashamed?"

For a while, then, there was a trial silence. Both nudged me

[171   ]

to look at one Creole mother who held a rosary in one hand, a switch in the other, and a child of about two, backside up across her lap, its bottom bare.

". . . *vobiscum*," said the padre, sweating as one who has run a race and won it, faster than sound, just as all the little lambs of God broke forth again.

Down the aisle came the choirboys jangling token francs in baskets, making the collection. The woman with the bare-bottomed baby covered it up, let it howl, dropped the switch, dropped the rosary between her bosoms, put a five-franc note into the basket, and took out four francs in change.

◦∾◦

Filled with godliness and good will, we could not have imagined that in this winsome comic-opera setting there was the starkest hate and fear awaiting us in our old Chinaman's shop, as we returned from the chapel. Wacapou seemed in every way a land of make-believe, where such grossness as murder had no place. Evil, like holiness, was too positive an element; evil would be assertive, offensive, rude, unimaginable here.

Ruth and I strode down the garden paths, admiring the friendliness with which the neighbors' gardens interwove, passing the goldsmith's shop in his thatched hut, like a child's tunnel in a bale of hay, where Ruth's wedding ring was at last being confected. We were talking with wonder, quietly, of the pure African survivals around us everywhere: the stilted peaked huts with untrimmed frond whiskers; the babies' charm lockets of cloth, much munched-upon; the singing in the wood, which was a high falsetto to fool the demons, and the duet singing nearby, which was contrapuntal, with two staggered, laminated melodies. This was West Africa, neat.

As we approached our shack, we saw Mohammed emerging from it at a gallop, flapping his arms like a wounded bird, followed by his dogs. He was drunk and terrified. We divined at last that he, the mighty hunter, had been ordered by Raphael to hunt, to prove his reputation. But after his passage through Ali's shop, where there was taffia, his vision had dimmed and he had brought home only one small but succulent tortoise, a *kono*, the very type, *mon capitaine*, which the French would give their eyeballs for. This, however, had not pleased Raphael, who flipped the tortoise in his face, drawing blood. There had been hard words spoken, including an allusion to death, and now he, Mohammed, the convict cook, enslaved to us by order of the administration, was resigning.

I "tut-tutted" him and sat him comfortably under a tree to sleep his troubles off. Nothing of note occurred during the rest of the afternoon except the quiet of it, for the gendarme Ferdinand was in "Benzdorp," seeking quinine injections for his mate, who was now so near to death that he did not even groan, and Raphael, to avoid discussion of the Mohammed matter, had disappeared. He wove home to work in the kitchen when we were on our third cocktail and getting hungry. Now he too was drunk. He was plastered. He had lost his shirt and sandals, and was wearing only blue denims. His brown sinewy torso staggered among the pots and astonishingly produced a pretty fair corned-beef goulash.

We pumped up the Coleman lantern, pulled our wooden stools to the table, and were about to enjoy this semblance of a meal when Mohammed sidled in by the back door and gave me the keys to the trunks in earnest of his "resignation." I was explaining patiently that his position as a servant, even as a bad servant, was a little special in that he was condemned for life to servitude — even to me if need be — when suddenly Raphael spotted him and with a leap and a roar, brandishing the bread knife dear Mother gave me, chased him out of the door.

"I'll cut his dirty head off!" he yelled. "He's one tenth white, he says to me! Hah, I'll slice the nine tenths of Arab off him and teach him his manners! Mohammed!" he yelled, lunging through the window. "Thou art listening to me, yes? I've slept enough by the puke of thee! Leave the door open so I can get my clothes!"

The trouble had begun, said Raphael, when they were visiting the bar of one Ali, a *libéré*, that afternoon, and though the bar was only a roof of thatch over an earthen floor, it purveyed genuine Marie Brizard *crème de menthe*, which so inflamed Raphael's sentiment and bonhomie that he gave first his shoes to Mohammed and then his shirt. He regretted this immediately. Could one imagine what Mohammed did? He refused to say thank you! By the name of God, Raphael urged him — first politely, then forcefully.

Mohammed, "*ce petit Jésus*," had stubbornly refused and, to make things worse, when he was in some pain beneath Raphael's suasion, he had the nerve, the temerity, not to thank him but to apologize! "I apologize," said Mohammed, "for accepting your God-damned shirt."

I could see how this might distress Raphael. We proffered him a glass of taffia, against the orders of his absent master, the gendarme, and backed him gradually into the kitchen, where he continued his complaints to the dishpan, swiping murderously at what must have been faces in the suds. I could almost hear the cogs of his mind gripping and slipping, gripping and slipping again. When he had spun a thought a little more than halfway round sufficiently to grasp its edges, he sprang to the doorway.

"But do you know what?" he demanded. Ruth and I looked up from our accounts and maps. "This little *Jésus* then had the nerve to say, 'But I will *not* apologize for accepting your God-damned shoes!' "

"*Mon capitaine*," said a voice through the window, Mohammed's. His brown wrinkled face, yellow-fanged and unshaven, burping *crème de menthe*, sneered at us all. With great restraint I pushed the flat of my hand against it. "Here are all the possessions, *mon capitaine*, which he left in my house." And in they came, smack against Raphael's stomach.

Then I saw a chilling display of the contrariety of the unfortunates who had spent some years in the colony called Devil's Island. Raphael put his white knuckles on the old, gray, wooden table, and said sweetly as a nurse lulling a

child in her arms, *"Vas dodo, mon chéri, jusque je te
viens. . . ."* ("Go to sleep, darling, until I come to you. . . .")

Mohammed's head bobbed like a marionette's against a
backdrop of dark green palm fronds and purple space. He
stammered, "Do you understand, *mon capitaine?* This spe-
cific phenomenon is only a *relégué*, a thief; I am a murderer,
a *transporté*. If I should fight with him I should have five more
years added to my sentence; he would have three months.
If I should kill him, I should be guillotined. I, who am remembered as a man in North Africa, must act like a woman
before this pickpocket pederast; I cannot fight back." He
sucked his bitterness through his foul gaping teeth.

Raphael's face was cadaverous as he strained across the
table toward the window; it was pure with hate. *"Vas dodo,
mon chéri. Je te visite. . . .Con!"*

"Inculé!" bawled Mohammed, and disappeared, as well he
should.

Raphael's lean tower of sinew twisted and leaped to the
kitchen, grabbed the machete — disdaining Mother's bread
knife now — and hurtled through the door to the path where
Mohammed had vanished. I believe I was delighted, for here
was the first physical crisis of the expedition and I had worried about my own reactions if it should occur. Had — *had*, I
said now to myself. You see how easy it is? How it always
is when the thing happens? You're getting up quickly and
quietly now. You haven't looked at Ruth, for it is purely
your affair. Down the three steps you go and into the dark
to stop this murder and bring Raphael back. . . . Not a quiver

in you. Remember your trespasses on the night patrols of Alamein? This is the restful way of action, and your head may be cut off, what the hell? Keep going, bub.

I kept going in the direction of the hut which Raphael and Mohammed shared, stumbling off the invisible path and flashing my light on briefly, aware that our maniac might turn and come toward it from a diagonal beyond the beam. I think I intended, since I was unarmed, to tackle him low when my outstretched hands touched his nude sweating back, twist him, get him in the groin, smash at his windpipe. It was tonic, it was good, it was ridiculous.

"Bill, here's the pistol," said Ruth just behind me. She had calmly followed and now I heard her squeaky sandals going deliberately back again. I held the flashlight in my left hand and shone it on the pistol in my right.

"Raphael, *halte-là!*"

Quickly I flashed the light up the path. There was no one ahead. The huts were tight-shuttered. I held the light on the gun barrel and turned slowly around with it. A voice close by said, "Careful, he's over there!"

I ringed an old native's head in a window, then snapped the light toward the river. There against a tree stood Raphael, his ankles crossed, his long blade swinging between finger and thumb, his face benign and smiling.

"You were looking for me, *capitaine?*"

"Give me that *sabre*, Raphael. Give me the handle of it."

Without uncrossing his ankles he bowed and gave me the machete. I didn't like his grin. . . .

[177]

"Get back to the house, Raphael, and leave Mohammed alone. You know I'm sending him down-river, and you are coming with me instead."

His thin lips lengthened, like worms stretching up one side of his face.

"Walk ahead of me." I talked to the brown oily leather of his back. "I am not a gendarme, Raphael, so I'm not going to beat you, but I'll damn well shoot you if you cause trouble. Do you understand?"

He turned his leer over his shoulder. "You are too good to me, *mon capitaine!*"

I prodded him in the ribs with the pistol, furious because I suspected that he meant just what he said. He had sized me up. He knew I wouldn't kill him. He knew already that we needed him. And he knew that this exact little knowledge could be a dangerous thing for us, as indeed it was to be.

❦

The last of the baboons had scarcely ceased howling when the notable events of the day began falling out of the dawn upon us. The Dutch on the opposite shore transmitted to us a telegram from Eastman Kodak reporting that the film we had sent back was good. Ferdinand, Mohammed, and the sick gendarme called Godspeed to us and set off down-river. And upriver came our three old canoes with our six same Boni paddlers, plus their omnipotent chief, the Granman Difoo.

He was truly a grand man — as his title implied — the

Granman Difoo. He had come upriver to meet death before our guns; death, he said, was implied by the bullet our former companion had sent to him. Here he was, he said, straightening someone's cast-off military jacket around his spare shoulders. His old hand, freckled and blue with veins, trembled a little as it reached to the tufts of his mustache. But would we tell him how he had been delinquent, how he had done any wrong to deserve the bullet?

We cleared this up rapidly, and before the half hour was gone we had agreed to pay our paddlers one hundred and fifty francs a day, and Ruth had trapped the batch of them in the storeroom and set them to packing our belongings. The crates, the hampers, the equipment cases, the duffel bags, the sacks of food, the tins of gasoline, the demijohns of rum were swung up onto the dark heads and paraded through the door to the high river bank where they were passed down through volunteers, including the padre, until Afokati stored them precisely in his canoes.

The women of Wacapou were already plaiting fifteen-foot coconut fronds to cover the baggage. Raphael, beaming, was installed in his kitchen canoe, the charcoal stove between his knees, the tea brewing on it, and all his pans in order. Spread like an ensign of heraldry was the blazoning of his blanket, gray and green and red, across the middle third of the canoe; this was the thick prickly prison blanket given to every convict. You might think it a shameful mantle, but you would be wrong. This was the one comforter, for all its harshness, the one rough comforting friend, the spiny womb of warmth which the prisoners clung to. It was their intimate retreat and refuge where finally they could lie alone.

"My children, I bless you," said our old padre, raising his hand above the canoes. "You are going to a land which I want never to visit again. Though the Roucouyennes are gentle people, you must distrust them; they are covetous. If you meet a band of them who perhaps have not seen me or other whites before, it is possible that they might not prevent your receiving an injury, an upset in the rapids, perhaps, so that they might get your goods without actually attacking you."

He leaned back against a short crucifix on the bank. It was not a Christian but a Boni device, with rags of someone's ancestor moldering on it.

"If you go far enough you will witness disturbing things. There are men among them who are telepathic. A few years ago I met an Indian who was fishing far down-river from his village. He couldn't possibly have known that I would be there. We exchanged presents of food, and as his canoe drew away he said, 'My daughter will be waiting for you on the sandspit.' And three weeks later, there she was, waiting at twilight on the only sandspit for miles around."

The padre took off his helmet and rivers of sweat ran into his beard.

"It will be cool in the creeks," he said, "beneath the great trees which are God's, and there you will hear voices, I think, but they will not be God's voices. They will be the evil tongues of Indians you will never see; at least I hope you may never see them."

"Oh? said Raphael, blinking.

"What's the name of this tribe, Father?" I asked, also blinking.

"They are the Oyaricoulets. Coudreau has mentioned them, and one other man. You have heard of him. It was he who came back, the only one of the party of fifty who had gone to survey the western Tumuc-Humacs. He had slept in a tree because he was afraid of snakes. So the Indians missed him. He wrote in his report to the Governor that for weeks his party had heard the voices in the bush around them, and from time to time they had found a white ball of kapok on a stick, which is a peaceful sign. It was the night after they saw the red ball, and ignored it, that the massacre occurred."

"Oh?" said Ruth.

"Oh!" said Raphael firmly. I judged that he had some antipathy to the Oyaricoulets.

One of the virtues of this expedition was that there was little time on it either for regret or anticipation, and it became increasingly evident that we must distract Raphael from both. That, for the most part, we succeeded in doing. With ruse and shock we learned to shadow these two thirds of his life, but the present, the current third was a bitch in the manger to us. I think we managed to ease the pain of his memories and his prospects, and in effect he said to hell with them, but it was his sharp, aching, actual every moment that tortured him.

For a while he seemed able to forget his past sufferings as a criminal and to ignore the future when eventually I should be obliged to return him to his cell, but pain had become his climate by now; he was unwell without it, he must speciously contrive it to be at ease.

By the end of the first day with Raphael on the river we knew we had with us a complex of prima donna and problem child. Somehow we were never very much aware of the tried and true assassin in him, and this was fortunate for us who came to doubt the loyalty of our paddlers, distrust our Indian guides, and suspect the twisted shadows behind the trees which were God's.

⟨⁂⟩

Raphael's trial balloon of temperament went up the first night out of Wacapou. We had hauled the canoes through three medium-sized rapids and stopped at Marepasoula, an outpost of the gendarmerie. But there had been no one in it, the office and the jail were locked, the corn grew old in the garden, so we picked the best of it and paddled around the bend to Inini which was the last customs post.

Everyone was weary by this time, including the customs inspector, whom we had roused from his malarial cot, and his luscious Creole wife who was about to burst with child. It seemed rather silly for the inspector to demand our papers this far up the river, before even offering us a drink, as though our considerable party might be sneaking through with contraband. But this was doubtless the only chance he had ever had to display his authority to official Europeans on his own ground.

Proof of my own certainty that I should never make an executive was obvious when our formalities were concluded and we sat down with our rum punches on the rickety veranda. The Bonis stood in a line before and below us, watching us reproachfully. Raphael leaned against a tree, drooping like one whose burdens were too great to bear. Pekein, the mascot, sat on the ground with eyes downcast, ashamed of us who were neglecting him. Our Fiji-haired Creole inspector laughed when I asked where our men should make their camp and ours. "Let them wait; you spoil them," he said, shaking so with malaria that he needed two hands for his drink. I envisioned the explorer, the fictional explorer, I had never managed to be, gruff, taking charge, flinging orders like banana peels over his shoulder. I gulped the drink and insisted boldly on making camp now.

This consisted of a tangle of shacks, in one of which we installed Raphael and his kitchen equipment, asking him simply to boil the corn; we should make a supper of that alone. The stove burned merrily, the water sizzled. It was half an hour later that I suspected something wrong and returned to the kitchen to see Raphael weeping. He couldn't boil the corn; he didn't know how nor how many minutes; we were slave drivers; we asked the impossible. I sat on the step beside him and put my arm around his shoulders. I'd straighten him out, all right.

"You're all alike!" he wailed. "You're against me too. So I'm a dog, am I? I prefer to go back to the cells!"

For one — and for the last — time, my sympathy won

him over, and before long we were working side by side, chuckling like old ladies at a church social as we shucked the corn and dropped it into the singing pot.

"Just needs a friend, poor bugger," I said to Ruth, risking my pivot tooth on that old corn. The monkeys from horizon to horizon howled their derision of my innocence.

❧

"Bee-hill!" came the call from the canoe behind me. I put aside the gun I was oiling and stood up, but it wasn't Ruth, it was her clown-paddler Eimo, a mimic of distinction. "Ex-kiss!" he said, which meant "Excuse!" Then he broke into hysterical laughter concluding with "Oo-la-la!"

This was in the dusk again, after a hard day with the rapids of Aiefiasoula and Soenajeue. We were passing Niam Creek, a slot in the aluminum sunset, and approaching the village of Antouka, the last of all, with a pointed island before it and what seemed a black hole in the island's center, framing an old white tree like a skeleton.

Raphael was standing in his canoe, to the annoyance of his back paddler, Toma, who couldn't see past him. Raphael, in fine humor, was expatiating on the pleasantness of the town and in particular on the charms of a Mademoiselle Victoire.

It was a kempt village of bordered gardens and sleepy old huts that looked as though their thatch had been washed frond by frond between caressing elderly hands. All of it was neat. The lanes had broom marks on them. In almost every garden there was an inner garden, like the heart of it, a child's canoe

[　184　]

filled with plants and held high in the air by four stilts rising from tin cans with water and oil in them to discourage that ravisher, the *fourmi manioc*, an omnivorous ant.

There were cashew and lime trees everywhere, with bird cages hanging from them. Old people moved silently along the lanes to the slow rhythm of an invisible primitive clarinet. It was a fairy-tale village, and Raphael's meeting with his Mademoiselle Victoire was equally unreal. She was a sweet old Creole of seventy or so who embraced that rock-hard sinner and graciously invited us to her house of leaves. "And this is my son, Victor," said Mademoiselle. Victor was a goblin, as round and fat and beaming as one.

First thing of all, Mademoiselle led Raphael to the canoe in her garden, and he exclaimed at it, for it was not, like the others, filled with flowers but with celery and scallions and a thorny vegetable called, I think, Christophine, rare plants anywhere in French Guiana.

Ruth said, "I didn't know that my mouth actually could water until now." We had had few canned vegetables and none fresh since St. Laurent.

Old Mademoiselle had a tiny shop in which she must have done big business. The gold-weighing scales occupied a third of her counter, its brass aglow in semi-darkness. The *bricoleurs*, the unlicensed prospectors, came here with their nuggets. Money was seldom seen this far upriver. Everyone had his sack of gold dust and little scales which he brought along to Mademoiselle, politely comparing the measure of his scales with hers and haggling over the difference.

We spent a busy few days at Antouka, mostly trying to persuade the people to part with fresh provisions. Mademoiselle sold us empty shotgun shells with caps, powder, and wadding so we could make our own ammunition. Raphael swapped our cigarettes for these, and gave the completed bullets to Afokati in exchange for his services as dishwasher, for Raphael was very lordly here; he had his position to maintain as a sort of vagabond prince since the day when he had staggered nude from the forest and sought refuge with Mademoiselle. The old dear had loved him because, as she told it, the house was surrounded with gendarmes while Raphael sat in a quiet corner repairing things, left and right. How Ferdinand of the *trompe* and the "boom-boom-boom" had induced him to come downriver was surely forgotten.

We were never to be royally entertained in French Guiana, in the spontaneous way of African or Asiatic villages where the stranger is a guest to whom a certain obeisance is due. The Bonis and the Creoles did not give things readily; they showed their esteem by demanding of you certain things and services which only you could give, a left-handed flattery. Thus at Antouka we were enjoined to visit the lame, the halt, the blind, the leprous, and the venereal, and to dispense to them our charms and nostrums. Equipped with the witch doctor's boxes from Ciba and Burroughs Wellcome, we went to the long hut of the volunteer schoolmaster, paralyzed these many years. He sat cross-legged like a tailor on a high dais of bamboo, overlooking the table where his bare brown students were drawing numerals and letters with charcoal upon pieces of plank. He hadn't moved, they said, for as long as they had known him, but he said no, that wasn't so at all, his wife moved him when there was no one to watch.

It was indeed a fine stout figure of a woman who lifted her husband, like a precious doll, and tipped him into positions so that we could massage the aching joints with plain Sloan's Liniment. His voice was of a deep sweet timbre, saying, "You are kind to me. I shall not wash until the last of this fragrance is gone, so that I may smell your kindness in it."

Mademoiselle Victoire led us down the path to the next patient's house. The front of it was a shop with a few fish-hooks and rusty cans for sale. The proprietor was a one-legged Hindu who had strangely made his way here from British Guiana, two jungles to the west, and he was less concerned with the fever and the pain which racked his new wooden leg than with the high cost of shopkeeping. The gendarmes, said he (the ones who had captured Raphael), had ruined his business by limiting the mark-up on his prices to only 60 per cent above the average at St. Laurent, whereas he actually needed 80 per cent to make a living.

"The sickness?" he said. "It is nothing. You should see my son!"

We did, by flashlight, in the back room. He was a hairless animal of about seventeen, whimpering in the dark. His legs were emaciated. There were smooth dead plaques of hide across his belly, and the nodules of leprosy across his brow. The only medicine we could give him was the flashlight.

Mademoiselle bustled us out of there, saying we must now

[187]

see a man about a dog, a bad case of *piay*, or witchcraft. His thatched hut was raised high on posts like all the huts at An-touka to keep it dry during the rains which were soon to come. He seemed a responsible trader and his dog impressed us favorably as one with no nonsense about it. It chased a cat beneath the counter, it accepted a piece of chocolate and leaned heavily against Ruth's knees expecting to be scratched behind the ears.

Monsieur Mouson, its Creole owner, said, "Listen to it, please."

We listened while he explained that it was a talking dog. "Lean closer, *madame*. Oh, if someone else could only hear it too!"

"Indigestion?" Ruth asked helpfully.

"But no! But no! Perhaps you don't understand Djuka very well. It talks Djuka from its heart! There's a *piay* in its heart! I do not like to believe such things, *madame*, but neither could I believe that my wife should do a faithless thing or that my own dog should threaten me. The trouble began a few months back when we were newly married and my wife be-came jealous of the dog which went with me everywhere and slept on the bed with us at night. The dog wasn't talking then, but he was so remarkable already, as a hunter, that a Djuka man from the other shore was always after me to sell it.

"One day I left the dog at home to go out fishing — no, *madame*, the dog didn't fish — and when I came back my wife gave me two thousand francs and told me she had sold

[188]

the dog. The Djuka had disappeared. For months I looked
for help up and down the forest and wherever I heard that a
Djuka was panning gold, as that was his business; and when
at last I came upon him in his sleep I left the same two thousand francs beside him and brought the dog back home."

"What did the dog think of that?" I asked.

"He didn't say," said Monsieur Mouson. "It was only in
the night that he began to talk. My wife — I had been
obliged to speak severely to her, you understand — lay in
the bed beside me, and by the moonlight through the window
I could see her eyes wide open. My dog lay between us, and
his eyes were open too. It was my opinion that neither one
was being very responsive to me.

"Then just as I was dozing off I heard the voice. It was
a Djuka speaking, and he was not in the room, for I searched
it. It was not my wife. I lit the candle and knelt by the bed.
The dog didn't move though its eyes were still wide open. I
put my ear to its chest to see if it was dead, and then, *monsieur*, I listened attentively! The Voice was in the dog!"

"Tell them what it said!" Mademoiselle Victoire was pop-
eyed with eagerness.

"It said, 'My flesh is Djuka. The dog is of my flesh which
you have rent apart, and its *piay* is on you!'" Now every
night I hear it, though my wife cannot. She too lies staring,
awake, while the dog talks on and on."

Such a problem as this is a challenge and a joy to witch
doctors such as I. Ruth eased the hound from her lap and
passed me the medical kit. I took six Phenobarbitol from it,

wrapped them in the silver paper I had saved from cigarette packages, and put them in the shaking cupped hands of Monsieur Mouson.

"One for you every night," I said, "and one for your wife, and" — I took the measure of the dog — "half a tablet for the dog. Now listen to me carefully: the dog must not lie between you but on the outside next to you. You must pat the dog and say good-night politely to it, then kiss your wife on each of her eyes. Every night, mind you, and you will never hear the Voice again."

"Don't forget," Ruth added, slinging her cameras on her back, "just half a tablet for the dog."

III

The Roucouyennes

WE LEFT Antouka in the nick of time, for the motherly influence of Mademoiselle Victoire upon Raphael was wearing him. He was drinking hard, and he was going to marry her, by God, or else . . . Somehow he saw himself as landed gentry, the good woman by his side, young Victor learning at his knee the while his vassals repulsed gendarmes. Maudlin in his cups, he was beginning to make pronunciamentos over the porch railing when I thought fit to lure him into his kitchen canoe by intimating that his blanket was already aboard and was getting wet.

More than Mademoiselle Victoire, the thick striped convict blanket was mother and wife to Raphael. It was his lonely refuge. Warmer, softer, deeper than the womb of the cell he both hated and loved was the striped cocoon of the blanket which was his very own to command, to embed him.

"Yo!" said Asa. "Yo!" said Afokati, swinging their poles to the rapids of Aoura Soula. My canoe zigzagged through them. Raphael's came next, with him hanging to the gunwales and sobering with every splash; then the lean canoe of Ruth, who stood fast like an ancient mariner with a movie camera ready for our possible capsizing. I wondered if it never occurred to her that the river gods, the Proud Ones, might like

[193]

her less than us others who knelt before them poling, paddling, or respectfully grinding our teeth.

❧

This was still the Aoua River, but the change in it, during the last slow few miles, was not imaginary, for all of us were aware of it — Ruth, Raphael who was sober and pensive, the Bonis who were oddly hushed. We may have rounded a bend into sweeter air blown through a valley of the mountains. The bird cries were more frequent; the flights of parrots and flamingos made mosaic against the sky. The water was warmer and the trees more massively packed. Lonely and lost was this land, but it was like a room of one's own.

❧

At the snarled entrance to a creek called Mattogou, where monkeys fled us, we stopped for an hour to dig through vines which were really almost impenetrable, to search for what long ago had been a camp where the essence of rosewood was distilled. We found it, the ruins of a once civilized race, our own: great iron shells of solid rust that once had been boilers, pipes twisted by the strangling vines, chunks of machinery squatting like idols beneath a hundred feet of interwoven vegetation. Even our gods, the slick machines, had reverted here and crouched leering at us through torn red lips.

With some fervor and shaking of the head I had been deploring the nondevelopment of France's oldest and probably potentially richest colony. There was gold in the creeks,

[194]

grazing land among the central savannas, wood for every use among the unplumbed jungles, a nascent energy in the earth that could fructify any agriculture. But in that lay the might and intransigence of French Guiana. Metal and plants could be torn from the soil, tamed, transplanted, and their mother the earth would eat her young.

I patted a rusty idol, which may once have been some sort of steam turbine, and my hand went through into its hot and wet and decaying bowels. I touched a coil of piping, and it disintegrated. I peered through a rusty hole in a boiler at what might be a nest of eggs; they were limes that had crashed through that carapace by their own small weight.

Respectfully, carefully, lest we crumble too, we moved back through the jungle to the canoes. The river seemed hard and clean in contrast to the porridge of vegetation we had left, and it was good to hear our voices clear and not hushed, furred, fearful. But it wasn't very long before fear came at us again, a thin bird-cry, like a needle falling. Our paddlers paused, muttering among themselves. It was the zombi bird, they said, and it was evil. It was the bird *aweeyo*, they said, pointing to the trees ahead; it would stick its bill through your heart at night.

❧

Suddenly this was the jungle of the old books which teased my childhood, those quartos full of rich engravings showing men no more important than insects against torrential cataract and towering wood. And here really was the toy canoe awaiting us beneath a bow that arched like a plume; and it held live Indians.

I was nearly as happy as when reading about them long ago. I looked back at Ruth, but her emotions were as usual tied to the practical business of photography; as I made a gesture without words to Afokati to move our canoe slowly toward the Indians, I saw that Ruth had maneuvered hers so that the light fell on a good angle shot of our meeting.

The Indians were blasé about it. They were painted a brilliant vermilion, and upon the long black hair which hung to their shoulders they wore red and orange coronets of woven feathers, placed squarely, as serious Caucasians wear their hats. I made an adjustment to mine.

The bow Indian said a guttural, "*Haliki!*" (which meant "Come here and listen," so I was later to learn) and Afokati said, "*Yepeh!*" which meant "Friend." I reached out my hand and my finger tips were taken by the rear Indian, who seemed to know something of what a handshake was. Afokati introduced him.

His name was Malfatti, a Roucouyenne; he had been the guide of the geographer, Richard. The other Indians had not seen white men before, but were not hesitant in accepting the half calabash of taffia I offered them, while by the magician's art of misdirection I managed to pour Three Star Hennessy into my own.

Malfatti fished around in the bilge-water of his canoe and presented me with a half-drowned bird, its legs tied together, which I couldn't imagine what to do with, as it seemed neither nutritive nor decorative; and I gave him a sort of chauffeur's cap, which he dropped carelessly into the bilge. We were beginning to understand each other already.

Raphael tipped his broad straw hat back onto his brown bare shoulders and returned the gawking of the Indians, who were more concerned with his half-nudity than with the scarlet French officer's cap and chest decorations which I had hurriedly put on. I was interested in the exaggerated height and protrusion of their Mongoloid cheekbones and the extraordinary cubic mass of their torsos. I shuddered to think of how a true anthropologist would *tchk-tchk* if I described them as elongated Esquimos.

They took the lead with their fine canoe of over-lapping, two-colored woods, and we wove through the spatter of islands at the juncture of the Aoua, the Itany, and the Maro-uini Rivers. Among these islands, slipping from one to another and back again, they had for generations fought off the enemy tribes of Jamares, Oyampis, and the blond and long-eared Oyaricoulets.

Just beyond, on the French bank, we came to the nomad village which for a week or a month or a year was Mal-fatti's, depending upon the pressure of other migratory Roucouyennes from the jungle behind. It was because these people were migratory and "changed waters" often that few had chanced to meet the very rare white travelers.

Negroes and Mongols react in quite different ways to the first appearance of a European. The Negroes either flee their villages or go into ecstasies of welcome or both, whereas

Indians of our hemisphere and Asiatic Mongols show no slightest sign either of fear or wonder. I had visited small villages in Nepal, deep in the Himalayas, where the likes of me had not only never been seen but not even heard of in legend, and the realistic Newars had simply accepted me, somewhat to my disappointment, as they would the arrival of an albino in fancy dress. I was just a blemished and benighted person whose ways weren't theirs, that was all, and so I was best ignored.

This was our experience among the Roucouyennes. We were classically welcomed by a troupe of braves rushing out and shooting enormous arrows straight into the sky, and so straight they flew that the Indians had to step aside when they returned to earth. This gesture of welcome, common among Indians, has been interpreted as an offer to shoot even the sun for the visitors' delectation. It was offset a bit by a gang of tough prepubic youngsters who made some show of shooting a flock of arrows into an old dead stump, as if it had been I.

We then were led to the largest of the conical thatched huts and left to our own devices.

It probably was the explorer Patrice (he who left his *dactylo* or stenographer with the Indians) who first saw the Roucouyennes. Crevaux points out that their own name for themselves was Ouayanes, from which perhaps the word Guiana was derived, and to which was added the prefix Roucou, the name of the berry they used to stain their bodies red. And that custom, they were to explain to me, served three purposes: it made them beautiful, it protected them from insect bites, and it prevented sunstroke, which was rather doubtful considering the brilliance of the red dye.

The early explorers of the nineteenth century, Crevaux and Coudreau, reported the presence or the alleged presence of other Indian tribes on the upper Awa and Itany Rivers, but they were neither seen by us nor by that infinitely more capable observer, Captain Richard. On the French side were the Emerillons, the Jamares of the long ears, and the Oyampis, who at one time nearly decimated the Roucouyennes. On the Dutch shore were Yapocoyes, Comayanas, and the fabulous race of white Indians with blue eyes and blond beards called Oyaricoulets — descendants, perhaps, of the diligent *dactylo*.

These, with the Galibis of the coast, the few Arawaks and lesser tribes, Coudreau estimated to number fifty thousand in 1877. Coeval estimates pare this down to twenty thousand, and I doubt that now, judging by the reports of gold-seekers in the bush, there are more than two thousand Indians in all French and Dutch Guiana, unless there should be a secret city of them, maybe El Dorado, somewhere in the uncharted wilderness west of the upper Oyapock River.

Unhappily for romance, such a dreamland would have been spotted by the many American planes flying across this country during the last war years. Aerial survey photos show savannas devoid of habitations and jungles as thick as the pile of a broadloom carpet. The shy Emerillons are certainly here, but not in sufficient numbers to cut plantations of manioc visible from the air.

I was sitting on a box in our hut, studying a United States Army Aerial Photo, when our mascot Boni boy, Pekein, rushed in to me shouting, "*Avion! Avion!*" and pointing to the roof of the hut. All the Indians and Bonis were looking at the sky, at nothing I could see, and listening to what I recognized some minutes later as the far drumming of an airplane motor. Raphael lay drunk in the sun amidst them, murmuring.

It was odd to think that probably we had friends up there, among the Pan American pilots who flew to Belém, and this prompted a notion for which I shall always be grateful to Pan American in addition to my gratitude for years of services which I unquestioningly believe were designed especially for me. I stood behind the half-dead body of Raphael, called Ruth to come look, quick, and pointed to the spot in the sky where most of the others' eyes were focused.

"A-ha!" I said in French for the Bonis' sake: "You see? Good old Panam! They're keeping an eye on us, all right! If anything goes wrong with us on the river there will be a plane down here full of food and medicine, and also" — I smiled at my Bonis — "full of men with 'bang-bang' guns, and also" — I beamed at the Indians — "with poison bows and arrows, I mean arrows and bows."

I wasn't sure that I could get away with this, but definitely I did. The Bonis said, "Eh?" The Indians said, "Oh!"

Raphael turned over and said, "*Quel toupet! Quel toupet!*"
meaning "What a nerve!"

It *was* a paltry ruse, but it was to serve us well, shamelessly, among the canyon creeks of the Tumuc-Humacs ahead,
when the light would leave us and we suspected shadows and
we should have to force our men to sunlit clearings where
they would hate us a little less. Panam would be watching
over us.

I attracted Raphael's attention by sitting him up and dem-
onstrating confidentially that we had our little secret about
dinner tonight, didn't we? The smoked alligator tail the Indians had given us while the Bonis were away?

"*Ah, les Bonis!*" he roared. "*Ils travaillent du chapeau! Ils
travaillent de la toiture! Je peux leur serrer la main!*" which
meant in his fine argot that the Bonis were nuts, like himself, that he and they might fittingly shake hands.

This was in respect to our clandestine acceptance of the
alligator, or rather cayman, tail. I had had trouble with our
paddlers before when I had wanted to try out Ben Holderness's Aqua-gun, which was designed primarily for underwater goggle-fishing, but was lethal on land at twenty yards.
The odd elements of this were a Duralumin spear with a
detachable barb and a motive power of a simple Sparklet
cartridge containing carbon dioxide, which is used for
charging soda-water bottles. When punctured by a pull on
the trigger the compressed gas projected the spear with a
force which decided me to take my grog with plain water
in the future.

The Bonis were wonderstruck when I captured a ten-pound *toukounari*, a golden fish with three black spots, with this infernal machine, but when once I sighted at a fifteen-foot boa looped gracefully over a limb, and when again I drew an intrepid bead on a cayman which was outstaring me, they yelled so hard they scared the beasts away.

I was, of course, furious, though somewhat relieved that my marksmanship would not have to be tested publicly again. But they explained. The boa was a god, the water god, and you must not even hack the root of a tree which resembled him. The cayman too was a god — a direct West African survival — and if killed would bring you bad luck in the shape of leprosy, as you could readily understand if you looked at the scaly, leprous hide of the beast.

So we ate secretly the smoked cayman tail of the Roucouyennes, who were in some ways sensible people, with Ruth's mayonnaise made of flamingo eggs. And it was good. It was something like whitefish and a bit like smoked eel, and it was somewhat spoiled by Ruth's whispering to me that she thought she saw the close-set eyes of our mascot Pekein watching us from the woods. They might, of course, have been the eyes of a lonely jaguar.

Unlike the Indians, I permitted my womanfolk to sit down with me at meals, which may have lessened my prestige but at least was a start toward shaking them from their complacence. Ruth's square shoulders and boyish hips encased in trousers probably added to the confusion, and the fact that I did any work at all, instead of letting the wife do all of it as the Indians did, must have been baffling. Gradually, through the weeks we lived with them, we broke down their apathy until at last a few of them would actually stare when I raised my voice or opened a case.

That was what we were waiting for, for the shucking of their proud reserve and for a realization that we were people like themselves, worthy of a neighbor's interest, that we were merely odd and not crazy, that we were harmless, generous, interesting, and sincerely interested in them. When their confidence was established we treated their lesser maladies, and had especial luck with "athlete's foot," which I cured with Mercurochrome and Desenex, miraculously. And when we rid their thick hair of lice by one squirting of an Aerosol bomb, it wasn't long before their social problems were being brought to us as well.

What, for example, was pretty little Culua to do? She had started menstruating, and was in love with Pierpan, who was a faithless youth. And now she would be confined for a moon in the hut where all menstruating women must live. How could she keep her Pierpan this while?

Pierpan, whom we too lusted for, professionally — trying by every means to lure him along with us as an actor in the film — talked about Culua frankly, in deliberate baby-talk and four-letter words which we were beginning to understand a little. He used a phrase which sounded like one from my childhood: "Ishkabibble!" — which was the equivalent of "So what?" or the French *"Tant pis!"*

"Ishkabibble!" said he, his eyes laughing at us and Culua.

They were blue eyes, fairly common among the Roucouyennes, and their lashes and brows had been completely
plucked out, like everybody else's. (My heavy eyebrows they
thought an obscenity on my face.) Pierpan sucked on his
thin ten-inch cigar and gave us to understand that Culua
was all right in her way, but that she wasn't the only one who
vied for his favors. And aside from that there were plenty
of the boys and even men who wanted him.

This was as we had suspected, not in Pierpan's case alone,
but almost generally. Bisexuality was completely normal
among the Roucouyenne males, though we found no instance
of it among the women and heard no talk of it. Indeed the
women seemed less demonstrative to one another than those
of the Bonis. The Indian men were flagrant; they were forever grabbing boys by their genitals or sitting with them
recumbent across their laps. Even the *Tamouchi,* the Chief
Malfatti, delighted in standing over our Bonis as they ate
and making pederastic gestures with his buttocks at them.

What surprised us was that the Bonis neither took offense
nor ridiculed this exhibitionism; they simply shook their
heads and said *"Anaboon!"* in their language and *"Hipokedah!"* in Roucouyenne, both meaning that for them this
wasn't good.

❦

By now, obviously, we were no longer strangers, we were
scarcely even strange, and because of constant surveillance
in a wall-less hut I am certain that our most cautious intima-

[204   ]

cies were common coin. Which was fair enough. They had as much right to study our customs as we had theirs. Earlier, whenever we had tried to photograph their work — the preparation of food, the care of babies, the mixing of *roucou* dye — they had not protested but simply fallen idle. Now they seemed to realize that our interest was flattering and worked harder and more skillfully when we appeared with our bug-eyed boxes.

We were welcome to any hut except that lonely one for the menstruating women. It was a pity we couldn't interpret the great gossip which came from it always. Every other house was as open as our own, no more than a peaked thatch on posts, with red hammocks, *roucou*-stained, slung from one to another. The doghouses, of which there was at least one per family, were fine structures floored about three feet from the ground and well shielded from the elements. The dog had a rope collar and a rope lead about five inches long — short enough so that he couldn't reach it with his teeth — which was attached to a two-foot stick of bitter wood to which a loop of rope was fastened. The dog could thus be led hunting at the end of the stick with no chance of his gnawing either his lead or his master.

There was good reason for this. The dogs were savage and kept savage through cruelty, and they were so immensely valuable that the Roucouyennes would go on forays as far as Brazil to raid other tribes, not for their women — since bisexuality had reared its pretty head — but for their dogs.

I had been told by old prospectors what was later to be

confirmed by the Indians themselves, that the dogs were not only trained to hunt certain animals but were drugged so that they were compelled to do so. Thus one dog, insentient to the spoor of all but jaguar, would frenziedly hunt only the jaguar; another would hunt only the peccary.

❧

Ruth and I had felt quite unwanted during the first days of perfect isolation beneath the huge dome of the chief's hut which he had evacuated in our honor, throwing out his one wife and seventeen sodomites. We had erected our cube of nylon netting around the two cots in the center of it, and lay on our backs at night admiring the spiraled truss-work of the roof and the ceremonial hats of basketware and feathers suspended like bright bells from the apex. Raphael, like a faithful rabid dog, slept somewhere near our feet.

Our first intimation that old residents were hard to lose came on a night when Ruth wakened me.

"Did you hear it?" she whispered. I said no. "Bill, just now, it sounded like one of the cameras dropping." This was preposterous; our precious cameras were slung securely from the eaves, but I was obliged to admire the conscience of such a photographer.

Her flashlight swept the ground first and jerked to rest upon the camera still fuming with dust motes across the beam. What she then said loudly would have been unfitting for the ears of an only child dropped upon its head. Her light swept up to the red crescent of a hammock idling in the space where the camera should have been. There was nothing to do, of course, but pick up our fledgling and give a clout to the bulge of the hammock as we passed by.

The next precipitating factor toward the repopulating of our hut was due to Ruth's embarrassment over being such a blond, with all the side embarrassments of Indians fingering her freckles and making obviously snide remarks. Her own remark, as she came up behind me when I was sweating upside down pawing into a duffel bag, did nothing to help my mood.

"I've just had the darnedest experience," she said, "and is my face red!"

I winced and grunted and kept on clawing through that invention of the anti-Christ, the duffel bag.

Behind me, she insisted, "But is it?"

"Huh?" I arose with the lost can of carbide in my hand. Her face was certainly red. She had succumbed before the blandishments of the village women and let them paint her as red as themselves with *roucou*. The golden curls frothed like melted butter around the salmon of her face.

"It's your honeymoon," I said. "Try everything once."

When the dizziness left me after my ascent from the duffel bag I saw that her make-up girls, quite serious, had followed her, and several of them were slinging their hammocks around our hut. Their young men helped them. We were done for. My greatest hopes, unfortunately, had been achieved. Without benefit of phony initiations or exchange of names or pin-prickings in a "blood ceremony," we had become definitely a part of the tribe. We were the mother-in-law come to live with the family, respected, indulged, thanked for services, imposed upon, casually catered to, but never really loved, an excellent position for studying such a group.

The younger folk turned in early as we did. The elders sat around the embers, drew doodles in the sand, and talked. Almost nothing ever happened. Many a traveler would have been impatient with such a placid life; he would have organized a dance and paid for it, and probably would have recorded a dance improvised to please him, neither spontaneous nor traditional. But it has been my experience that dances paid for are dances phony.

Almost nothing ever happened, which was the way of those Roucouyennes, and it was their normal way of living which I found of interest. We were to see a dance, in their own good time, when we came down-river, but it was to be the traditional accompaniment to a torture ceremony, and nothing specially done for us. Similarly one night we witnessed a very odd performance which I tried vainly to have repeated so we could get it on film; but no, they said, they might not feel like getting that drunk again in quite some while.

They were, indeed, already pretty drunk on *cachiri*, a mild, gritty corn wine, when I wandered past the open hut where a dozen of the middle-aged men were squatting, and was asked to join them. I drank as much *cachiri* as I could out of gourds and felt very little better. They drank quantities, swilling it down through open throats until their stomachs distended like balloons. Then they took a chaser of *sakoula*, a stronger brew made of manioc, and leaned back to gossip in undertones. They were understandably short of breath. Though by no means cheered by these intoxicants, I felt well enough to attempt a witticism or two in Roucou-yenne, and was pleased when everyone laughed.

Then everyone got up and stood in a line outside the hut and vomited, but not, mind you, as you and I might vomit from drink or a white man's wit. A more serious investigator than I would take off his glasses, wipe them, reflectively fill his pipe, and state that this was Ritual Degurgitation; for there they stood, the red Indians, in a row, and simultaneously opened their mouths and spewed, not as you and I, sporadi-cally, but in a series of thick golden streams across the moon. The wine came forth in solid liquid arcs, unbroken, continuous, lasting at least a quarter of a minute, and the man who shot farthest and longest won.

I refrained from joining these wine-shooting contests, which went on for some hours that night, reminding myself sternly that I was not here to learn new games, but to dis-cover, among other things, the significance of native customs and how they might be employed to tighten the cultural re-lations of all mankind.

The custom of that evening gave me little to work upon. Ruth had come to sit quietly beside me by now, and I knew the burning questions she would have to answer for her friends the psychoanalysts back home, so I asked them.

"Why do you get drunk like this? What are you escaping?"

Old Soukalou looked around him hurriedly, saw nothing, and served us both a drink. He then shrugged his shoulders and used the Boni word for "witchcraft," which I understood.

"Is the *cachiri* a *piay* in your country to help you escape the Evil Ones?" This was like asking, "Is it true that you have stopped beating your wife?" So Ruth just grumbled and gave me a kick.

I leaned forward and tapped old Soukoula on the knee. "Is it true," I demanded, "that this bocal ejaculation of wine, the pleasure fluid, has some sexual and psychological significance?"

Soukoula drank deep and passed the gourd down the line. He could barely talk when he answered with what wind was left above his bulging belly.

"I do not understand," he said, "but I think we drink just because we like it. And we blow it out because that makes fun, eh?"

I nodded, taking another sip, but I had my duty to my stern colleagues to perform, so I asked, "Do you have no legends about this? When your father, Gan, was tired of your mother, didn't he . . . ?"

Old Soukoula was near to tears, and I knew that I had probably talked myself out of an invitation to his next party.

"No, no, no!" he wheezed. "We just do it because we like

it! And I invented it! Why must you think it a twisted thing to do?" He made a sign to his men and lined them up with dignity, and the golden flood of their pleasure went streaking across the moon.

☙

The bed manners of savages, or hammock manners, were a matter of intense concern to us as we slept amidst them or tried to sleep while the invisible orgy pulsed around and above us. Wearing the exotic pajamas Ruth had whipped up on a Chinese sewing machine, and tossing on the striped sheets she had confected brilliantly with elastic loops to hold them on the cots, we looked up at the dozen Indian hammocks slung variously from the cross-timbers of our hut. All were hooded with a homespun material, barely porous, to keep out the mosquitoes as well as the gaze of earnest students like ourselves. Roughly they were of three sorts: the double hammock in which older husbands and wives slept crosswise; the single hammock in which children slept, sometimes three together, diagonally, their pert faces defying the mosquitoes outside and their long hair streaming down; and the hammocks of the young mixed couples and the homosexuals.

None of them were ever still. Through the cloth we would see the quick movement of Mama's fist as she scratched her old man's back, or the sly movement of fiancés. It was as good as counting sheep to count the imprints of feet in the hammocks, close our eyes to sleepily review them; then, if

[211   ]

that didn't work, to look up again and count them again in their changed positions.

We would lie peacefully, sucking the little breeze through our nylon net, listening to the *teo* birds, like two people talking in the dark of the confessional, one like a little nun confessing her sins, the other like a shocked but admiring priest, the nun-bird giggling, the priest-bird replying with a *whoo-wee-ooo!*

Raphael, drowsing drunk at the foot of our cots to guard our privacy, started up once and shook us, "*Capitaine*, do you see what I see? In the hammock over there? *Five feet!* Count them!"

"Now! Now!" said Ruth, lighting a cigarette. There were five feet, all right, only one of them upside down, and whenever we wakened that night there were still five feet, though in different positions; and thereafter none of us drank *cachiri* wine.

☙

Thus we slept, or tried to, on the hot nights among the Roucouyennes, during the pregnancy of the rains. I would waken panting, my arms spread wide against an air that was almost palpable, confining an urgent rain. And I would sit up in terror of the knowledge that our work was far from finished, that the Tumuc-Humacs were far away, that the great rains were soon to burst upon us, that our film was perhaps half done, and whether this was good or bad we still didn't know, for there it was beneath our cots, dried in the desiccant silica gel and cooled by damp cloths around its airtight tins. There was no way to send it back for development; we had to keep it with us all these months and trust that it would come out well.

Knowing Ruth's quiet competence to deal with anything photographic, or anything at all, I could say blindly, Yes, it will be all right, unless a canoe capsizes or the film is carelessly left in the sun. And I would turn, assured, to watch her sleep and look above her at the little gray bodies suspended like moldy cheeses from the thatch: the vampire bats churning their courage to brave the light of the India oil lamp and descend upon us. One would let go, drop, straighten, veer toward a hammock, and flip back to the thatch again, a test flight. Before dawn they would be whirling around us on wings of stinking velour, and if your toe or hand should touch the mosquito netting, and you asleep, you would waken to the "pit-pit-pit" upon the ground of your own blood. Will Beebe, a more inquisitive explorer than I, tried this deliberately, and wrote of it so well that I felt no need to copy him.

By now, we said one morning as the mist over the village was drawn to the river and absorbed by it, we had filmed the basic elements of our Indians' lives; the more dramatic perquisites could wait until we came back from the mountains. And we had to move fast. There was a sharp cry of pain from a hut near ours, and the smell of Raphael's charcoal stove was tingling up our noses. I cut my chin in shaving with someone's going-away present, and across my shaving mirror, which was affixed to the outside thatch, I saw a flight of arrows. The children were shooting at a *cuata* monkey which some progressive-school parents had tied high in a tree.

"*Les crêpes, madame!*" said Raphael. His pancakes, rolled over a layer of native peanut butter, were ready.

While eating breakfast, with the arrows whizzing over us, we heard again that cry from the adjacent hut.

"Labor pains," said Ruth.

We returned to the marvel of Raphael's pancakes, built on a recipe we had taught him despite his loyal French conviction that pancakes were only thin, sweet, flaming desserts. He was improvising now and proudly. Since he couldn't bake bread he was inventing pancakes, some crisp, some foamy, some large enough to fill the pan, some in heaps like golden coins, some rolled around jam or fish or cheese, some thick and serious and square, or triangular.

The noise of what Ruth thought was labor pains came from the hut of Pierpan's father, who had mistimed things slightly and was rolling in his hammock with a raw baby clutched to his sinewy breast. This was the odd custom known as "couvade," which was common in Pharaonic Egypt and is practiced by many Indian tribes in South America. The mother bears the baby, right enough, but it is the father who takes to his hammock and groans as if the pangs of birth were his, and must convalesce, furthermore, for a month after his baby is born, abstaining from wine and intercourse, and eating lightly as befits one in his condition.

The mother rests for a little while in her hammock, too, for the strain of worrying about Father is hard to bear. She is comforted by a steam bath. A fire is built under her hammock, a pot of water is put on it, and the steam rises directly to her loins. There is not much time for such self-indulgence, however, as Father must be cared for. Someone must chop the wood and do the gardening and prepare the little dishes that Father likes. He meanwhile lies languid, the baby cuddled to him, and receives visits of congratulation on the fine job he has done.

There is always a scene when Mother takes the baby from the dry breast to nurse it at her own. You can see the worry in Father's face, his concern that Mother, in her well-meaning but clumsy way, might not hold the darling right, or might drop it on its head. If it is a boy child, Father makes a game of bellowing for meat, and when his warrior friends bring it to him, he pretends to stuff it down the throat of his heir, until Mother takes it away again.

Being a father among the Roucouyennes is quite a trial.

I asked our young Pierpan why his father was still groaning, since the child seemed satisfactorily born, and that young man of the world replied that this was only the second baby his father had had, so the old one didn't know much about it. He should have shut up long ago.

"Are you coming with us, Pierpan?" Ruth asked. Neither of us had ever seen such a beautiful boy, and though Bob Flaherty had his Sabu I knew we would have made the old master jealous if our paragon could be lured into the film.

"Can't," said Pierpan, indifferently. "Father's sick with the baby, so I'll have to do his work." By now we knew it was no use. We had offered both the boy and his father our most precious trade goods — money meant nothing to them — and they weren't in the slightest tempted. Ruth tried them with a Navajo beadwork bracelet, which was surprisingly like their own, but that was the most dismal failure. They sneered at it, pointing out what any idiot should be able to see, that the red eagle on it was quite the wrong red. In our eagerness to get Pierpan, we offered everything we had that was red, including other pieces of some value from Ruth's small stock of jewelry — but it was useless; the wrong red. With the exception of some red cotton we had brought for loinclothes, we could trade nothing that was red. We offered half the bolt of this and were still refused.

"Perhaps if my father is well I shall go with the other party," said Pierpan pertly.

"Other party? What party?"

"The big one that is coming up the river very soon."

That chilled us. "Who told you this, Pierpan?"

"Manu told us. He just came up from the Boni village. There is a big party of Frenchmen with ten big canoes. They are going into the Tumuc-Humacs to cut down trees so that airplanes can go there."

This was an awful blow. It certainly was of interest to us to be the first to see this group of Roucouyennes and to explore unknown parts of the mountains, but if there was another expedition on our heels, with ten canoes, it would be awkward in many ways; one way would be that the party would surely have cameras, probably more resources than Ruth and I, and might very well get out their films before we did.

The report sounded in many ways true. There had indeed been a mysterious group of Frenchmen who arrived in Cayenne as we were leaving, and it was said that they were going into the interior to look for gold, bauxite, and so forth. And there was indeed some talk of one day establishing an air base in the Tumuc-Humacs. And the boy Pierpan did know what an airplane was, for Pan American did fly high over this country, though it didn't land within five hundred miles of it.

We felt rather sick. We had sunk every cent we owned into this expedition, and every franc I had managed to save during five years with the Free French Army. If we didn't pull it off we would be in a damned bad way. I had the gloomy view of returning to other people's expeditions, of Ruth doing studio portraits again, of the future we had planned exultantly together washing down the drain of the Maroni River.

Ruth, standing beside me, slipped an arm around my back and hugged my short ribs hard.

"Raphael!" I called. "By God, he's sober!" I said to Ruth. He was, and genial as any cutthroat you ever met, beaming beneficence.

When he was this way I was fond of him and showed it, and like any Fascist gangster he took generosity for a sign

[217]

of weakness. I gave him a pack of Pall Malls, which I should pay for later.

"Go get Afokati and Chief Malfatti. We're leaving. Open up the box of trade goods and put a demijohn of taffia beside it. Don't bother to break the seal."

Afokati came to our hut with the entire crew. Malfatti brought half a dozen of his Indians. The rest of the village packed around the two groups while Ruth and I sat in our deck chairs and passed rum to the chief personages of the tribe, including the women. I swapped a cigarette for one of Malfatti's foot-long tubes of hand-rolled tobacco, and said that we were continuing upriver tomorrow and into the Tumuc-Humacs. We needed guides and porters. So what among our trade goods would the Indians want as payment for their services?

Like an auctioneer, Raphael held an object high and the Indians grunted in approval or shook their heads. We took him out occasionally to pass the taffia in a single glass, from which each one drank very accurately his share, or to pull from the equally fascinating red box a bit of magic to make them laugh and wonder. It has been reasonably said, though with charity, in magical circles, that no one has ever had less talent for the black art than I, but that has in no way daunted a passion which has grown since school days when I first learned to change water into a noxious fluid which my mother patiently sipped.

This hobby had, however, stood me in good stead during a number of years of living among primitives who were easier to baffle than my friends. It had made me witch doctor throughout Africa, a sort of unfrocked priest in the South Seas, and almost a minor lama in a village high in the Himalayas on the border of Tibet. Before leaving for this Guiana expedition I had become such a devotee that I actually prepared a book of magic for children, which appeared with real apparatus for tricks in it. These were made by the S.S. Adams Company, whose Chief Wizard, Jules Traub, had given me this trunkload of wondrous effects to try out on the natives.

They were eminently successful. Even the adults howled with glee when I produced litters of rubber rabbits from their fists, so we returned to our trading and I to my cardinal mistake of giving them complete and not half payment before we started. It might have been that, with half of it still coming to them, they would not have left us in the bad Indian country a few weeks later; it is also possible that, had their greed overcome their fear and had they continued with us, we might, none of us, have come back.

I was trading for the service of four male Indians to serve as guides and porters for a month and a half, and paid for them generously in goods worth about forty dollars.

From my notebook the list, for each Roucouyenne, is as follows:

One thin aluminum tube which you could blow pebbles or
    beans through

One metal file
One small mirror
One Camillus paring knife
One handful of beads — blue, red, or mixed
One useless insulated bag of tinfoil
Three different-sized fishhooks
One and a half yards of red calico
One paper and cellophane raincoat (army surplus, gas-protection covering)
Three galvanized staples
One sheet of carborundum paper
One sheet sandpaper
One yard of elastic cord
Forty yards of fishline
One medium machete
One comb
One pack of twelve candles
One box of army water-resistant matches
Three boxes of regular kitchen matches
One bar of brown soap
One large cup of rice
One cup of salt
One and three quarters large cups of flour
One cup of beans
One half-cup of cooking oil

In addition we gave a bonus to Chief Malfatti of several special items, including one we had picked up in a Chinese store, a comb with a mirror in the handle of it, and Malfatti nearly crippled his arm trying to use both at the same time. We were so happy with the appreciation of our largesse that we also donated a stock of foodstuffs to the villagers who could not come with us.

I stood up at the end of the business, shook hands with Malfatti, and made certain he understood that what we had given was in payment for the services of himself and three men for a period of six weeks. I also got his assurance that he and his men would be ready to leave early in the morning with sufficient food to see them through. And as an afterthought I asked Afokati again whether he had ample stocks of dried manioc and fish, for one month and a half — a moon, like this; and a half, like this.

Everything was dandy, and so we went to bed.

❧

I thought it was just hangover which was responsible for the sulking of Malfatti and Papa, his brother-in-law, next day; but no, it was in one case the water-resistant matches and in the other the cellophane raincoats. Malfatti brought me the matches and whanged them against the box, rubbing their noses up and down it. They didn't light. They were fireproof now. They had resisted long enough since the war and had given in to the seeping humidity of this climate. I saved face as well as I could by drying them over the fire. But the raincoat was irreparable: Papa, trusting me, had wrapped his arrows in it and they had come straight through. I saw I was getting off to a bad start as a dealer in shoddy merchandise.

It looked for a while as if we should not start that day at all, what with the human and material impedimenta of Malfatti's crew. Six canoes were going with us now, laden with the entire contents of our four Indians' huts — their food, their baskets, hammocks, steels, dogs, wives, children, grandparents, and a supercargo of a vicious parrot named Papagai, which Ruth moved to her canoe, hoping it might do tricks in the film. She also adopted a small boy named Aliman.

Our seven canoes shoved off toward the Sauts Yaktokou, breached them bravely, with the women and children doing most of the work as usual, and entered the Itany River, a continuation of the Awa we had been traveling on. The dogs, half of them in my canoe, took the rapids standing, giving a little at the knees when we bumped over domes of white water which I expected momently to stave us in. I patted them and felicitated them on this, and got nipped for my courtesy. Ruth's passenger, Aliman, was behaving all right, but the parrot was no mariner. He leaned over the gunwale, beak open, but nothing issued; unabashed, he walked up and down, defecating neatly.

Eimo swung a wallop with his *takari* at the bird, which sidestepped smartly; Eimo swore by Massa Gaddu that the parrot would go overboard if it kept on fouling his canoe. A little cloud, a foetal rain, covered the sun appropriately when I looked at Raphael's canoe. There he sat immobile, straw hat, brown back, blue denims, talking straight to his charcoal stove, not drunk but merely mad again.

"Species of stove," he said, "thou hast heard them laughing at me, the Bonis. Thou art witness to Toma calling me a violator of my mother. It is time for us to leave. We will make the *évasion* together." His long pointed chin snapped up and pointed like a witch's at Toma. "Species of mother violator that thou art!"

I too was talking to myself by now, and the gist of my mumbling was, "O God! O God!" Raphael's newest grievance was that the boys were calling him names in French, very fancy names which, as I vainly pointed out to him, were not at all the same in Boni; they were of argot so elaborate that they never could have been picked up during brief visits to St. Laurent. They were, therefore, names which Raphael had so constantly called our paddlers that they had been learned and turned against him. Though the Bonis didn't know what they meant, there was no mistaking their effectiveness. Raphael's bowman, Toma, who looked like a country parson in blackface, took particular delight in paying back Raphael with his own dirty coinage because it was he who had the heavy work of loading and unloading the kitchen canoe under Raphael's snarling tyranny.

At one point I thought his madness might be catching. It was during a slight attack of fever on the second day out from the Indian village. I had been drowsing, filled with a delicious but heavy lunch of pancakes which Raphael had rolled around crushed coconut. No matter how angry he was, his pride in good cooking never altered. I was awakened by the impact of Ruth's canoe against mine, and her hand shaking me. I saw the sunlight through her hair and smelled the odd frangipani scent of her skin.

"*Toi aussi, tu es fou?* Are you balmy, my Bill?"

[223]

"Uh-uh. Maybe. Why?"

"Do you know what you've been mumbling over and over again? 'Never, never! Not once in a blue womb! Not once in a blue womb!'"

"It wasn't 'moon'?"

"*Womb!* I said, 'Whose?' You said, 'Whom?' I said, 'Womb.' You said, 'Whose?' Maybe I'm going crazy, too. Let's send Raphael's canoe ahead so we won't have to listen to him."

I tried to shake the specks from before my eyes, saw they were Ruth's freckles, close-up. I ordered Raphael's canoe to take the lead, and got a baleful glance from him. Toma, strangely, didn't respond at all. His eyes were on the *moko-moko*, the inverted heart-shaped leaves which usually indicated good fishing grounds. I was about to gird myself for another weary lecture on dawdling and our need to reach the Tumac-Humacs before the rains, to add that I ate fish only once in a blue womb, when all the canoes of Bonis and Indians came to a stop and the personnel plunged overboard with their bows and arrows.

Galloping through muddy water up to their waists, weaving through the *moko-moko*, suddenly twanging a bowstring and diving after the arrow to catch it almost as soon as it struck the fish, gallumphing back to the canoes with their knees high in silver spray, yelling like banshees, our sportsmen loaded us to the gunwales in ten minutes with perhaps a quarter of a ton of flopping fish, the coumalu, *coulamara*, *ayamara*, and *comoto* with its blood-red sucker mouth. Chasing after the bowmen came Ruth with her Filmo and me with two still cameras, trying to photograph, to avoid splashing, and to plant our feet solidly on neither mud nor hysterical fish. Ruth ran out of color film; there was no time to reload; she kept on with the black-and-white camera.

This put everyone but Raphael in excellent high spirits, and we went on again singing through a long stretch of river, agreeably smooth, and into a range of hills on each side of us where we heard the cries of the macaque and the *cuata* monkeys.

Afokati stopped the canoes with a gesture. "*Fusil*," he whispered. Our paddlers sneaked out their antique firearms and slipped ashore. Afokati asked for my cousin Robert's precious shotgun, but this time, I thought, I would carry it myself for the moral effect of the thing. Ruth and I hurried up the slippery hill trying to keep pace with the boys and at the same time keep our cameras from slapping into trees. There were various matters I forgot at the moment, my leather-soled low shoes, my right knee which had been ripped in the war, and the discretion of forewarning Ruth that it was bad policy, when with our natives, for her to bound up the hill like a chamois while the old man skidded at the tail of the hunt. Grimly I clutched the swinging Medallist with one hand, cousin Robert's treasure with the other, and advanced ten steps to slip back two or fall on one elbow, hoping frantically that no one, particularly Ruth, was noticing. There was little to fear there. From half a mile ahead I heard the calling of many monkeys. They were the boys, imitating our prey. Ruth was barely visible as an occasional flash of khaki backside. I placed the right leg firmly before the left and its knee crumpled. Picking myself up with the help of the gun barrel, which got clogged with humus, I put the left foot forward and skidded on its city-slicker sole. I disliked to yell for Ruth, but this was hopeless.

"Hopeless," I said with a smile, as she came floating ethereally back to me — no trouble at all — which I justified in knowing that the boys were by now half a mile ahead of even her.

"I thought so too," she said faithfully. "We would never catch up with them." I turned around toward where the river should be, but though the hill slanted toward it, there was not even the light of its valley below. The gray-green boles of lizard-skinned trees rose in a wall around us, interlaced with so many liana vines that it seemed impossible that I could have stumbled through them with gun and camera. Because we had zigzagged up the hill I now had no vaguest notion of where the canoes lay.

"Right down there, no, a little farther, there. . . ." I said with a confident smile.

"Not over there, a little?"

"Just follow me, darling."

Boldly I led on, downhill, slipping only once, too proud to call out to Raphael and his stove. The canoes were exactly there, so Ruth gave an affectionate clutch at my ribs and I felt somewhat better.

But as we went on, with the Explorers' Club flag hanging limp before me, and the dead *cuata* monkey lying across the prow with its hands trailing in the water, I found myself rationalizing, remembering jauntier journeys on which I had done very well, recalling night patrols along the cliffs of the Quatarra Depression, defending my failure on the hill, and wishing I had a friendly stove to talk to. This was not helped by the giggling conversation of the boys, who obviously were describing over and over again how the *bakra* had skidded on the hill and how *madame* had far outdistanced him.

Forget it, I thought, with no effect whatever. Think of what you're going to do about Raphael. With fine restraint, I thought — because Ruth had recently taken me to task for yelling at delinquents — I stopped the giggling of the boys and got them to paddle smartly.

Smartly for half an hour, until we landed between the bastion rocks of an island where it had been decided that we should spend the night. The urgency of this was that both Bonis and Indians must smoke their fish. The Indians enthusiastically built us our usual *carbet*, or hut of leaves, while the Bonis made trellis platforms propped by four sticks and put the split fish upon them to smoke over smoldering fires. Small birds like hummingbirds dive-bombed them, burned their beaks, and flew away again.

This was a bad day, with no light in it but a sullen sun. Ruth noticed now, as she was filming the fish, that our film was unevenly dated and that our emulsion numbers were not

[227]

continuous, which might easily mean that exposure and quality would be uneven, presuming, of course, that we had anything left on film when we got it back several months from now for processing.

And I noticed that Raphael, his blanket, and his stove were reclining placidly against a tree. The cots, kitchenware, chairs, mosquito netting, and other personal paraphernalia lay untended before him where Toma had abandoned them.

Raphael sighed. It was obvious to the understanding observer that eight hours' conversation with his stove had given him a thirst and that he had been at our rum again. No, said he, he wasn't going to work tonight. This was Sunday and he had a right to his repose. As a matter of fact, he was going to repose from now on, forever. I could have my choice; shoot him, or take him along as passenger, or tie him to a tree and leave him there.

Fine, I said, I'd decide that later. I had business to do and couldn't be bothered with him now. Fine, he said, that would give him time to get the Bonis with a *"coup de sabre."*

I went over to the Bonis and the Indians who were sitting in a council of war around the smoking fish, and they too were talking about the *"coup de sabre,"* a phrase they understood by now. Abbibal leapt to his feet shouting that his blood was as red as Raphael's, and slit his black arm with the fish knife to prove it. And old Afokati, without saying a word, held out his palms to me; they were pink as my own; he lifted a black foot and its sole was the same as mine. That was something to think about.

I returned to Raphael and was starting to tell him to give me back immediately the pants, shirt, tobacco, machete, sun glasses, matches, and other stuff which I had given him in such loving-kindness some weeks ago, when Ruth told me that he had already done so. There was the neat packet. I had only to add that if he was going on strike he wasn't going to eat, whereupon Ruth popped the cork of a Martell bottle, glugged it into glasses, and we sat comfortably in our chairs with the Totelites pointing at Raphael through the sudden dark, talking cheerfully but wondering what we had better do.

The choices Raphael had suggested as to his disposition were quite reasonable, but none would help us much. To take him up the river and down again as a nonpaying passenger was unthinkable; to tie him to a tree and leave him for the ants might be frowned upon; to shoot him, said Ruth with a *moue*, was vulgar. We finished the cocktails and prepared supper deftly and effortlessly with a pair of Hotcans, those magical tinned dinners which heat through self-combustion by the simple poking of two holes in them — no fire, no water necessary, wait twelve minutes, open and serve.

We had meanwhile come to the decision that the only thing to do with Raphael was not exactly to throw him to the Bonis, but to ostracize him, forget him, and let him have his war alone, come what might. This notion was gaining piquancy by the minute as from the direction of the Bonis' fish fire there came increasingly the chant of "*Coup de sabre, coup de sabre*," and it looked as though they might be the aggressors.

It might have been this in combination with the perfume of our dinner and the lack of tobacco, rum, and mosquito netting that eventually got Raphael to his feet.

Quite as though he had forgiven everybody he set about making camp, whistling while he worked. This touched me so much, in my innocence, that I gave him back his packet with a fatherly lecture, and offered him my hand. He gazed at it for a moment, wiped off his, and shook mine gingerly. No one, probably, had shaken hands with him in twenty years. But he did not smile; no tears welled from his dark eyes. They just measured my stupidity with little twitches like inward winks, Raphael telling Raphael that he had my measure now.

I sat snarling at the fire for a long while that night, wishing I had brought along just one person whom I could sock in the teeth from time to time, without jeopardizing the whole expedition. Every explorer should have one.

❧

The thinning river, the slot in the forest, made an excellent channel for the wind, which whipped the stench of half-smoked fish up and down our caravan of canoes.

Malfatti was far in the lead, running his private expedition, no longer helping to pull our canoes through the rapids. Now he stopped and waited for us patiently, his chin lifted, his lips protruded, tolerant, shamelessly mercenary.

We were beginning to dislike and distrust Chief Malfatti, and when he said we should make camp here, for fear of the bird *aweeyo*, I ordered the Bonis on. It was too early to stop, and again I was faced with the problem of who was running this expedition. But there were no *carbets* farther on, they said (the *carbet* was an Indian hut used during their dog-stealing forays). The tension between the blacks, the Indians, and ourselves stretched till it nearly hummed; if the bird should cry again it would puncture it. But we went on until I spotted a *carbet* among the trees and ordered a halt as the sun went down.

It was only because the *aweeyo* or zombie bird was need-ling us again that Afokati and Malfatti came to us with pres-ents to make peace. Afokati gave us an *agami*, a tough and flavorless fowl. Malfatti slowly and with ceremony presented me with a piece of honeycomb, saying that I should eat it, that it was rare and a delight.

Apologetic as usual for my severity, I examined it appre-ciatively, noted the fine plump white maggots in every cell, and to show that I was as good a sport as you could hope to find hereabouts, I bit into it and chewed. The sensation of the mouthful of maggots was quite unusual, and I tried quickly to kill them all, concentrating hard on the sympa-thetic eyes of Ruth, but once again I was doing the wrong thing. Malfatti, because he was afraid of the *aweeyo* bird, did not laugh out loud, but with a restrained smile he took the comb from my limp hand, carefully extracted the maggots on the tip of a lime tree thorn, and ate them individually.

The truly tender heart of Afokati must have quaked at the bitter pill of maggots I had swallowed, for he came into

the lamplight suddenly, leading by the hand an unknown
Indian, and swished the mist of little "fee-fee bugs" from between us.

Ruth was swishing too, for clearer vision. "Where did
that Indian come from? He's another one we didn't hire. I
hope he brought provisions." Our band of Indians had already intimated that they were running short of food and
would enjoy our rice.

Afokati got his man to tell us why he had come after us,
and then interpreted. He smiled pleasantly with the gift of
good news, as indeed it was. The Indian had come to say that
that other party of ten canoes, the great expedition we feared
was following us, was *Davis-bakra* — our own selves.

Except for minor differences, the Indians and the Bonis
were, to use an appropriate phrase, as thick as thieves. When
our Camillus cutlery and kerosene and taffia dwindled notice-
ably, the Bonis blamed the Roucouyennes and vice versa,
begging forgiveness for the poor souls who lacked both light
and cheer. They shared each other's viands, or mine, and were
cheerfully amicable, as I was, unaware of what Warner
Brothers were later to insist on calling "Jungle Terror" when
they distributed the film of this expedition. The Boni Negroes
were the more intelligent, and their Granman was titular head
of the Indian tribes, according to the government, but this
seemed to be unknown to the Indians, and it is doubtful that
the Granman cared. The Indians' superiority lay in their

simplified living. They had learned, for instance, to keep their skins free of infection by bathing frequently, as the Bonis did not, or by painting themselves with red *roucou* when at work in the woods. They had learned not only to feather their arrows but to do it spirally, whereas the Bonis still used the unelaborated stick. The Indian canoes were sleek and graceful in comparison with the crude Boni boats, and their houses were not hermetically closed like the Bonis', but open on all sides to wind and sun and neighbors.

The Bonis, however, did not think them very bright, as on one morning after a night when I, tired of the constant plea for laxatives, gave a small jar of Epsom Salts to Malfatti with the understanding that he divide it equitably among the wives, children, and livestock whom we had not invited on this party. I should have known the cupidity of our Indian better by now. He returned the empty bottle to me in the morning, admitting that he had drunk it all, because it was very good, it was like the *sauts* of the river. But this, he said, with a smile which chided me as a joker, this — and he left the sentence unfinished as one who hesitated to imply that his boss had poor taste.

This was a sheaf of sandpaper which I had given him thinking that it would be most useful in polishing the shafts of arrows. Malfatti laid it down on the box which served us as table, while all the Indians looked at me as though the last of their faith was gone.

Malfatti pointed to a roll of toilet tissue which we were using as napkins.

[233   ]

This, said he, dropping the sandpaper like an objectionable thing, might be all right for the likes of us, but not half good enough for him.

❧

October was here again. It lay again on the river, a yellow effluence, a golden, pounding sunlight which you knew anywhere in the tropics to be the precursor of the rains. The trees were quiet and you saw scintillations around them that were heat and the souls of trees escaping to the river again. Parched and sober as October were the trees.

From time to time our boys spotted a *comu* palm, always high on the valley edge of our river, and nothing would stop them from climbing to it and mounting it to tear off its golden beard of twigs where the gray *comu* berries grew. They would toss the mass of them over their shoulders like capes and swing them into our patient canoes. The Indians' red chickens roosted nicely on them. They were somewhat edible when beaten into a juice which resembled burned malted milk or rye with peanut butter. And the only suitable accompaniment to the nightly fete of drinking the *comu* was the same incredible but actual singing of the anaconda, the whooing, whiffling sound which the natives steadfastly maintained were gods' voices. It was a high sweet voice with such an urgency of desire as Adam must have heard in a world scarcely more primeval than this. It was evil; the red howler monkey which usually lulled us with his chanting would

[234]

quieten before the voice of the boa and be small in his top leaves.

This was odd enough; but the feeling we had increasingly of tension among our known and unknown personnel was accentuated even more oddly when we became certain that though all of our party, even the strays, were asleep, yet punctuating the serpent's song was the clear but incomprehensible conversation of other Indians, just beyond the nimbus where the beam of our flashlight abruptly stopped. Our Roucouyennes admitted this in daylight: we were being accompanied, and by no kin of theirs — and no kin of theirs meant hostile folk from whom our boys had probably stolen dogs.

October turned to November as we poled slowly into the Tumuc-Humacs, and our neighbors still were with us, leaving fires smoldering at each camp site we would have chosen, chattering behind us but close on our heels as we launched our canoes early in the morning and took to the middle of the stream.

We went quietly forward, and I saw us as I would later in our film: Ruth kneeling, her upraised knee obscuring half of her, her elbow and camera the other, Raphael, the zombie, bent over his familiar stove, myself sliding pink from the *pomekari* of my canoe to teeter erect when there was a voice among the trees or the canoes slowed down.

There was an astounding lack of birds, flowers, serpents, monkeys here — of everything but trees. The visible animal life consisted mostly of scorpions, which invaded Ruth's canoe and lurked in her more intimate garments, such as panties and bathing suits. Sometimes in bright daylight the bats would come veering from the forest, and as though drawn on elastic threads they would swerve suddenly back to the bole of one tree. They were like the voices of our invisible Indians. Our Bonis would exclaim, "O-oh! O-oh!" and the buffalo bullfrogs, as big as your head, would grunt, "Wow! Wow!" in stentorian surprise.

"Bird," said Ruth, who was being thrifty with words, one evening; above us passed a bird called the "aha" because it said "aha!" sometimes. It swooped like a comet, and its back was butterfly blue, its underwings orange. Its long tail had a puff of feathers like a poodle's and its beak was a parrot's. I noted this conscientiously for ornithologists such as Jimmy Chapin of the American Museum of Natural History, who dismissed it with something less than a shrug.

It was in approaching the Alama River, a confluent of the Itany, that the first signs of mutiny became known to us. I had started some time ago to prepare our rivermen for the work they would have to do when we came to the end of water, the end of the creek which we would take through the mountains to the Brazilian frontier, when they would have to walk on their feet and carry baggage. This lacked appeal to both Indians and Bonis. Afokati made me a life-sized drawing in the sand of the little load which he, a riverman, could carry on his back when obliged to use feet for transport, and Malfatti, our Indian chief, gave us an example of how he was going to run ahead of us when we should take to the woods. Like this, he said, while Ruth and I sat on a couple of jerry cans, dehydrating our film with silica gel. Like this, he yelled, and we looked up to see him running in the strange way that these Indians have, erect, head high, crooked elbows moving like pistons by his ribs.

We were very firm. We explained again fruitlessly that in the first place we didn't run like that in New York, and that also we couldn't see much if we did. We had to see much, we said. I was opening the jerry can beneath me — taking out handfuls of silica gel and thrusting them at Ruth, who put them in her film cans — and flipping shut my can again lest the humidity reach it — when I saw behind us, in our hut of palm fronds, another sign of dissidence: the occupation of Raphael.

"What is that thing?" I asked Raphael, pointing to the stick in his hands. He had wound on it what at first I had thought was our nylon cord, a ball a foot thick. I went over to him and he smirked at me. It wasn't cord; it was spaghetti, cooked, wound round and round the stock like a fisherman's line.

Ruth admired the pattern of its winding. "But what is it for?" she asked amiably.

"For the *évasion*," he replied as to a child. "I've had enough of it, both the prison and this river where we'll get our heads cut off. You can come with me if you want. I've made enough spaghetti for three."

"No meat?" I asked sternly. He drew from every pocket a bundle of smoked fish wrapped in banana leaves.

"I'll take those," said I, "and put them in the silica gel."

We went up the river, and on our left at last was a slight depression in the woods which was the entrance to the creek Coule-Coule, which had been reached by the geographer Richard. Now there was only a point of water leading to a dry stream bed, and though I had hoped to follow Richard's route along it I was happy that our Indians themselves considered it with suspended paddles and suggested that there was another creek, the Ouaremapan, a little farther, which would take us to the path they used when raiding Brazil for hunting dogs.

Our river, the Itany, was now diminished to about seventy feet across; the dry entrance to the Coule-Coule was twenty, and I wondered how we would navigate on the Ouaremapan with canoes thirty feet long, for if the Coule-Coule was an example of what we were to expect — choked with fallen trees — the Ouaremapan would require portage. Even the Itany here was choked with logs from the last rains.

And the new rains were coming on. We had brought them on, said the Bonis. We had washed the Explorers' Club flag, number 127, in the river, which of course would bring on the rains. Eimo pointed to the flag which Ruth had spread to dry on the *pomekari* of her canoe. "Rain," he said; so it rained. The first rains — to confound us who had no business here and should never have washed a flag in a female river inseminated by the male seeds of rain — sluiced us mightily.

The nights were cold thereafter, and hard on Ruth, who was feverish. Softened, diffused through the mosquito netting, her legs drawn under her, her arms stretched with fingers interlaced, she slept preciously and terribly for me who typed these notes on an up-ended box at the periphery of the lantern's light. I would come to my cot beside her and with one hand touch her forehead lightly for its temperature and with the other spread the low-fronded roof until I could see several stars and watch them move across my minute horizons, deciding whether I should awaken her for more quinine.

And this was terrible to think about: the fragility of what one loved. The old bold sun was corrupted by rain; the words for writing at one's fingertips were dissolved in the fever of a pattern of a girl.

I would hold my eyes wide open to watch my several stars.

We probably seemed, said Ruth, like people peacefully punting on the Thames, except for the increasing arguments among the canoes of Bonis and Indians, and the constant counterpoint of voices in the forest. By wishful thinking they seemed echoes at times, and I would quieten our paddlers to listen; and they were voices certainly. Then our own would rise in argument again, and it was simple to guess that the Indians were not for going on with us, and that the Bonis were afraid to go on without them.

Even more ancient than the rumor of El Dorado in the

Tumuc-Humac Mountains, was the legend of this region —
that it was haunted; and I talked with Ruth of the men here,
the amphibian people, who were said to live beneath the
river, breathing water, as the Moors of African Mauritania
maintain, with fair evidence, that they do today.

One day, almost like any other, became burdened for us
by Raphael being chucked under the chin by a low branch,
which Toma had probably designed for him. Over went his
kitchen, scalding in his lap. The branch swept on to leave a
bald spot on his plaited *pomekari*, and even our invisible companions of the shore were silent before Raphael's rage.

This so exacerbated Malfatti that he ordered all canoes
ashore, where they went while I was trying to understand what
he was up to. We landed on a sandspit, half an arrow's flight
from the jungle wall; if you were smart, you could see an
arrow coming. Now, said Malfatti, cockily, roosting on a
rock, he was going to turn back with all his canoes.

"And you, Afokati?"

The gentle Afokati, nominally the chief, became limp before the glowering of the crescent of Indians and Negroes
who had us backed to the river, where we might be better
targets for the ghosts. Afokati had lost command; the suasion
of his councilors was too great for him, and he looked like an
old man as he reached down to pour sand between his toes,
and without looking up said that this was very difficult for
him, that everyone was against him, that if the Indians left
us his Bonis, who were rivermen, could not carry our baggage through the woods.

This was the moment for the firmness of which pioneers are made, and I saw myself — pink and white, in bathing trunks, surrounded by magnificent black and brown natives who, by the simple color of their skins, seemed neatly clothed; and I remembered Ruth's saying only yesterday that she hated me when I yelled at them. So I set to imagining the three pips on my epaulettes and the ribbons over the left breast pocket (which were always falling off), and spoke to my mutineers in a tone well-modulated for Ruth's appreciation, without much hope that it would be effective.

I had learned long ago that you mustn't sneer at natives or make fun of them, so I told them in baleful terms, calmly, what I thought of men who broke faith — keeping an eye on Ruth, who was pretending to dig a chigger from her foot. I mentioned offhand to my audience that I'd be triple damned and a beggar's ulcer if any of them would ever again transport honest white folk on this river. Ruth on the side lines now seemed to have become sincerely interested in the chigger; she had dug out three white sacs of eggs from her toe, and wasn't worrying about me.

And oddly enough the blacks and the Indians were, as she had said they would be. They paid heed, took council, deliberated, and were, I felt, on the verge of capitulation when my thunder was stolen by the rumble of a plane coming from the northwest. They heard it before I did, and muttered, "Panam! Panam!" And Raphael came out from behind a rock and pointed with a doomful finger at the sky, bawling at them, "You see? It is as we said! The administration has sent another plane to watch our expedition! *Bande de couillons, vas!"*

I shrank modestly into my pink skin and suggested that we return to the canoes. Afokati and Malfatti seconded me, and away we went, vigorously — for a hundred yards or so.

❧

We had — as noted above — taken no tents with us. A tent in the jungle is as silly as a sun helmet. The slight air is baffled by it; insects seek its refuge; and in the Bad Lands such as ours, where one could remember without false dramatics the numerous trusting souls who had gone to sleep and not wakened again, in these Tumuc-Humacs of glamorous and evil legend, the tent was a trap. So each night the Bonis built for us a house of fronds, and after dinner we received. The Bonis came first for their shot of taffia, then the Indians joined them to watch me practice my legerdemain, a form of solitaire which improves with audience participation, even if it goes wrong.

The soft, grinning sausages of Malfatti's lips should have warned me one night when out of the dark he, in turn, produced egg after egg, iguana eggs, a rarity, and a fine gesture for a recent mutineer. We went to sleep talking of the good, the reformed Malfatti, and in the morning sat around the breakfast fire eagerly while Raphael broke egg after egg into the skillet, and flung each one over his shoulder at the rising sun, until I stopped him at the ninth. That egg like the others contained a baby iguana which had been on the verge of birth and was warmed to wiggling life in our frying pan.

"I would take a dim view of that so-called gesture," I said to Ruth, who was philosophically mixing egg powder into a noxious mush, "and I would reproach Malfatti for it, if I wanted to spoil the joy of the morning."

"What joy?" she asked. "And what morning? Do you know?"

"The joy, darling, of seeing my first Tumuc-Humac. Look. That." A few miles up the river and seeming to block it was a gray-and-green rounded mountain, the Knopoya-moye, said our guides. In the Andes it would have been called a hill, but it had dignity here, though without much allure. It was like a hunchbacked footman before the estate of El Dorado where lived the noble peaks of Timotakem and Temo-mairem.

Narrowly we saw before us our El Dorado, and the legend's end.

∽

Once we camped above the river, on a bank of clay. The Indians at their fire were whispering among themselves, and the Bonis at their fire were whispering also. Our Raphael was no whisperer, thief and murderer though he might be, so Raphael said aloud, "Those parts-of-female-genitalia who are traveling with us and watching us from the shore seem particularly cheerful tonight."

We listened. Surely not more than thirty feet away from

us in the dark there were men talking, but I had tried before to rush them, and tripped on roots, and clutched at slim limbs, as I fell with their laughter gurgling another thirty feet away.

By morning we had still not slept very much and there was a crick in the back of my neck where a ghost's dull machete had sawed back and forth on it. When the sleep was shaken from us we still heard voices, still gay. We took to the canoes, rounded an amphibious tree which held beans three feet long above our heads, and with a twist of canoes to left, then to right, went straight into the woods, into the thin vein which was our creek, the Ouaremapan.

Almost before we could get out from under, our boys had torn the *pomekaris* from above our heads and tossed them into the stream that was littered with decaying wood and laced by branches which our canoes would have to slink beneath. We insinuated ourselves another hundred feet, like leucocytes following blindly the stout red corpuscles of our natives along this vein, and stopped in a clear space of water. The gushing of red sunlit water still came from the paddles which had abruptly arrested us. No one spoke, or looked from left to right, or made any gesture. There was suddenly not a sound from our neighbors in the woods, while I, also quietly, was looking around for the reason of this strange stop.

Nobody but I looked at it, when I found it at last. I whistled to Ruth, and she and Raphael did look. It was a ball of white kapok, about six inches in diameter, on the end of a four-foot stick planted in the southern bank of the stream.

The glaring white of it was shocking against the green. It hurt the eyes. It was as flagrant as a scream in the dark.

And yet I was relieved to come upon it at last, as evidence of the intentions of our invisible hosts, and confirmation of the honesty reported by Coudreau. There should be, from time to time, a white ball as signal that strangers might continue in the country of the Oyaricoulets. Whereas a red ball, such as the one which had caused the massacre of the party of forty-nine Frenchmen, meant distinctly that one should go no farther.

"That's clear enough for my taste," said Ruth, as we backed up our canoes to film the Indian sign. "But why do they leave a white ball permitting you to go on, if they won't even talk to you, or come out to trade?"

"Name of God!" said Raphael, closing one eye, grinning, nodding knowingly. "*Madame* cannot be so naïve. They will lead us up the garden path with their damned white balls, like they did the other party, to murder us when they're tired of your pretty face." He doffed his straw hat gallantly: "That should take some time, *madame*."

The only clement answer that I could guess at was a village somewhere farther along this creek Ouaremapan, which might be interested in trading with us, or at least in regarding us as a diversion. According to the tales we had heard there should be several white balls after the first one, but following from one to another was like chasing the sixty-four-dollar question of radio; you would be winning at every white ball with little more virgin country to your credit, but at any moment, instead of the white ball, there might appear the red one. Then you would lose, abruptly.

Now Raphael was behaving no better than usually, but because we were far away in a land that wanted none of us, and because no one — neither among our Bonis nor our Roucouyennes — was on our side now, we took some pains to make Raphael understand that he was our friend, that I should do my best to get him pardoned when we returned to St. Laurent, that we should spend a family Christmas together with pleasant presents and such. But it was no use. When I offered him one of the rare sausages from my own plate he had fits again: we treated him like a dog, flinging our ordure at him. It became plain that, should we have active trouble with Indians, Raphael would take to the woods.

What he would do there was beyond my imagining, for the woods were cavernous and hostile. Even our creek was a tunnel lighted by speckles through the filigree of branches and leaves, a place where shadow was substance and light ephemeral, like the latticed passages of an Arab bazaar. Unseamed huge rocks rose in a wall to form the fundament of the mountain on our right; on our left was impenetrable liana; beneath us was a maculate water of black and gold where long-legged insects floated like the stars in opals, their reflections rounding them; in front of us there was always a log.

The log would be a tree from thirty to fifty feet long, fallen athwart the stream, and impossible to move. The Indians would throw up their hands; but the Bonis would chop valiantly and in an hour or so we would have a passage made which permitted the passage of our canoes for another few yards, to another barrier, two feet thick, of fine hardwood, much prized by cabinetmakers. Sometimes we made a distance of half a mile in a day, hacking and hauling, sliding under snarls of branches as we lay flat with our dear cameras in the wet bottoms of the canoes, or seesawing them over half-sunken logs which were impossible to cut.

"Good going," Ruth said often, with complete sincerity, to cheer my morale, while we lay on our backs in the cool stream at night.

"Brazil," said I, "can't be more than three hundred logs away."

We could hear the angry jabber of our Indians, and when they quieted we could hear the equally ugly mutter of the Bonis, and when they too were silent we could listen to the soft voices of the invisible Oyaricoulets in the forest.

The stream flowed over us, when we bathed, cool and caressing, and so strong was it here that we had to crotch our arms around the boulders. The fireflies, called by the Indians *kukri* and by the Bonis *kimonimoni*, were elaborate with green eyes and golden belly lights, and beneath and around us must have been the same school of piranha we had seen in daylight.

The piranha is the explorer's bugaboo, the "man-eating fish" of the lecture platform, the little assassin with enormous pointed teeth that would tear you limb from limb if you fell overboard in a South American river. Even if carelessly you dangled your fingers in the water they would be eaten to the bone. There are explorers, the intrepid type, who tell tales of seeing Indians rush across a shallow stream to crumple on the farther shore with not a shred of flesh up to their skeletal knees. This gives a lecture audience the shudders.

But we got on well with the piranhas, frequently eating them, to their surprise. It is true that if you throw the gory entrails of a monkey into the stream they would rather eat it now than wait for a better meal farther down, and if you poke a bleeding finger into a school of them, and beckon with it, they will pay it some heed, but my experience of many rivers full of them was that they were just as timid as sharks and lions; keep moving in their presence so they won't bump into you, and they will politely shy away.

It was the men in this wilderness who were incalculable if not yet dangerous. We returned one night from such a bathing, a respite from worry and hot fatigue, to find Asa casually leaning on a forked stick I had cut to hang our cameras on. He leaned a little harder on it and the stick leaned with him until they both bent in the direction of the Boni camp and suddenly were gone.

We were bedding down for the night, ill at ease because the Bonis and Indians had not come for their usual nightcap, when the one we called Abracadabra arrived alone, for treatment of his leg. He had been coming faithfully every day since St. Laurent, and Ruth and I, who are less than amateurs in medicine, had despaired of healing an open abscess above his ankle. We had tried the antiseptics, the salves, the sulfa drugs, we had dined him on penicillin.

I had cut away the slough within the abscess, and this would have been torture for all but heroes.

"Doesn't that hurt, Abracadabra?"

He would shake his head and smile, and I would notice how his nose was flattened and his cheeks were puffy.

I disinfected the wound with straight alcohol, and he didn't flinch. Curious. I tried iodine, and he calmly smiled. This was beginning to worry me, for it looked less like heroism now than like deadened nerves, and that was of evil omen in French Guiana. Yesterday, to be sure, I had packed the abscess with salt enough to make a mummy squirm, and had bandaged it tight. During twenty-four hours it had been soaking into the raw pit. It was dissolved by now, and the wound looked clean and scarlet.

"And that didn't hurt?"

Abracadabra, whose face was always limp with innocence, looked at me craftily. I poured into the wound a slug of straight limejuice, an excellent antiseptic and a torture of the Inquisition.

My patient had no reaction but the broadening of his leper's leer; by a dozen signs about him, which I might have noticed any evening as he sat with the light full on him, drinking taffia from our glasses, I should have seen that he had leprosy, the Guiana *cocobai*.

"I can't go back alone," said he. "There is no small canoe for me. The others will take me back. We have no food left.

We can't go on. The others are not afraid of me, but I am afraid for madame."

This was the threat direct, reinforced by the arrival of the other Bonis, led by the wrestler Abbidal who had been surly for two days since Ruth told him to get his arrows the hell off her tarpaulin. I offered no taffia now, and got in return a chorus of *"Taffia tant pis! M'en fous de taffia!"* Then the Indians came and squatted, looking big as butchers to me.

They had no food, they said. Were they men of the woods or of the villages? I asked. There was no game here, they said; this was no place to take one's stomach. But the Indians had sworn to me that they had food enough, I said, and the Bonis had been paid 2400 francs' advance money to buy food down-river. But the Bonis, they said, had given half their food to the Indians, and Toma — the sea lawyer of this combine — inadvisedly piped up to say that French money was no good anyway, and Malfatti with equal unwisdom stated that if the French didn't treat him better and send him arms and a hat, he would take all his men, numbering fifty, and go to live on the Dutch shore.

"Aha!" said I with a bound, the District Attorney coming out in me. "Ruth, you are witness to those two statements, and you, Raphael!"

Ruth hesitated but a moment. "Hanging evidence," she said.

"C'est chouette!" yelled Raphael. *"On les aura!"* He reached for his machete and drew its razor edge along his thumb.

I whipped a sheet of my fancy stationery into the typewriter and began writing a REPORT TO THE GOVERNOR, reading

[250]

aloud my accusations against the mutineers, particularly Toma and Malfatti, quoting their treasonable statements. I folded this and put it in an envelope which I adorned with stars, dollar signs, and exclamation points.

Only Asa, my savage bowman, stirred. *"Finis!"* he said, adding the equivalent of "Nuts!" — and glided into the woods. Toma and Malfatti looked distressed. Afokati was near to tears. He came close to me, shaking his old head.

"Captain, tear up the paper," he begged me. "They are children when they are excited like this."

"The captain never flinches from his duty," said Ruth, sighing in sympathy with the culprits.

"A hard man but just," said Raphael, rolling his eyes as at the tortures I personally had inflicted. *"Tiens, on connait la musique!"*

I snapped off the Totelite. Its long fluorescent bulb glowed orange for an instant, then sucked all the dark of the night around us. We didn't move. The Bonis and the Indians stumbled away from us, dazzled by darkness; there was a smashing of leaves and small branches and a terrific plop into the river as an anaconda, the Bonis' god, slipped from his limb in sleep.

We didn't laugh at the perfection of this climax; there was to be no laughter any more. We sat still and sweated until the wowing frog, the *mo-aima*, began to howl that everyone but he was asleep.

❦

We usually were wakened at dawn by Malfatti. Pekein, the Boni mascot, was striding up and down against the glint of the stream, singing, "Blu-blu-blu-blu . . . " in a cheery way; it had been some time since he had been friendly with us, for his moods reflected those of his elders faithfully. In the good old days a month ago, when we all loved each other to distraction, Pekein had been a pest with his hot, hard, dirty body pressed like a poultice against one or another of us while we tried to eat or to film.

Ducking through the low doorway of the hut and gouging another furrow in my back, I saw that the "Blu-blu-blu-blu . . . " of Pekein was probably due to his joy over break-fast, for in his small hands he held a monkey's head larger than his own, and having ripped loose the maxillary muscle and swallowed it, as one would a whole snake, he was now plunging a pink tongue into the eyes.

Ruth stirred in the house of our green mosquito netting and asked where her soul had gone, but I was busy trying to inter-pret the song of Eimo and Abbibal, trying to catch the pulse of my mutineers. The black balls of their heads were nodding toward each other from their opposite white hammocks, and they were singing cheerfully too: "*Je m'en fous de taffia . . .*" which meant with asterisks that they could get along without my rum.

I wondered with asterisks what we were coming to, Ruth and I alone with this band of poisonous people. If there had been any way of making contact with the Oyaricoulets, I should have joined them gladly now, and founded a Sunday-

[252]

supplement Empire of the Great White Chief and lived prof-
itably on the bounty of my fellow members of the Explorers'
Club; anything, I thought, to get away from these black and
vermillion bandits upon whom we were so exasperatingly de-
pendent.

Eimo had the best baritone among them, and when he
yelled *"Finis"* at the ends of cadences it rang like a gong along
the creek. And all his cadences were built craftily toward the
apex of the decision, *"Finis."* Eimo was the sort of tough
hysteric you knew in the war, who cracked up quicker than
the fragile, subtle people like Toma, who would hold his gun
straight at the enemy because he was afraid to be afraid.

Eimo fell from the hammock on his round black head, and
went tearing around in circles through the bush, singing,
beating the air, yowling, *"Taffia! . . . Finis!"* leaping over
phantoms.

At the entrance of our hut I reached behind me for the
brass knuckles and saw that Ruth was asleep again. Eimo
wouldn't be dangerous until he ran afoul of opposition; and
his *kitta*, his madness, his trance, led him safely past the
hammocks and the looping vines and close before me while
he chanted, *"Finis! Finis!"*

He was still zigzagging like a bumblebee when old Afokati,
bent with his problems, came to me to say that a special,
extra problem which he had neglected to mention last night
was Aliman. Aliman was the little Indian mascot whom we
had rented for three yards of red calico and a mosquito net
in the hope that he would add a grace note to the film. He

had traveled in Ruth's canoe, and they had become fast friends. Outknitting the Indians, she had made him the sort of fringed legging which great warriors wear, and which he wore with pride.

Afokati mumbled with much shaking of the head that his paddlers had decided that either Aliman must work or that I must pay his passage; he was not in our contract either as passenger or baggage.

This was the limit. I spoke very loudly. Ruth woke up and to my amazement smiled at the tirade I was delivering. This threw me quite off stroke, for I knew she suffered when I raised my voice to the boys nearly as much as when I spoke justly but angrily to them with "that tone" (well modulated and disguised, I thought, and a hell of an effort) which meant that I was unpleased.

Marvelously she stood beside me now and reminded Afokati that we still had the parrot, Papagai, to which Eimo objected, and would Afokati like us to pay passage for him? Or should we put him to work?

There's the darling! I thought, with such delight and consternation that I lost the train of my tirade, and my anger guttered out, and with renewed good cheer in me I shouted that we would continue up the creek immediately.

An hour or so later, and three logs cut through, I was sitting without a shirt in my canoe, hugging the remembrance of Ruth's fealty, when Malfatti, at the head of our flotilla, rose and faced us and made a gesture meaning that we should stop.

There was a mountain on our right, to the west. I learned that it was Mount Ga Mongo, unlisted on my maps. We should go up it, said Malfatti, and look into Brazil.

While I was considering this and remembering my last ignominious mountain climb, I was also covering the soles of my bare feet and the bottoms of my toes with adhesive tape. This I did craftily and unseen by the boys. I sprang ashore in a sprightly fashion and went up the hill like an antelope, barefooted to all appearances, and with my knee by good luck functioning because the floating particle of ligament had fallen into its groove again. Ruth, who walks on air anyway, sprang along even nimbler than I, while the boys lost time in wonderment.

We knew we were at the top only when we started to go downhill again. I was content to learn that only a few yards from the river, where there was less moisture in the soil, the forest, the jungle of the books, became clean as the woods of a park, with no undergrowth because the majestic pillars of trees, which propped the "jungle cathedral" of the books, impeded the sunlight.

From the top of Mount Ga Mongo we saw practically nothing, because of the speckling of the leaves before us on every side, and as it would be the work of hours to clear a passage for a view I agreed with Malfatti that there was Brazil just yonder, sure enough. So far as we could see through the speckling leaves, there were blue hummocks to the south with yellow-white cubes like old teeth rising amongst them: the great, the legendary, the sinister Tumuc-Humacs, where

Lake Parimé and its golden cities shone in the dreams of the old adventurers, and would always shine for me.

So we went down through that docile jungle to the boats again, and as we continued up the creek, hacking our way every thirty feet or so, I kept thinking of the jungle and how like a lion it was, superficially ferocious when you met it at the water's edge and timid in the darkness beyond. On the high ground above the creek you could stroll anywhere. It was only the swamplands you had to fear.

Malfatti was angrier than ever because he couldn't say, "Hah, Ga Mongo was too much for you, my fine white friends. You will never reach Brazil. We shall go home now."

All afternoon the clouds were curding gray. They began to rain toward evening, and in our naked canoes we sat despondently beneath plastic ponchos, sweating gouts, knowing that our film was finished, that the rains had beaten us. And we felt no cheerier when we came to another white ball of kapok on a stick, indicating that we might go on. I began to suspect that this was a clever ruse of the Oyaricoulets to get us to do the work of clearing the timber from their creek.

The Oyaricoulets, walking invisible beside us, were talking louder now. They laughed. They no longer seemed to care whether we heard their machetes cutting the undergrowth. And that silenced even Eimo. At sunset, or about the time of it, for we couldn't see it through the rain, we still had found no possible camp site. The creek had become a canyon with granite walls.

"We'll sleep in the canoes," I said to Malfatti. He turned

in his canoe, which seemed inextricably entangled in lianas, and, without quite focusing his eyes on me, said that soon we would come to a hut, a *carbet*, which he had built as a base for his dog-raiding in Brazil.

"When is 'soon'?" I asked suspiciously. The measurement of time and distance is elastic to an Indian. Malfatti flicked his head, the black lank hair swinging in the rain. "Soon" was somewhere in the vines ahead of us.

"How about it, darling?"

Ruth's voice came muffled from her poncho. "The Bonis will be happier under shelter, and we'd better keep them happy now."

"Soon" was amazingly sooner than I expected. We cut through a tangle and found a clearing in the creek, where it was three or four yards across. There were two tiny *carbets* on the sloping bank, simple roofs perched close to the ground. We took one, the Bonis the other, and the Indians, grunting in the rain, quickly constructed for themselves a splendid house of thatch. I protested that ours was not large enough for us and our baggage, and where was Raphael with his kitchen to go?

I saw then that we were in the midst of pure revolt. Neither Indians nor Bonis would budge to extend our roof or patch the holes through which the rain jetted as from a dozen faucets. There was no use arguing now. In a few minutes it would be too dark to see. While Ruth arranged baggage, storing film and cameras cautiously, Raphael and I hacked a short twisting path to serve as lavatory — the woods were so thick that there was scarcely standing room outside the hut — and made props for the tarpaulins to cover and extend the roof.

"Toma!" I yelled in frustrate fury. "Where the hell's our wood and water?" It was his job to supply these to Raphael every evening.

"Wood and water? Wood and water?" echoed Toma from his hut. "The water is all around you, and the wood is wet!" Neither they nor the Indians had a fire.

At that moment of misery Raphael became heroic. Swearing like the apache he was, he waded into the creek and hauled out logs from beneath the surface. We were certain he was beginning one of his mad crises again as he carefully examined them, chose certain ones, ripped off the soaking bark of them as though to make a fire. The Bonis were laughing and describing him vividly.

But there was a super Boy Scout in Raphael, and with the initial aid of a little kerosene he soon had a blaze as high as the hut and the logs themselves were burning.

"Oil in them," he explained with a snarl. He could have cut them on shore, but for the Bonis it was more impressive that he bring them from the depths of the creek. Angrily he made a bigger and bigger fire, and as the Bonis and Indians, agog with wonder, approached it he drove them back with his machete. Only our one nice Indian family would he allow to dry themselves. They squatted with us before the whopping, rolling flames, and old Oulua, the wife, said that the word for fire was *waput*, and Papa Alibon said that sand was *hamut*,

[258]

and Ali-hali, the boy, rubbing his eyes, said that sleep was *tinikeh tinikeh.*

Because they were good and we were lonely we gave them presents of razor blades, food, and soap, which was observed against the firelight by the others in the rain and the dark, for we heard their growling. They would either become angrier, I thought, or realize that there was profit in co-operating with us. Then Malfatti began to yell and a few minutes later I heard a canoe being put into the creek. It went past us swiftly bearing one of the younger Indians and his family. I hurried with the flashlight to the other side of the fire and demanded an explanation from Malfatti. It was simple, said he; he had not enough food; he had to send some of his people home. I had not contracted for this family anyway.

"Don't you remember," I shouted, "that I said yesterday I would give you food until we reached the border?"

"*Oui, oui,*" he replied.

"And don't you know that you'll never get any presents when we return, if you don't do as I say?"

"*Oui, oui,*" said he.

God give me patience, I thought. For days this brute had answered all my questions with his smirk and his prim "*Oui, oui.*"

"Malfatti, would you like to get a bullet in the guts, right in there?" I jabbed his fat belly with the flashlight.

"*Oui, oui,*" he said.

I returned to the fire and the smell of Ruth's biscuits. Papa Alibon was telling her that "no good" is *hipokedah,* leaning

[259]

over her shoulder to watch her write it. Oulua was peeking under the can where the biscuits cooked; she laughed the laugh which was called *tawakeh*. Ali-hali, wakeful again and helpful, pointed to his fringed leggings, which were *waipu*, and his loincloth, which was *camisa*. The water, the rain, was *tuna*.

But old Alibon smiled sadly while I still stood there, admiring the coziness of this little group, surrounded by discomfort and menace. Alibon reached up and drew a circle in the air, enclosing all of us and the Bonis' and Malfatti's camps; and he said, "*Tanetsep* — finished."

Raphael wakened me in the morning and I parted the thatch to look at the creek where he was pointing. The canoe with our good Indians was drifting by; they were gesturing to us dispiritedly, to say that there was nothing they could do. We ate breakfast without much conversation, watching our journey fray before our eyes. There were no more Indian canoes along the shore, only our three long ones. All the Indians but Malfatti had gone, and his canoe with them. The Bonis sat in their hut saying nothing. Malfatti, who usually was sociable with them, sat alone in his, with his long bow and arrows on his knees.

When Ruth and I went over to them we were greeted with grunts from the Bonis, and Malfatti simply turned his head to stare into the woods. He stared so long that finally I went to the spot where he seemed to be looking.

I found what I suspected, the red ball of kapok on a spear.

We returned to camp, told Raphael, and spent that day in cleaning guns, dividing baggage into two heaps, one of which could be abandoned if we had to get away fast, and deciding alternately, over and over again, that we should push forward anyway or that we should return. Here, in the midst of the mountains, with Brazil close enough to shoot a bullet into, it seemed disgraceful to be forced to return, and if we should do so there was every likelihood — as we were to confirm later — of our being ambushed by Malfatti's men. If we pushed on, we had the Oyaricoulets to worry about, and they had already given us notice.

I called to Afokati and Malfatti to come over and discuss this, and they called back, "Later on." At last, later on, I had to go to them.

Malfatti, looking never at me, said straight that he must return to his village. He fiddled with his long poisoned arrows.

The Bonis, to my amazement, said that they were willing to go on, but not by the creek; the chopping was too arduous and would take too much time. They would carry a little of our baggage on their backs and we would cut through the woods until we joined the Indian path of which Malfatti had spoken, the path to Brazil which the dog thieves used. I preferred to follow the creek, knowing that the path ran up from it surely not very far away, and suggested that we should start as soon as they had woven their carrying baskets. They were adamant: we must go through the woods. I saw no possible hope of finding the trail without Malfatti's guidance, but I left them then, encouraged by the fact that they were starting their basketware.

I was at a total loss as to what to do. I thought of trying to force Malfatti at pistol point to guide us, but there were too many dangerous intangibles. As we ourselves were being threatened with war by the Oyaricoulets, it would be imprudent to declare war against my own men. Ruth could help me somewhat, and courageously, but I couldn't count on Raphael, and it looked like an insuperable ordeal to struggle up the creek with a camera in one hand and a pistol in the other, to guard my guides by night and day. We were so deep in the forest by now — much farther than any white man had ever been — that with the slightest lack of vigilance on our part we could be knocked on our heads by our guides, and forgotten about. The authorities could never prove that it was not the Oyaricoulets who had done us in.

Late on that gray afternoon I went to see how the baskets were coming, and found only three of them made, ridiculously small, not large enough even to fit our movie cameras. Abbibal shrugged; he wouldn't be able to carry more than that. And savage Asa growled that as a matter of fact they weren't even going to carry that; they were rivermen, not porters.

Ruth had moved up beside me. "So you're not coming with us?" she inquired softly.

They were taken aback by this, but they said no.

We were in for it now. There was no use bawling at them

[262]

any more. I stated that Ruth and Raphael and I would continue alone tomorrow morning, and they could wait for us
to come back this way if they wished. This would be to their
advantage, in that they would be paid for the trip down-river.
However, if they wished to leave us, I would appreciate their
not forgetting to store our provisions well. Pan American
would pick us up, of course; and I should be obliged, of
course, to report their bad faith to the Governor, who would
deal with them as traitors. The *bagne*, the penal settlement,
was full of traitors, I pointed out.

With that I turned to them my back, and felt the shivers
run up it. Before we had time to reflect on our folly we had
told Raphael of it and found him incredibly enthusiastic.
The very thought of leaving the Bonis behind was wonderful
to him.

"They won't leave," he prophesied. "They'll sit and
stew and worry themselves sick till we get back, or until
the Indians get us." He grinned as though that were a
joke.

The rain came on again that night, bringing with it the
fireflies we loved, with luminous green eyes and golden
belly lights. When Ruth was in her cot and Raphael sharpen-
ing his machete, I also sat and stewed for a while, and I worried, for I had seen Malfatti talking fairly amiably with the
Bonis again. There was nothing, I thought, to prevent that
combination from quietly massacring us in the night, getting
and dividing our baggage and telling the authorities that there
had been the quite common upset of our canoes in the rapids.

It had happened, just like that, and much closer to civilization.

I got up and brought a boxful of empty bottles from one of the canoes. These, in my loving-kindness, I had been saving as presents for the Roucouyennes when we should return to their village. Fumbling in the rainy darkness, I lay the bottles along the edge of our hut, feeling that prowlers would slip on them. And as I was placing them carefully in strategic positions I knew suddenly that I was being followed. I squatted on my heels beneath the thatch and got the pistol in my hand; for its moral effect I had been wearing it these past few days.

I had often wondered in other countries, and in greater wars, at the irrelevance of thoughts and perceptions at moments when I was seriously worried about survival. Here I knew that my pulse was carefully slowing down. I tasted all right to me. I thought of the adrenalin being flooded through my system, but felt nothing of it. I saw my fireflies' bright green eyes and jewels of bellies, and just at my back I heard the slightly roughened whisper of Ruth, breathing sleep.

It is rarely at such moments that you have had the sense to take your flashlight with you, so I waited, listening to something brushing toward me around the fringed thatch of the hut. And suddenly there was a clanking of glass and the crash of a bottle that broke and a banshee howl.

Ruth's awakening was almost instantaneous with the broad beam of her Totelite, and in it was seated Raphael on broken bottles and clutching like babies an armful of whole ones.

We bent him over a flour keg and crisscrossed his buttocks with Band-Aids while he ranted at fate and the fact that low, suspicious minds, such as his and mine, ran together. For he, it appeared, had had the same notion as I, and without knowing that I was ahead of him, had circled the hut, placing bottles in the dark a few feet beyond my defenses, of which he was unaware.

❧

It was five in the morning when Raphael wakened us. The rain was tickling our tarpaulined roof, and the sky was the color of an unwashed zinc sink.

"Look," said Raphael. "Get the pistol."

I got the pistol first and leaned on an elbow to peer beneath the thatch. In the creek a few feet below us was an Indian canoe I had never seen before, and standing in the stern of it was the thick statue of Malfatti, cautiously paddling away.

I couldn't imagine what Raphael wanted me to do with the pistol: shoot the Indian, hold him up, bring him back alive? And to what good end? Ruth had slipped from her cot to mine and was leaning painfully across my ribs, watching Malfatti. "That's the shot I've been waiting for," she said, referring to photography, not ballistics, "but let it go."

We watched it go around the bend, ate breakfast thoughtfully, prepared cameras and knapsacks, and, taking one Indian dog named Chew along with us, went to say a few curt words of parting to the Bonis. These were elaborated on by Raphael at the top of his voice as we hacked our way for fifty feet or so up the creek. He then had no more breath, and I was able to remind him of the red ball of kapok on the spear, and Ruth to remind me that since we had seen it we had not heard a sound from the Oyaricoulets who had accompanied us for so long. That did not, as the saying goes, put stomach in me.

There was another thing I had been wondering about. I panted it to Raphael. "Where could Malfatti have gotten that canoe? He had none last night."

We were emptying our rubber boots of water and scraping black mud from our legs. Raphael turned his leer, upside down, upon me. "I asked my friends, the Bonis. Malfatti told them that not far up the creek here was the Indian path to Brazil, and a little beyond it was a place where the Roucouyennes sank their canoes, to hide them from the Oyaricoulets while raiding in Brazil. He borrowed one of them. The next man returning will borrow someone else's, and so on until someone gets stuck without transport. It's a game, like Musical Chairs."

"That's encouraging, because he got the canoe sometime last night, which means that the entrance to the path can't be too far away. If we miss it we'll probably stub our toes on the canoes."

"Or on an Oyaricoulet," said Ruth.

❧

All day long we trudged, hacked, enlarged openings in vines. As the creek had no definite edge here but spread its

[266]

morass gradually to the sopping ground, the entrance to the trail would be hard to find.

The alternate pelting and dripping of rain added to the obscurity when we got too far from the main creek bed, but we stuck to the gummy shallows because, although the stream was far from "teeming" with caymaus, we had occasionally seen them, of respectable proportions. I shot at them only once, and regretted it for the racket I made. I didn't want our hosts on shore to get the notion that I was attacking anyone or anything in their fair land. Another regret was the presence of the dog Chew, who was as unhappy as we were and constantly barked or whined as he slipped to his ears in that black slime.

We made camp in a daze that night, around inflatable Vinylite mattresses protected by tarpaulins. The hot soup and pancakes made of dried eggs and buggy flour were heartening. We wrapped them around slices of Borden's portable cheese and ate them in our fingers.

The next day was no improvement on the first. It is possible that we managed a mile, and still no canoes and no bloody Indian trail. Still, however, no trouble with Indians. The mosquitoes tasted their first white meat, despite our repellents, and Raphael became so enraged by them that he caught one alive and lingeringly bit it in two. He was holding up admirably, old Raphael. He hacked hard, carrying three quarters of the baggage, and sometimes smiled, more brightly than we could, at our adversities. I had never thought that he might be actively dangerous to either of us, but I was always cautious with him for fear that one night when the confusions were in him he might take us for Bonis in our sleep. Such caution is, I think, reasonable when traveling alone in the woods, far from the nearest gendarme, with a Devil's Island convict condemned for life. It required our utmost democracy to treat him as friend and equal.

He had a slump during most of one afternoon, because he had tied a piece of string around his finger, and it was too tight, and he wouldn't take it off until he remembered why he had put it there. This made him so nervous that when Ruth, with no malice, asked him if there were any pancakes left over from the night before, his persecution complex reasserted its ugly head. We were accusing him of stealing, were we? We were denying him even our ordure; we were treating him like a dog; let the dog carry some baggage then.

It was cold in this mountain stream, despite the proximity of the equator. Our feet chilled and chafed in the rubber boots which were usually filled with pounds of slime. Even the sting of the mosquitoes had a cold sharp bite to it, unlike the burning of their northern kin. Ruth plodded and stumbled forward magnificently, trim and lovely from upwards of the waist. Even now she never complained of physical circumstances, unless, perchance, they were I. When Raphael ranted she turned a tolerant deaf ear to him. The defection of the Indians she could condone. The Bonis' cold war on us was perhaps a matter of ideological necessity. Wind and water and what looked like proximate famine only stirred her to the making of better film, before it should be too late.

The possibility that we might never return down-river, because of the various human agencies against us, evoked in her only solicitude for all that good lost film.

❧

By now we had surely gone as far as Malfatti could have gone in the night to steal his canoe, but we had rations for another day and so kept on to a clearing above the creek where on each side of us were thin, straight virginal trees crushed in an orgy of green. It may have been Brazil. Our vision was limited by the sky and a horizontal periphery of nearly twenty feet. The rain deployed like toy silver soldiers along the creek, while the mosquitoes blitzed them, for they had nothing else to do until they discovered us. We leaned against roots, our knees in water, munching chocolate. The dog Chew, a traitor, gave out his signal to the Indians that he was guarding us for them. All around us, whirling, sometimes getting into the chocolate, were pterodactylian dragonflies, the females dragging the corpses of their lovers whose jaws were closed on their tails; it should be a lesson to us all.

We had found no path by nightfall, and no canoes. The rain jostled us. Our footing was so unsure that I chopped my hand with the blade intended for a liana. We lay us down to sleep with the exquisite decision that in the morning we would go back — back to the Bonis, the Indian village, to Mademoiselle Victoire, to old Cayenne, to 226 Fifth Avenue where the books would be warm about us and the deep rugs dry.

❧

Out of the creek and back on the River Itany again, we stopped briefly to weave our canoe cabins, our *pomekaris*, as we would have no more low branches before us. Our boys were unsociable, but at least they were with us. They had faithfully or fearfully awaited our return from the vain search for the Indian path. They had been huddled in a knot when we reached them, back to back, each one with his bow and arrows and homemade blunderbuss between his knees. The Oyaricoulets, they said — perhaps imaginatively — had been making faces at them from the bush, and would I kindly give them back the powder which I had taken away from them one day when they had been obstreperous? With the exception of my savage bowman Asa, they were glad, I think, to see us. Asa's rump had been bitten by a fish, and he gave it a snide jerk at us as we arrived, and urinated lengthily.

The only evidence that they might actually have seen the Oyaricoulets, the tribe which I presumed had put the red ball on the spear, was that they described them as "the long-eared Indians," the same phrase used by Coudreau when he met them farther east. They also agreed that the ears were stretched by circles of bamboo in the lobes.

Despite the work of clearing we had done on the Ouare-mapan, we made scarcely better time on the way out than

on the way in. With the rains, the waters had swollen tremendously; there was a rise of eighteen inches, and the bridg-
ing logs we had slipped under before now had to be cut
through at water level. This, with the hot breath of the Indians on our necks, was not much fun. The Bonis swung
their axes with enthusiasm, which was doubled when once
we saw a string of pink flamingo feathers swinging from a
limb. Akofati opined that pink was still red, though less
violently, and that perhaps, Massa Gaddu be praised, we
would come to white feathers if we worked fast, and then
to none.

Afokati and Asa had put the last layer of banana leaves
and the last of fronds to hold them on the roof of my *pomekari*, tucked in the ends, secured these with vines, and now
almost without breaking motion pushed the canoe from shore
and started paddling. The river beneath the rain was like a
rough gray worsted stretched tight from shore to
shore.

There was no sign on the surface of the mighty current
which hauled us away and flung us off downstream. In this
area which had been strewn with visible sharp rocks on our
way up, there were now none above the surface, but they
couldn't be far down, I thought, as I stood up in the rain to
make sure the other canoes were all right. We traveled like
torpedoes, and nearly as fast, before a seething wake. The
paddlers didn't paddle; fore and aft they steered adroitly,
descrying with their X-ray eyes the subfluvial rocks which
might have shattered us. Ruth was standing too, wonderfully

[271]

balancing with the Filmo to her eye, shooting beneath a poncho. She would have made a good Boni.

The rain sizzled quietly against the river, and there was no other sound for days excepting once when a *bofu* with a loud "Wow!" plunged into the water from the forest ahead.

"What is a *bofu*, Afokati?"

"Sit down! Sit down, *mon capitaine!*"

"Was it a pig, a *sanglier?*"

"Massa Gaddu, will he please sit down?"

I recoiled into my cabin and opened the thatch behind me so that I could see Afokati's old and excellent body straining against the current.

"How big is it, Afokati?"

Down, deeper and deeper, went his paddle, steering, until his face was level with mine. His jaw muscles were tight as he replied, "About like a horse, or two horses."

We came to a bend in the river and the paddles chop-chopped the water, slishing it toward the bouldered shore where the current was tugging us.

❧

It would have been rude to interrupt Raphael's monologue to his stove. His personal dragons had got him again, and he confused us with them. Huddled bare-backed in the kitchen canoe, his old straw hat set rakishly above a lock of hair which obscured one eye, he resumed his intimacies with the stove that had been interrupted by his protracted sobriety on the creek, when he had been too busy worrying even to drink.

"Thou art aware," he shouted at the stove, giving it a wallop, "that I work twenty-five hours a day for them, cooking, scrubbing, washing the garbage of their linen, and what do they pay me with? Bonis! I'll stopper the beaks of the bastards, the Bonis!"

I had had enough of this and was about to tell him to stopper his own, when from one of the other canoes came the shout of "*Bofu! Bofu!*" We swerved in our tracks and went upriver prodigiously, trying to intercept a huge black head which was making for the Dutch shore. Afokati passed me his paddle and snatched my cousin Robert's gun, he being the mightier hunter, and as we ran across the back of the enormous animal he shot five cartridges at it while the other boys hacked it with machetes, nearly upsetting the canoes.

The animal went under, dying, and when it rolled over Eimo grabbed it by its genital structure, which was considerable, and held it fast, screaming like Priapus before a sacrifice. We got a noose around its neck and towed it to a rock in midstream.

It was a giant tapir, known in native as *bofu*, or *maipuri*, as big as a cow and shaped like one with the exception of its snout, which resembled the trunk of an elephant truncated. This was the four-toed tapir. Now the four-toed tapir is a beast herbivorous, non-belligerent, adipose, amphibian, and of small repute. It is mocked by the cruder hunters because

[273]

of its modesty. When it is known that a tapir is in a certain patch of woods, the Bonis surround it, sling their hammocks, and wait until the animal returns to the river and sits in it to defecate or urinate, when it is killed by the hunter there.

Our boys cleaned it on the rock, throwing the entrails into the water. We waited for the piranhas to come milling in their myriads, churning the water to a bloody froth, lunging at the rock to rip our bare toes from us. We waited eagerly with our cameras and filmed a couple of piranhas, or maybe three, which rose languidly as catfish to the floating tripe, snapped at it, showed their truly terrible fangs to us, and spurted away when Ruth's pink toes splashed water in their eyes.

We were safely out of the bad lands by now and had time to enjoy the tapir, basted over a fire that sizzled sweetly in the rain. The cutlets were delectable, and the liver as tender as mushrooms, with that taste and texture of silver and velour that the best *pâté* has.

"With a few truffles," I remarked, "you could have a Pâté de Foie Gras de Tapir which would make gourmets like Silas Spitzer tilt their noses at a goose."

Ruth, with a slice of liver as large as a pancake flapping between her scarlet nails, was looking at the one rough and largely hypothetical map we had of this region. "Where do you suppose we are?"

I asked Afokati, who was eating toasted skin with fur on it. As I expected, he looked not at the white line of rapids ahead but at those behind us. "That is the Saut Krabai Soula," he said surlily. And Ruth, locating it on the map, said that that left us sixty-three of our eighty-four rapids to go.

"And as for you, Afokati," she added, "if ever you take a subway with me in New York, and ask me what is the next station, as you might want to get off there, I won't tell you the name of it until after we have passed. For fear of offending the subway gods, you know."

Slipping from side to side in the current, quivering like compass needles, our three long canoes raced down the river. The rain was so thick here at the beginning of the season that it was sometimes hard to tell where it ended and the river itself began. The boys guided the canoes with their long poles and the helmsmen's paddles. It occurred to me that our paddles had been used only for steering, both upriver and down; they had never paddled. We had pushed our way up with poles, and returned with poles held like knights' lances to break our flight and fend the rocks from us. The river was rising several inches a day.

The boys remained surly and it helped not at all to talk of Christmas presents in St. Laurent, and bonuses for the co-operative spirit. The canoes of Ruth and Raphael lagged far behind mine on the even stretches, while the paddlers conversed. In revenge we took our time at filming, holding all boats up for half an hour at a time until we were certain that we had enough takes and retakes to assure the shot. I had hated the disciplining of men in the army; I hated it now, but we were too close to the end and fruition of our work to let it scatter before us. I envisaged every conceivable catastrophe between here and St. Laurent, and attached the jerry can full of precious film with a length of nylon cord to a log which would float if we were accidentally or deliberately upset.

∾

What I did not foresee was a bend in the river at a *saut* called Doichine, and a group of rocks in the middle of it with a huddle of Indian women and children on them. When we came closer through the rain I saw that these were the families of the Roucouyenne guides who had abandoned us. The queasy, irrational feeling that tells you something is wrong walked with cold sharp claws along my spine. I yelled to Afokati, Eimo, and Abbibal to stop. They dug in their poles but the current pulled us forward toward the bank, and we had nearly reached it when I saw the Indian Malfatti half hidden by a tree, with a shining machete swinging from his hand. Behind him, against the green, were other patches of red *roucou*-dyed Indian bodies.

This is the sort of moment which should make you feel like a dyed-in-the-wool old-time explorer, but actually leaves you with bile in the esophagus. The sensible thing would have been to order Ruth's Eino to paddle her like hell downriver. I assume it is a compliment to her that this never occurred to me, that subconsciously I felt she would fight adequately by my side.

I stood up in my canoe, making an excellent target, and poured half a bottle of good cognac into the water. This alone astonished the Indians and Ruth — and me. I cut a notch in the side of the cork and without too much fumbling found the can of carbide, pried it open, poured half of it into the bottle, stoppered it, and flung it overboard in the direction of Malfatti.

Time stood still as death while I examined the cartridge clip of my pistol. Ruth, standing up, was doing the same, and Raphael was whetting his machete on the sole of his sandal. I was considering how thoughtful it was of the Indians to put their children and womenfolk on a rock, out of the way of war, when there came a deep submarine "boom" as the water, seeping into my bottle, formed gas with the carbide and exploded.

Bubbles burst at the surface. There was a stink of brimstone. Great fish and little fish heaved up, stunned. I took a pot-shot at one of them and hit it.

I think our paddlers were as scared as the Indians, for they shouted angrily. With a howl Malfatti realized which side his war was buttered on. He jumped into his canoe, followed by four so-called braves, whipped to the rocky island, collected the nonbelligerents, and shot down-river before I could even ask Ruth if there wasn't another bottle of cognac somewhere. And that was fast.

I began to shake when I saw Afokati shaking and the hands of the wrestler Abbibal trembling on his pole.

❧

The Indians had had a nice idea, whether with or without

the complicity of the Bonis. If the Bonis had played along with them, they could have divided the pillage while the piranha were overcoming their terror of us and we drifted gracefully in our bones through the rapids. But even if the Bonis had not wanted to co-operate, it is certain that they would have done nothing in defense of their white cargo.

The effect upon Raphael of this contretemps was curious. Loyally he had whetted his blade; the excitement was good and he would fight for an underdog like me; he was prince of assassins again. But when I displayed something resembling force, though it was only trickery, he remembered the *bagne*, the forceful *surveillants*, the noise and echo of punishment. If we had not bluffed the Indians quickly, it is possible that he would have gone over to them. However it was, he now began to drink again and to hate us all.

Though it rained I had to tell him to sleep elsewhere than in our shelter; we couldn't sleep for his monologues and the whishing of his machete against the dangling fronds of our roof. So he slept "like a dog" in the rain, carefully wrapped in ponchos or in my army hammock, waking frequently to emit a blast of invective against those bastards who had dropped his blanket in the mud some months ago, his blanket, the only mother he had.

Only when I raised my voice to him would he reply with any cheer. "Aha, I knew it," he would say. "Your promises are vapors, *mon capitaine!* You will not see me liberated! You will send me back to the cell in St. Laurent!" And this

[278   ]

he said wistfully. "*Trente jours de cellule!*" Thirty days of solitary confinement, which for Raphael was bliss.

ᐇᕲ

It was just beyond the Saut Doichine that we camped with a lone black lady gold miner. She was rich with gold and ulcers, and I cleaned out a sore on her leg so deep that I could tap the bone with the scalpel. I packed it with sulfanilamide, bandaged it cleanly, and gave her penicillin tablets.

As she was a fat and ugly harridan we couldn't understand why Raphael should spend that evening with her, even in decent conversation before her open fire. Even the Bonis were worried, as their names were mentioned occasionally, including that of our mascot, Pekein.

"It is true, I did call him a decayed pederast," said Toma, "but not intentionally. He called me that. I didn't know what he meant by *inculé*, but since it was good enough for me, I've been calling him the same thing ever since. Afokati just now explained it to me."

Those were not the exact words of Toma, who spoke in talkie-talkie, but they are essentially what he meant. Eimo came into the firelight, and his skin with the rain on it looked like moiré black silk.

"It is Pekein we are worried about," he said. "The *vieux blanc* may get him in the night." A *vieux blanc* was Raphael or any convict, "old white man." And it was true. Even the twenty-year-old convicts, after a short while in the *bagne*, became old white men.

I gave Eimo a whistle. He was to blow it if Raphael should appear in the night. I then taught him a few blows and twists of jiu-jitsu, which might discourage Raphael without utterly destroying him, as the Bonis had threatened to do, with their *sabres*. Like the products which I had taken along to test in the jungle for the American army, I felt obliged to return Raphael, a product of the *bagne*, to his proprietors, who would be interested in whatever physical and moral changes had occurred in him during those fairly active but rather comfortable months when he had been subjected to the complete democracy of our expedition. Psychologically it was an experiment of interest, but I feared that the changes would be negligible.

"Come here, Eimo," I said. "I will show you another thing to do if Raphael should attack Pekein."

He hesitated, as I had once bent his joints a little more than necessary for demonstration. We needed, for ourselves, a good deal of propaganda just now.

"Look, put your finger here." I put the tip of his forefinger in the hollow beneath his own ear. "And the other finger on the other side." I placed it for him, right on the pneumogastric nerve. "You do this, see? Push in hard and Raphael will stop fighting. Push!"

Eimo pushed and screamed. He kept on pushing and jumped up and down. "Oh-oh!" he yelled. "Oh-oh!" Stupefied by pain, he got his directions wrong and kept pushing in ius fingers instead of pulling them out. He leaped with anguish until I seized him and with some effort pulled his fingers from the nerves.

He collapsed, the tears in his eyes.

"Nice, eh?" I said.

He shook his tough young face. "But why should I do this to me when the *vieux blanc* has his knife in the air? It spoils my forces; I am as a child like Pekein, and he will kill us all!"

~

It was very odd, Ruth said next morning, that she couldn't find the sulfanilimide powder and one bottle of penicillin tablets, and a roll of bandages — the equipment I had used last night on the gold-digging lady's ulcer. And it was doubly odd, I thought a little later when Ruth showed me a small packet of gold dust and a couple of nuggets, that Raphael had given this to her to give to me as a Christmas present in St. Laurent. There was a fine sense of fair dealing in the dishonesty of Raphael. He had helped the poor woman, repaid me more than ten times the value of the articles stolen, and unquestionably reaped a neat profit in gold for himself.

But he was hopeless. As we went down-river gaily in the rain, his spirits sank to unplumbed levels, for he was convinced that not only would I not try to get him freed, as I had sincerely promised, but that I would recommend special tortures for him when I flung him back to the gendarmes. The level of the taffia lowered with his mood, and there was nothing I could do about it; I couldn't take a twenty-gallon demijohn to bed with me.

Ruth, on a misty morning, blew a whistle from her canoe, which was some distance behind mine. Afokati, after deliberation, drew in to the bank, for it was impossible to stop in that current. While waiting for Ruth to catch up with us he passed the time by cutting another notch in the red stick he used as calendar and account book. Every notch was a day and a hundred and fifty francs for each of the six Bonis.

"How many now, Afokati?"

"One hundred and five."

Ruth's canoe came swirling beneath an arbor of dangling two-foot beans, called by the natives *asekasi*. She was standing up, filming through the hole in her poncho until the beans knocked her against the *pomekari* roof. Like a sheeted ghost she returned valiantly for a closeup of a bean; damnedest cameraman I ever knew.

An orderly type was Ruth; she checked exposure, consulted the factors she had written on slips of celluloid, shot her scene, checked footage, and finally turned to me.

"My boys want to land on that island. Both of their paddles are broken, and they've seen the right trees there for whittling new ones. How are you?"

"I'm wet and fine, and you're a great darling of a gal and a cameraman. How are you too?"

"The second camera jams. The shutter. Rust or fungus probably. I'll beat you to the island."

But the Bonis wouldn't race any more. Our days of levity

were done. With dignity we swung to the island and landed on the round gray boulders of its shore.

Ruth went to the right to film close-up the pellets of rain on the water. I went amidst the trees with the Bonis, looking for the fromagers with great flanged roots from which paddles could be made. The mascot Pekein was ahead of me. The others followed in single file.

∾

Somehow I was the first to see what thriller writers would call The Thing ahead of us. It lay asleep in a slight declivity, a gray and purple mass of monstrous coils, an anaconda about twenty-seven feet long and a good twelve inches thick. Such a reptile I had never seen, not even in a zoo, and I was so excited that I shouted, "Boa!"

Pekein and the others looked and fled, jumping, flailing their arms, howling horribly. The anaconda didn't budge, being full of food and confident that even in sleep it was master of the jungle. Alone and a dozen feet away from it I gawked, saying to myself, "Migod, we're in luck at last; this is it, this will make the film."

I tiptoed back along the route of flight the Bonis had taken, reflecting that the boa (anaconda) was their god. Ruth, in a bathing suit, was crouched between the rain and the river, filming spurts and circles.

"Ruth!" I whispered from too far away to be heard. I wove to her through the tall thorny grass. "We've got a boa, a colossus. Over there. Wait for me."

She looked up quizzically and nodded. I climbed down the bank to the canoes. My whole crew of Bonis was sitting on the shore with their backs turned to me and the boa, their heads in their hands.

"Gun!" I whispered. "Gun, gun, gun!" They didn't move. Raphael had succumbed to taffia and was lying mostly nude across the kitchen boxes in his canoe. His mouth was open and filled with rain, which ran in a thick stream from the corner of it.

"Raphael!" He swallowed, choked, went to sleep again. I waded to my canoe, decided on the pistol, and hurried up the bank past the immobile Bonis to meet Ruth moving quietly toward the boa nest.

We stood above it. The boa hadn't moved. Ruth adjusted the shutter aperture and reached for my hand, which she closed over the back strap of her bra. With the other hand I picked up a five-pound rock. "I'm shooting," she murmured.

Slowly, holding to the back strap, I steadied her as she leaned over the edge of the pit. The camera whirred at twenty-four frames per second, as fast as my heart. The great snake didn't move.

"Throw your rock," she whispered. I tossed it onto the head of the boa. His sigh was audible, but he didn't move.

"Don't jerk, darling. I'm shooting above it. Pistol." The three shots wakened the boa. He didn't look around. King and idiot that he was, he ruffled his scales against the grass, slipped over and under his coils, moved through the bush and disappeared toward the river.

"Great, great! How did it look?"

"Great."

Foolishly but spontaneously we shook hands and then hugged each other. We returned to the river and the Bonis and the canoes. Afokati was standing up, facing us, smiling for the first time in weeks.

"You did not shoot him, *capitaine*," he said, almost as though, at last, he were proud of me.

"I did not. I have told you often that I would not shoot your gods, either the cayman or the boa. But he would have been good to eat, Afokati. The boa is fine eating, for you who complain that you have no meat, and the gods don't worry about their flesh."

The other Bonis, still not moving, were looking at me queerly. Abracadabra, the leper, said through his pouted lips, "Since you have not killed him . . ."

Afokati continued, " . . . You might know that just beside him, over the ridge of the pit, his wife is lying." The boys put their heads into their hands again.

This needed no consultation. We stepped in time together, gently, like people in a slow-motion picture of a barn dance, and looked over the ridge. The mate of the boa was sleeping there, as big as her spouse, on a grassy slope which fell off toward the rocks and the river.

Ruth moved to a position below the snake, set her camera, tossed the hair from her eyes, and raised her hand. I had a long stick and reached down slowly with it to tap the snake's head. She was complacent. I tapped more heartily and she constricted, twined within herself — there's a good bowline, I thought — and got my stick caught in the bush, I thought. I tugged at it. I couldn't see the snake because of the bush between us. The rain let up suddenly and I could hear Ruth's camera whirring. There was a pause and it whirred again, a pause and a whir, while I tried to disengage the stick. Then Ruth called to me.

"Be careful. The snake is on the stick!"

Jiggling the stick foolishly with one hand I reached for my Browning with the other, pointed it toward the Tumac-Humacs, and squeezed the trigger. It squeaked; lack of oil and lack of bullets. But the good Massa Gaddu had placed another long stick just beside me. I seized it and loved it and batted it down on Ruth's side of where the boa should be. The camera whirred. I batted again, blindly through the bush, and saw twenty-seven or -eight or thirty feet of ir-ritated boa gliding over the rocks and into the river.

Throught the arched fringes of the bamboo which had dropped its itchy dust upon me, I saw Ruth too at last, following action to the last flick of the anaconda's tail.

❧

It was some days later, on a morning with a sky like pewter scratched by rain, when Ruth, dissolving Klim in a cocktail shaker, flipping it deftly from hand to hand, bared her con-science.

[286   ]

"It was a hard decision to make," said she, "when that boa came after you along the stick. Sentimentally, I was concerned, of course; but professionally I couldn't help but see what a dandy bit of film it would be if the boa climbed up and up and almost got you."

❧

"Downgo," said Afokati, meaning "Now we go down the river," and we pushed into muddy waters, the drainage of the swamps, and the glutinous, khaki-colored shores. For a while there was an oval of blue sky between the clouds, and across it, like sparks, came a flight of parrots. There was light enough in that space to see the green and red and gray of them.

We veered and twisted, spun halfway round, straightened with a jerk and slid silently through the Mama Saut. Asa turned round in the bow of my canoe and shouted, "*Gran tankee! Tabaka!*" in gratitude to Mama Saut for letting us pass.

A hideous laughter came from the canoe behind me. It was Raphael's, and he was dipping up the river in his straw hat and putting the hat on his head. The water sluiced into his mouth.

"Raphael, stop that!" I shouted. "You're driving me crazy too."

"I can't help it! I can't stop! It reminds me so much of the good old days at Cayenne, when we had to unload cooking oil from the ships, and when the *surveillants* weren't looking we would siphon it with a rubber hose into the bottles we had in our shirts, and sell it for a good price, naturally."

"Naturally. It was an excellent idea, but don't make that noise about it."

"But that wasn't the best of it, *mon capitaine*. When we got a cargo of sugar once, we unloaded it from the boat and piled it on the wharf for the next crew to take to the warehouse. Ha, ha, ha, ha!"

"Pretty funny," I said, looking at the map on my knees which indicated that Malfatti's village was just below the next *saut*, which was called Granman Ponsou. This *saut* had been troublesome when we came up; it should be worse now. And I looked forward with no enthusiasm to the passing of Malfatti's village. It was quite possible that his annoyance with me had increased.

"Funny?" howled Raphael, and clapped his hand over his mouth to hold in the laughter. "But that isn't the half of it! You know our convict clothing, the pajamas?" Suddenly and as though surprised he glanced down at himself. "This, of course. Long sleeves, long trousers. Half of us dockers had tied strings around our sleeves at the wrist and our trousers at the ankles, and that half of us became afflicted with dysentery. The *surveillant* was a soft old bastard; he was recovering from a crisis of dysentery himself, so when one after the other of us asked for a moment off to relieve ourselves, he would permit us to go under the wharf.

"There, *mon capitaine*, *mon cher capitaine*, we had pushed up a knife through a crack in the planking, so that it penetrated a sack of sugar. You understand? You are beginning to laugh now, eh? So when a colleague would go down to take care of his needs, he would open his shirt at the neck to receive the trickle of sugar from the sack. It would fill his shirt and sleeves and he would loosen his belt so it ran down his trouser legs which were tied at the bottom. Then he would fill his shirt again.

"At the end of the unloading that night we were pretty tired men. We staggered back to the cells, where of course we regaled ourselves with sugar, for a change, and later we sold it dear. Ha, ha, ha!"

❧

Just ahead of us was the cold boiling water of the *saut*. Ruth's canoe was beside mine. She said, "Ha, ha, ha!" as she hurried to get the cameras into plastic bags which were attached one to another and all tied to a couple of inflated rubber pillows.

Laughing like mad things, and whistling even, and holding tight, we plunged through the pass of Granman Ponsou, our small ships vibrating until I felt their thwarts must burst, the water heaving in by bucketfuls. We bailed furiously, sitting in the bottoms of the canoes and in the bilge for balance. The spray whipped like knotted cords against our eyeballs. Edges of gray-blue water, like slices of tin, slashed at us, to leave our faces welted. The thunder of the *saut* became a hissing and a whisper finally, as we reached the exhausted pool below it.

[289]

"*Gran tankee!*" I said to the *saut*. "*Tabaka!*"

❧

There was no one in Malfatti's village, not a dog. We slid with quiet paddles along the shore of it, watching it carefully, waiting for the vagrant arrow, but there was no one to resent us now, so far as we could see. Our old hut with its great round roof looked an inviting refuge from the rain, but I didn't trust it.

"We'll go to the other side of the river," I said to the paddlers, who had slowed up, wistfully eying the good shelters, for it was getting dark.

"Malfatti is afraid," yelled Toma. "You should have heard what we said to him," said Toma, that old sea lawyer. "He has fled into the bush with his people, and the village is ours."

"Get to the other side," I said temperately. We made slow progress there while the boys argued among themselves, softly punctuated by Afokati's sighs.

I stood up, letting the accumulated rain trickle from my shirt to my pants like Raphael's sugar. Ruth, indefatigable, was filming again. Ralphael had lost his laughter as the taffia wore thin, and was huddled over his only friend, the stove, cursing it.

"Afokati, where is the next camp site below?"

"Three *sauts*," said he. "Are you afraid to camp in Malfatti's village when you have that fizz-foop with you?"

"Fizz-foop? What?" I kept on bailing.

[290   ]

He referred with respect to my carbide explosion in Malfatti's ambush upriver.

"I am afraid a little, for Madame Davis, and you, and maybe me. And certainly for the film. Sabotage, you know?"

In his good innocence, he didn't know. He might naïvely have been capable of it, but he didn't know. I let it go at that and stopped bailing, with the water in the canoe at the level of my ankles. The baggage on the cross-slats was above it.

"I think we'll camp on that island," I said. "But now look. There's a *comu* palm. There. Look and you'll see even three of them. We'll stop at the island, and before the sun goes out I want you to get me a heart of *comu* palm. We shall eat it tonight, all of us."

The canoes were tied to mangrove roots and the Bonis went up the slope. We sat side by side in the *pomekaris* and poured ourselves each a cognac, and one for Raphael, who spilled it. From above us came the clunking sound of axes, and I was whetting my palate for the boiled heart of *comu* with the last of our butter and hot pimentoes and thin strips of ham, when the boys returned carrying slabs of wood cut from fromager roots, and no *comu*.

There had been no time, they said, before the sun should go. Most of their paddles had been split in the *sauts*. They would make new paddles now.

We went ashore to the island which I had chosen in preference to the abandoned village, and walked across it, up to our knees in quagmire. It was a very poor choice. The Bonis ignored us and fiercely attacked their slabs of fromager. We came back from our inspection and sat ourselves like apes on the limbs of trees, wishing that we had light enough to film the paddle-carving. They were all equally expert at it, slashing with two-foot-long machetes at the raw pink wood, and the wood melted before their violent blows. The shape of a paddle was in Asa's hands. Behind a gray tree, whacking privately, was Abbibal, his paddle already thinned to its oval edges; and Eimo, cheating, had already carved designs on his before thinning the edge.

Afokati, looking at us on the limbs with a sort of compassion, said that if we went back up the river past Malfatti's abandoned village (if we were sure that we really didn't want to stop there), and took the *bistouri* to the right around another island, we would find the village, on the Dutch shore, of another Roucouyenne chief, Yana Mali, who was not Malfatti's friend. No more than a kilometer, no *sauts*, said he.

This, like anything else seen through the hazy lens of our fatigue, looked like a trap. We could have slung hammocks in the branches above the marsh, but I still distrusted the army hammocks, covered and zippered, in these purlieus of Malfatti's hunting ground. They would be hard to get out of fast.

"Good. Let us go to Yana Mali," I said, sliding off my limb, ripping my shirttail. "All right, Ruth?"

She took her cameras from the knotholes where she had neatly deposited them, and swung down accurately, with her strange assurance, into her canoe.

"I was wondering, but let's try it. With your fizz-foop I'm unafraid."

❧

The head of Yana Mali, blurred through the mosquito net as we wakened in the morning, was not prepossessing. It was more Mongoloid than the others, with higher cheekbones and heavier hair, which was cropped fairly evenly at ear-length, unlike the long lank tresses of the other Indians.

He brought us gifts of dozens of eggs, all rotten, and a piece of smoked cayman tail which he passed to me surreptitiously when the Bonis' backs were turned. He obviously knew a good deal about us, and probably had heard from Malfatti himself of our troubles with that wretched renegade. Whether through fear of the fizz-foop or the intelligent realization that we were really quite nice people, he and his villagers accorded us their greatest compliment: they neither bothered nor bothered about us. We were like house guests of long standing whom one need neither solicit nor entertain.

The tremendously pregnant woman, with messages written in mud on her belly, brought us loads of firewood. The urchin with the fledgeling birds in a calabash consulted us as to whether worms were better than small fish for them. The sorcerer called me brother.

It was in this spirit of pleasant relationship that one afternoon Chief Yana Mali, holding the hands of Ruth and me

[293]

as we walked through the village, said, "That smoke over there may change the whole life of a man."

We took the outer path around the thatched huts and went through a tunnel in the forest. Half a dozen Indians were holding torches beneath a large wasps' nest, swiping at the tougher wasps which fled from it. But these soon went away to a clearer air, and when the rest of them were drugged with smoke, the Indians cut the wasp nest down and returned to the village with it.

We squatted in a circle around Yana Mali as he dug the doped wasps from the nest. They wiggled a little. His very red-painted son had woven a mat of green and yellow rattan, and into the interstices of this Yana Mali put the wasps. He would slip their fat tails into feather quills, push the quills through the holes in the mat, carrying the tails through, then remove the quills, leaving the wasps caught, alive, by their slender waists. They were huge beasts, an inch and a half long.

When hundreds had been trapped in the mat like this and I was wondering if ever I had seen a more useless-looking machine, Yana Mali said, "This is to test the courage of a man."

"How?" I asked politely.

"They sting," said he, "and they bite. Look."

The wasps were wide awake by now, shaking the smoke from their eyes. Yana Mali put one on his tongue, and I could see the stinger plunge viciously in. He turned it around, with the head to his tongue, and the mandibles cut into the quivering flesh, drawing blood from it. Remembering that real ethnologists with diplomas did test their findings in the field, I plucked another wasp from its nest, waking it and annoying it, and placed it on my quivering forearm. It bit and stung me simultaneously.

"You will have fever," said Yana Mali thickly, as his tongue was already swelling. I was convinced of it.

Ruth had of course been filming the whole fabrication of the wasp-mat machine on the chance that it might make sense eventually, while I wrung my hands at the thought of the little film we had left, saying, "Darling, we're poor people! Damn it, we haven't the film to spend! Save it, for God's sake, save it, until we *know* we have something we can use!"

She took her eyes away from the view-finder and winked with it; I had said this so often before.

"Look," said I, lowering my voice to the well-modulated level she approved, but it trailed off, for I couldn't keep it there.

"What are you going to do with it?" Ruth asked Yana Mali practically — "that mat?"

I had the feeling that our Indian chief was repenting of putting the wasp on his tongue, for those of his words which should have begun with s now issued with a *th* instead.

He explained, and I nodded my apologies to Ruth. He explained that every boy of the Roucouyennes at the age of puberty must undergo the test of manhood, before he could be accepted as a warrior. This consisted of a torture by wasps or ants, whichever was the handiest. Trapped in the mat, they were placed upon his chest by the oldest woman of the tribe, first the side they stung with, and then the biting side, and then alternately for hours until the youngster fell with fever and pain. If he had not cried out he was accepted as one fit to fight for dogs in Brazil.

"But now," said the chief — his Mongol eyes, like horizontal commas, looking at me with an intensity which seemed strangely personal, as if I were involved — "now we prepare the wasps for a different matter, which is very much the same."

And he went on to talk of warriors who sometimes were thought craven by their fellows in the battles with the Oyaricoulets. These were few, he said proudly, but when the case was proved against them, they were shamefully forced to submit again to the test of their pubic youth, to prove them men and warriors. There was such a person among them now. Malfatti was his name.

"Eh? Malfatti? Our, so to speak, Malfatti?"

Everyone talked at once, which made a difficult explanation even harder for me to grasp. I feel them to be speaking in embarrassed and formal phrases, such as "It has come to our attention . . ." and so on, but finally it came out that the village of Yani Mali was noted for a number of things: its courage in battle, its low incidence of homosexuality, and its fealty to the French administration, which had once sent it a supply of fishhooks.

It had come to their attention that the renegade Malfatti, in his relations with my expedition, had breached Roucouyenne honor on these three points. It was regrettable, and Yani Mali apologized in the name of his people, lisping over his sore tongue.

By now all the interstices of the mat were filled with live and kicking wasps. It itched and ached me to look at it.

Ruth said, "But we don't want Malfatti punished. . . ."

I added, "All I insist on, and what I shall advise the *préfet* at Cayenne, is that Malfatti shall not guide another French expedition."

While we were walking through the village, soberly as inquisitors, it was pointed out to me that the wasp test was not punishment at all. It was simply necessary that Malfatti prove, by courage, his right to reinstatement in the tribe, for he had been, in his time, a respectable warrior and a fine bush citizen. Such a man should not be lost. He should endure a little salutary pain and prove to the world of the Roucouyennes that his pecadilloes up-river with us were temporary aberrations. Such was the law of Yolok.

The anthropomorphic god Yolok, blue-eyed and hairless from forehead to feet, running knock-kneed everywhere and screaming capricious orders, had frequently disturbed our matter-of-fact expedition when, always at awkward moments, he had been conjured.

This was one of them, I thought, as we came to the center of the village. The tethered dogs were howling. The sun had a whole clean heaven to itself at last and was scorching the earth so fast that you could see cracks form in the clay. No one was about but an old squatted woman, her breasts laid out on her knees to dry.

From some sort of special hut which had been previously closed, just behind the menstrual hut, came strange, monotonous sounds of fluting, followed by two drunken Indians who spilled through the door, arm in arm, tootling on three-note flutes made from the tibias of jaguar. One of them was Malfatti, the other his nimble lieutenant whose name I had never known.

No one but ourselves, the inquisitors, and the squatted hag stood there in the sun to watch the antics of their preparation for the trial. They danced forward and back together, approaching and recoiling from the hag, tootling on their flutes, taking a nip occasionally from their gourds of *cachiri*, the raw corn wine.

Malfatti may have recognized us, but he gave no sign of it, even when we sat on the ground a couple of feet from him to film his frenzy. Up and down he went with his partner, up to the hut where the old woman was standing now, holding the wasp mat which Yana Mali had given her, and down to the river and more slowly back again.

"There are only twenty feet in the camera," said Ruth. "Will you get me two more reels? Color."

Even the Bonis had disappeared. Raphael, who had obviously been drinking *cachiri* with our oppressed and exploited Indian chief, tried to come through the door of the hut, hit his head, turned, and backed out on all fours. For the rest of the afternoon his lean figure in striped convict pajamas stood diagonally across the doorway, smoking the rare Pall Malls which I had not given him.

❧

When I returned from our round hut with four of our still cameras loaded, and Ruth's color film, the ceremony of Malfatti's trial, in a terrible silence, had begun. He was leaning against the thatch of an empty house, his arms spread out like a man to be crucified. The old woman, the oldest of the tribe, was slowly and gently touching his arms and his face with the mat, the stinger side, and as the wasps felt flesh behind them their whole bodies writhed with the effort of blind piercing and excretion.

Malfatti trembled. At least half the wasps, perhaps a hundred, had stung him, and he knew that the wasp, unlike the bee, does not lose its stinging needle in the wound. They would sting him again, but not immediately, for the old torturing woman, who had probably been doing this for many years, now turned the mat against his nipples and with a little smile and a modest closing of the eyes, applied the other side. We filmed the wasp tails wiggling in ecstasy as the mandibles sank in. And when the mat was lifted away there were little gouts of blood on Malfatti's chest.

His face had twisted, green-blue veins had swollen at his temples, but he had not yet cried out.

Holding the bright reflector before him, flinging light into his tired and tortured eyes so that Ruth could get close-ups, I felt ashamed that we must photograph this, as I had very often felt when filming native rituals before. But it was something we must do. If it was important to the Roucouyennes, it was important to us, to UNESCO, to France, to all cultural or military organizations which someday might meet these people. One economic geographer, whom I knew and trusted, Earl Parker Hanson, had seen a similar ceremony in Brazil, employing giant ants instead of wasps, as our Roucouyennes occasionally did. But neither he nor anyone else, I believed, had filmed it. It probably was indigenous to and unique among these related tribes of South American Indians, and the sort of thing which one of their putative ancestors, the Incas, might well have invented.

I knew perhaps as little about the Indian anthropologically and historically as I did about the Brooklyn Man, but the notes of Pizarro and the tomes of Prescott had led me to believe that these Roucouyennes were more likely the descendants of some Incan hegira than the refugee sons of Caribs, Arawaks, or Galibis. Physiologically they seemed more similar; sociologically it was difficult to make comparisons owing to the complete decadence of the Roucouyennes, but there was one point — to be disdained by my betters probably — in favor of my assumption: the point of these Indians' distrust and hatred and fear of gold, as if the tribal memory retained the fierce and faithless image of the gold which had led to the Incas' ruin.

❦

"Need a new reading," said Ruth, "and the haze filter."

I held the Norwood meter to the back of the torturing hag, who smiled at me demurely and continued her work. Flick . . . flick. She pressed the mat, one side and the other, against the blood-flecked chest. Malfatti's arms were spread against the roof and his blunt fingers were tearing thatch from it. I hoped the studios would not neglect to dub in the grinding of his teeth. Sweat poured slowly, because of its oiliness, over the wrinkled flesh where his eyebrows had been shaved, over the lashless eyelids, and down his cheeks to follow their furrows to his twitching upper lip and drip upon the limp lower one.

"Pig of an Indian," said Raphael behind me. "He has something in the abdomen, after all. If I had seen this first I wouldn't have tried to bluff him with the fizz-foop. You are lucky, my son, I mean *mon capitaine*."

He offered me one of my cigarettes, which I accepted graciously, exchanging it with Yana Mali for one of his, a thin tube of native tobacco the width of a pencil and a foot long. It had the titillating taste of old pine needles and Borden's excellent and ripest Liederkranz.

Yana Mali, holding my cigarette awkwardly as a schoolgirl between forefinger and thumb, his other fingers genteelly lifted, remarked that it might be hours yet before Malfatti fell. It was over three hours now since the trial had begun; the sun was setting, bronzing Malfatti's black hair, brazening the palm thatch behind it. The immensely pregnant woman had brought a calabash full of some revolting pink gruel to the torturing hag, who ate it with her left hand, letting her right hand never stop in its dreadful work.

All around the oval of huts the dogs were howling, not for Malfatti but because their dinner was late. It was the prelude to a symphony of hysteria. Far away, it seemed, was the voice of a woman crying, and some red howler monkey, despairing of the sun, began to crow and keen in his two voices.

Ruth's hand was shaking as I took it from her camera; she was more tired than the man writhing beneath the wasps. She had been at this for four hours now, moving forward and back and in semicircles, on her bare feet which were surer than shoes. It couldn't have yet occurred to her that her sound prevision had recorded from its beginning a ceremony which singly justified our long travel. She sat on the ground quietly, with her camera and tripod folded against her chest like some great dead bug.

"Billo, stop me if I try to film any more."

"There's no light, darling." We had been shooting in color, which you shouldn't do when the shadow of a man in the evening becomes longer than himself. Ruth's shadow lay long and humped before us, and she flung sand upon it.

Dragging our shadows behind us, we went to our own hut and pulled our cots close together so that, as we sat at the ends of them, we could understand how good was our fortune, and how much we deserved it, and how fond we were, and how soon we had better be leaving Yana Mali's village.

The moon, as if pulled on a cord around the earth, ascended as the sun went down. There was darkness suddenly, sprinkled by the lights of fireflies. We put our baggage together, listening. We packed the tape recorder in rubber sponge and sealed it. We discarded unnecessary baggage around the circumference of the hut. We added the desiccant silica gel to the jerry cans where our film was stored.

We stopped often and listened to the village, waiting for Malfatti, whose twisted silhouette we still could see, to scream or collapse upon his bloody shadows. But the hag kept on, eating gruel with her thin left hand, flicking her right hand with its mat of wasps. Malfatti held to the fraying thatch, drooping a little.

Yana Mali may have felt that we suspected him. He went around our hut collecting the junk we had thrown out and the occasional surprise of a useful thing with which I had hoped to hold his vague allegiance for half an hour more.

He sat on the ground squarely between Ruth and me and the heaving, drooping silhouette of Malfatti, and told us in detail, slowly, of how else the wasp mat was used.

When a Roucouyenne couple wished to marry, he said, they were placed in a hammock together, nude, without even a *calambé*; and the top cover of the hammock, which served to keep out rain and mosquitoes, was sewn down tightly all around except for one small opening. Into this was pushed a basketful of live wasps and ants. Then the opening was sewn shut with some fine sadistic petitpoint, and the loving couple was left for the night. The elders sat around them or slung hammocks nearby, watching the vibrations of love inspirited by wasps and ants.

Yana Mali smiled. "*Hipok?*" he asked. "Good?"

"*Hipokedah*," I answered fluently.

He turned his head, listening. "Then," he said, "if in the morning the two young people still love each other they are married. If they don't . . ."

He was listening again, but for which of various noises in that troubled night, I didn't know. The nearest was that of Raphael at the edge of our hut, burning his hands as he plucked plantains from the embers of his kitchen fire. "That this should happen to me," he growled. "I'll get the black buggers in their beds."

Sighing, probably, I moved behind him and took the machete he had stuck in the sand. I stuck it elsewhere, through a shadow. I could hear none of the usual sounds of Indians talking as they ate, and this was surely dinnertime. Malfatti was still erect, mute, defying the wasps. Ruth had neatly walked Yana Mali to the hut of his wife and left him there. When she returned, I said, "We're getting out, darling."

She said, "And soon."

On the river edge by the canoes the Bonis were chanting as they had not done before during all this expedition. It was good sound; we would record it later; not tonight. The only disturbing element of it was Eimo's shrilling voice, a noise we knew when the *kitta* possessed him. He would be running through the night, through the village, to the forest, screaming melodiously, pretending he was a zombie, a jaguar, an ape.

Ruth told Raphael to pack up his kitchen fast; we were leaving. I trapped Eimo with a dose of rum in an aspirin bottle, and prodded my six men to the hut and the baggage so fast that they had no time for thinking.

As the Revere tape recorder went away on the head of Pekein, when I was bending to pick up a film dropped from my pocket, I saw the red apparition of Yana Mali, who must have sluiced himself with *roucou* only a few minutes ago. He was more purple than red in the blaze of our fluorescent lamps, and he looked distressed. He said he was distressed, as I buckled on my paltry pistol. He had wanted to have a good long talk with me, and I felt he was still intending to make it long. Now that we were going away, said he with a grimace such as Malfatti had not yet shown, now that we were returning to Cayenne and would see the *préfet*, didn't I think that I might suggest to the *préfet* that he, Yana Mali, should be considered chief of Malfatti's village as well as his own?

Malfatti, he said, could not last much longer beneath the test. He had once cried out as a warrior never should.

The three of us were walking toward the canoes, Yana Mali between us. He stopped once, and I listened too, to a low keening, a terrifying woman's song. It rose and fell like a bell ringing alternately in deep and shallow water.

"Why is she singing now?"

"Her husband died, last night . . ."

The rain came down, whisking like the little metal flyswishes that dance bands use upon their drums. Ruth climbed into her canoe. The dirge of the woman stopped; there was silence; and when my ears became accustomed to sound again, as one's eyes become pitched to perceive grayness in the dark, I could dimly hear a concerted mumbling from the hut where Malfatti had prepared for his ordeal. It was mean and fierce as small thundering.

I stepped into my canoe and stayed standing. The Bonis pushed off. Ruth's hand was on the thwart beside me. I liked the good small knuckles and the coursing veins of it.

The rapids were silver ahead of us, with rain and a strangely piercing moonlight. My canoe, Ruth's, and Raphael's were abreast. Eimo's song had depth in it, a healthy baritone. Raphael was talking fondly to his stove.